NEW DATA

FOR

V. I. LENIN'S

"IMPERIALISM, THE HIGHEST STAGE OF CAPITALISM"·

Edited by

E. VARGA, L. MENDELSOHN

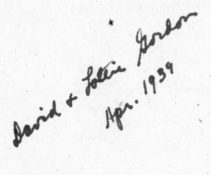

David + Lottie Gordon
Apr. 1939

NEW YORK
INTERNATIONAL PUBLISHERS

Printed in the Union of Soviet Socialist Republics
B-44815

CONTENTS

V. I. LENIN—*IMPERIALISM, THE HIGHEST STAGE OF CAPITALISM*

NEW DATA FOR V. I. LENIN'S *IMPERIALISM, THE HIGHEST STAGE OF CAPITALISM*

I. CONCENTRATION OF PRODUCTION AND MONOPOLIES

IV
CONTENTS

CONTENTS   V

CONCERNING NEW DATA FOR V. I. LENIN'S *IMPERIALISM THE HIGHEST STAGE OF CAPITALISM*, BY LEO MENDELSON

DIAGRAMS

V. I. LENIN

IMPERIALISM
THE HIGHEST STAGE OF CAPITALISM

A POPULAR OUTLINE

With New Data

PREFACE TO THE RUSSIAN EDITION

The pamphlet here presented to the reader was written in Zürich in the spring of 1916. In the conditions in which I was obliged to work there I naturally suffered somewhat from a shortage of French and English literature and from a serious dearth of Russian literature. However, I made use of the principal English work, *Imperialism*, J. A. Hobson's book, with all the care that, in my opinion, that work deserves.

This pamphlet was written with an eye to the tsarist censorship. Hence, I was not only forced to confine myself strictly to an exclusively theoretical, mainly economic analysis of facts, but to formulate the few necessary observations on politics with extreme caution, by hints, in that Æsopian language—in that cursed Æsopian language—to which tsarism compelled all revolutionaries to have recourse whenever they took up their pens to write a "legal" work.[1]

It is very painful, in these days of liberty, to read these cramped passages of the pamphlet, crushed, as they seem, in an iron vise, distorted on account of the censor. Of how imperialism is the eve of the socialist revolution; of how social-chauvinism (socialism in words, chauvinism in deeds) is the utter betrayal of socialism, complete desertion to the side of the bourgeoisie; of how the split in the labour movement is bound up with the objective conditions of imperialism, etc., I had to speak in a "slavish" tongue, and I must refer the reader who is interested in the question to the volume, which is soon to appear, in which are reproduced the articles I wrote abroad in the years 1914-17. Special attention must be drawn, however, to a passage on pages 119-20.[2] In order to show, in a guise acceptable to the censors, how shamefully the capitalists and the social-chauvinist deserters (whom Kautsky opposes with so much inconsistency) lie on the question of annexations; in order to show with what cynicism they *screen* the annexations of *their* capitalists, I was forced to quote as an example—Japan! The careful reader

---

[1] "Æsopian," after the Greek fable writer Æsop, was the term applied to the allusive and roundabout style adopted in "legal" publications by revolutionaries in order to evade the censorship.—*Ed. Eng. ed.*

[2] *Cf.* pp. 248-50 in this volume.—*Ed. Eng. ed.*

will easily substitute Russia for Japan, and Finland, Poland, Courland, the Ukraine, Khiva, Bokhara, Esthonia or other regions peopled by non-Great Russians, for Korea.

I trust that this pamphlet will help the reader to understand the fundamental economic question, *viz.*, the question of the economic essence of imperialism, for unless this is studied, it will be impossible to understand and appraise modern war and modern politics.

Petrograd, April 26, 1917

PREFACE TO THE FRENCH AND GERMAN EDITIONS

I

As was indicated in the preface to the Russian edition, this pamphlet was written in 1916, with an eye to the tsarist censorship. I am unable to revise the whole text at the present time, nor, perhaps, is this advisable, since the main purpose of the book was and remains: to present, on the basis of the summarised returns of irrefutable bourgeois statistics, and the admissions of bourgeois scholars of all countries, a *general picture* of the world capitalist system in its international relationships at the beginning of the twentieth century—on the eve of the first world imperialist war.

To a certain extent it will be useful for many Communists in advanced capitalist countries to convince themselves by the example of this pamphlet, *legal, from the standpoint of the tsarist censor*, of the possibility—and necessity—of making use of even the slight remnants of legality which still remain at the disposal of the Communists, say, in contemporary America or France, after the recent wholesale arrests of Communists, in order to explain the utter falsity of social-pacifist views and hopes for "world democracy." The most essential of what should be added to this censored pamphlet I shall try to present in this preface.

II

In the pamphlet I proved that the war of 1914-18 was imperialistic (that is, an annexationist, predatory, plunderous war) on the part of both sides; it was a war for the division of the world, for the partition and repartition of colonies, "spheres of influence" of finance capital, etc.

Proof of what was the true social, or rather, the true class character of the war is naturally to be found, not in the diplomatic history of the war, but in an analysis of the *objective* position of the ruling *classes in all* belligerent countries. In order to depict this objective position one must not take examples or isolated data (in view of the extreme

5

complexity of social life it is always quite easy to select any number of examples or separate data to prove any point one desires), but the *whole* of the data concerning the *basis* of economic life in *all* the belligerent countries and the *whole* world.

It is precisely irrefutable summarised data of this kind that I quoted in describing the *partition of the world* in the period of 1876 to 1914 (in chapter VI) and the distribution of the *railways* all over the world in the period of 1890 to 1913 (in chapter VII). Railways combine within themselves the basic capitalist industries: coal, iron and steel; and they are the most striking index of the development of international trade and bourgeois-democratic civilisation. In the preceding chapters of the book I showed how the railways are linked up with large-scale industry, with monopolies, syndicates, cartels, trusts, banks and the financial oligarchy. The uneven distribution of the railways, their uneven development—sums up, as it were, modern world monopolist capitalism. And this summing up proves that imperialist wars are absolutely inevitable under *such* an economic system, *as long as* private property in the means of production exists.

The building of railways seems to be a simple, natural, democratic, cultural and civilising enterprise; that is what it is in the opinion of bourgeois professors, who are paid to depict capitalist slavery in bright colours, and in the opinion of petty-bourgeois philistines. But as a matter of fact the capitalist threads, which in thousands of different intercrossings bind these enterprises with private property in the means of production in general, have converted this work of construction into an instrument for oppressing *a thousand million* people (in the colonies and semi-colonies), that is, more than half the population of the globe, which inhabits the subject countries, as well as the wage slaves of capitalism in the lands of "civilisation."

Private property based on the labour of the small proprietor, free competition, democracy, *i.e.*, all the catchwords with which the capitalists and their press deceive the workers and the peasants—are things of the past. Capitalism has grown into a world system of colonial oppression and of the financial strangulation of the overwhelming majority of the people of the world by a handful of "advanced" countries. And this "booty" is shared between two or three powerful world marauders armed to the teeth (America, Great Britain, Japan), who involve the whole world in *their* war over the sharing of *their* booty.

III

The Brest-Litovsk Peace Treaty dictated by monarchist Germany, and later on, the much more brutal and despicable Versailles Treaty dictated by the "democratic" republics of America and France and also by "free" England, have rendered very good service to humanity by exposing both the hired coolies of the pen of imperialism and the petty-bourgeois reactionaries, although they call themselves pacifists and socialists, who sang praises to "Wilsonism," and who insisted that peace and reform were possible under imperialism.

The tens of millions of dead and maimed left by the war—a war for the purpose of deciding whether the British or German group of financial marauders is to receive the lion's share—and the two "peace treaties," mentioned above, open the eyes of the millions and tens of millions of people who are downtrodden, oppressed, deceived and duped by the bourgeoisie with unprecedented rapidity. Thus, out of the universal ruin caused by the war a world-wide revolutionary crisis is arising which, in spite of the protracted and difficult stages it may have to pass, cannot end in any other way than in a proletarian revolution and in its victory.

The Basle Manifesto of the Second International which in 1912 gave an appraisal of the war that ultimately broke out in 1914, and not of war in general (there are all kinds of wars, including revolutionary wars), this Manifesto is now a monument exposing the shameful bankruptcy and treachery of the heroes of the Second International.

That is why I reproduce this Manifesto as a supplement to the present edition and again I call upon the reader to note that the heroes of the Second International are just as assiduously avoiding the passages of this Manifesto which speak precisely, clearly and definitely of the connection between that impending war and the proletarian revolution, as a thief avoids the place where he has committed a theft.

IV

Special attention has been devoted in this pamphlet to a criticism of "Kautskyism," the international ideological trend represented in all countries of the world by the "prominent theoreticians" and leaders of the Second International (Otto Bauer and Co. in Austria, Ramsay MacDonald and others in England, Albert Thomas in France, etc., etc.) and multitudes of socialists, reformists, pacifists, bourgeois-democrats and parsons.

This ideological trend is, on the one hand, a product of the disintegration and decay of the Second International, and, on the other hand, it is the inevitable fruit of the ideology of the petty bourgeoisie, who, by the whole of their conditions of life, are held captive to bourgeois and democratic prejudices.

The views held by Kautsky and his like are a complete renunciation of the very revolutionary principles of Marxism which he championed for decades, especially in his struggle against socialist opportunism (Bernstein, Millerand, Hyndman, Gompers, etc.). It is not a mere accident, therefore, that the "Kautskyans" all over the world have now united in practical politics with the extreme opportunists (through the Second, or the Yellow, International) and with the bourgeois governments (through bourgeois coalition governments in which socialists take part).

The growing world proletarian revolutionary movement in general, and the Communist movement in particular, demands that the theoretical errors of "Kautskyism" be analysed and exposed. The more so since pacifism and "democracy" in general, which have no claim to Marxism whatever, but which, like Kautsky and Co., are obscuring the profundity of the contradictions of imperialism and the inevitable revolutionary crisis to which it gives rise, are still very widespread all over the world. It is the bounden duty of the party of the proletariat to combat these tendencies and to win away from the bourgeoisie the small proprietors who are duped by them, and the millions of toilers who live in more or less petty-bourgeois conditions of life.

V

A few words must be said about chapter VIII entitled: "The Parasitism and Decay of Capitalism." As already pointed out in the text, Hilferding, ex-Marxist, and now a comrade-in-arms of Kautsky, one of the chief exponents of bourgeois reformist policy in the Independent Social-Democratic Party of Germany, has taken a step backward compared with the *frankly* pacifist and reformist Englishman, Hobson, on this question. The international split of the whole labour movement is now quite evident (Second and Third Internationals). Armed struggle and civil war between the two trends is now a recognised fact: the support given to Kolchak and Denikin in Russia by the Mensheviks and Socialist-Revolutionaries against the Bolsheviks; the fight the Scheidemanns, Noskes and Co. have conducted in conjunction with the bourgeoisie against the Spartacists in Germany; the same thing in Finland, Poland, Hungary, etc. What is the economic basis of this historically important world phenomenon?

Precisely the parasitism and decay of capitalism which are the characteristic features of its highest historical stage of development, *i.e.*, imperialism. As has been shown in this pamphlet, capitalism has now brought to the front a *handful* (less than one-tenth of the inhabitants of the globe; less than one-fifth, if the most "generous" and liberal calculations were made) of very rich and very powerful states which plunder the whole world simply by "clipping coupons." Capital exports produce an income of eight to ten billion francs per annum, according to pre-war prices and pre-war bourgeois statistics. Now, of course, they produce much more than that.

Obviously, out of such enormous *super-profits* (since they are obtained over and above the profits which capitalists squeeze out of the workers of their "home" country) it is quite *possible to bribe* the labour leaders and the upper stratum of the labour aristocracy. And the capitalists of the "advanced" countries are bribing them; they bribe them in a thousand different ways, direct and indirect, overt and covert.

This stratum of bourgeoisified workers, or the "labour aristocracy," who are quite philistine in their mode of life, in the size of their earnings and in their outlook, serves as the principal prop of the Second International, and, in our days, the principal *social* (not military) *prop of the bourgeoisie.* They are the real *agents of the bourgeoisie in the labour* movement, the labour lieutenants of the capitalist class, real channels of reformism and chauvinism. In the civil war between the proletariat and the bourgeoisie they inevitably, and in no small numbers, stand side by side with the bourgeoisie, with the "Versaillese" against the "Communards."

Not the slightest progress can be made toward the solution of the practical problems of the Communist movement and of the impending social revolution unless the economic roots of this phenomenon are understood and unless its political and sociological significance is appreciated.

Imperialism is the eve of the proletarian social revolution. This has been confirmed since 1917 on a world-wide scale.

N. LENIN

July 6, 1920

IMPERIALISM, THE HIGHEST STAGE OF CAPITALISM

DURING the last fifteen or twenty years, especially since the Spanish-American War (1898), and the Anglo-Boer War (1899-1902), the economic and also the political literature of the two hemispheres has more and more often adopted the term "imperialism" in order to define the present era. In 1902, a book by the English economist, J. A. Hobson, *Imperialism*, was published in London and New York. This author, who adopts the point of view of bourgeois social reformism and pacifism which, in essence, is identical with the present point of view of the ex-Marxist, K. Kautsky, gives an excellent and comprehensive description of the principal economic and political characteristics of imperialism. In 1910, there appeared in Vienna the work of the Austrian Marxist, Rudolf Hilferding, *Finance Capital*. In spite of the mistake the author commits on the theory of money, and in spite of a certain inclination on his part to reconcile Marxism with opportunism, this work gives a very valuable theoretical analysis, as its sub-title tells us, of "the latest phase of capitalist development." Indeed, what has been said of imperialism during the last few years, especially in a great many magazine and newspaper articles, and also in the resolutions, for example, of the Chemnitz and Basle Congresses which took place in the autumn of 1912, has scarcely gone beyond the ideas put forward, or, more exactly, summed up by the two writers mentioned above.

Later on we shall try to show briefly, and as simply as possible, the connection and relationships between the *principal* economic features of imperialism. We shall not be able to deal with non-economic aspects of the question, however much they deserve to be dealt with. We have put references to literature and other notes which, perhaps, would not interest all readers, at the end of this pamphlet.

CHAPTER I

CONCENTRATION OF PRODUCTION AND MONOPOLIES

THE enormous growth of industry and the remarkably rapid process of concentration of production in ever-larger enterprises represent one of the most characteristic features of capitalism. Modern censuses of production give very complete and exact data on this process.

In Germany, for example, for every 1,000 industrial enterprises, large enterprises, i.e., 'those 'employing more than 50 workers, numbered three in 1882, six in 1895 and nine in 1907; and out of every 100 workers employed, this group of enterprises employed 22, 30 and 37 respectively. Concentration of production, however, is much more intense than the concentration of workers, since labour in the large enterprises is much more productive. This is shown by the figures available on steam engines and electric motors.

CONCENTRATION OF PRODUCTION IN GERMAN INDUSTRY

(In the broad sense, *i.e.*, including commerce, transportation and communications, etc.)

	1882	1895	1907	1925	1933[1]
Number of establishments per thousand employing 50 persons and over	3	6	9	12	8
Number of persons per hundred employed in establishments employing 50 persons and over .	22	30	37	48	38

[1] The diminution in the proportion of big establishments in 1933 was due to the crisis: owing to the diminution in the number of persons employed many establishments were transferred to the smaller size groups.

SOURCES: The figures for 1882, 1895 and 1907 are quoted from Lenin. Those for 1925 and 1933 have been computed from the summaries of industrial censuses published in *Statistik des Deutschen Reichs*, Bd. 413, I. Teil, S. 252, 276-279 and Bd. 462, H. 2, S. 5, 58-61.

If we take what in Germany is called industry in the broad sense of the term, that is, including commerce, transport, etc., we get the following picture: Large-scale enterprises: 30,588 out of a total of 3,265,623, that is to say, 0.9 per cent. These large-scale enterprises employ 5,700,000 workers out of a total of 14,400,000, that is, 39.4 per cent; they use 6,660,000 steam horse power out of a total of 8,800,000, that is 75.3 per cent and 1,200,000 kilowatts of electricity out of a total of 1,500,000, that is, 77.2 per cent.

Less than one-hundredth of the total enterprises utilise *more than three-fourths* of the steam and electric power! Two million nine hundred and seventy thousand small enterprises (employing up to five workers), representing 91 per cent of the total, utilise only 7 per cent of the steam and electric power. Tens of thousands of large-scale enterprises are everything; millions of small ones are nothing.

In 1907, there were in Germany 586 establishments employing one thousand and more workers. They employed nearly *one-tenth* (1,380,000) of the total number of workers employed in industry and utilised *almost one-third* (32 per cent) of the total steam and electric power employed.[1] As we shall see, money capital and the banks make this superiority of a handful of the largest enterprises still more overwhelming, in the most literal sense of the word, since millions of small, medium, and even some big "masters" are in fact in complete subjection to some hundreds of millionaire financiers.

---

[1] *Annalen des Deutschen Reichs (Annals of the German Empire)*, 1911, Zahn.

CONCENTRATION OF PRODUCTION IN GERMAN INDUSTRY

(In the broad sense, *i.e.*, including commerce, transportation and communications, etc.)

	1907	1925	1933[1]
Total number of establishments	3,265,623	3,489,374	3,541,809
No. of big establishments (empl. 50 and over)	30,588	43,099	29,004
Proportion of big establishments (%)	0.9	1.2	0.8

No. employed

	1907	1925	1933
In all establishments ⎱ millions	14.4	18.7	14.6
In big establishments ⎰	5.7	8.9	5.5
Proportion of big establishments (%)	39.4	47.6	38.0

Total motive power directly transferring energy to machines:

	1907	1925	1933
In all establishments ⎱ million h.p.	9.95	19.9	25.3
In big establishments ⎰	7.51	15.7	18.8
Proportion of big establishments (%)	75.5	78.9	74.2

Non-Electric Motive Power: [2]

	1907	1925	1933
In all establishments ⎱ million h.p.	8.8	6.7	6.8
In big establishments ⎰	6.6	5.1	4.7
Proportion of big establishments (%)	75.3	75.8	68.9

Power of Electric Motors:

	1907	1925	1933
In all establishments ⎱ million kw.	1.5	9.7	13.6
In big establishments ⎰	1.2	7.8	10.4
Proportion of big establishments (%)	77.2	80.4	76.2

No. of small establishments (employing up to

	1907	1925	1933
5 wage earners)	2,970,000	3,109,194	3,254,906

Proportion of small establishments to entire industry:

	1907	1925	1933
According to no. of establishments ⎱ (%)	91.0	89.1	91.9
According to amount of steam and ⎰ electric power employed	7.4	7.6	11.4

[1] *Cf.* footnote to page 13.   [2] Lenin terms it steam horse power.

SOURCES: The figures for 1907 are quoted from Lenin; Lenin gives the proportion of small establishments according to steam and electric power employed in the round figure of 7%. The figures for the power of all motors were computed by adding together the power of non-electric (conventionally steam) and electric motors, the kilowatt power of the latter being converted into h.p. (1 h.p. = 0.736 kw). The figures for 1925 and 1933 are taken from the industrial censuses published in *Statistik des Deutschen Reichs*, Bd. 413, I. Teil, S. 252, 276-279 and Bd. 462, H. 2, S. 5, 58-61. The power of electric motors for 1925 and 1933 given in the censuses in terms of h.p. has been converted into kilowatts.

ESTABLISHMENTS IN GERMAN INDUSTRY EMPLOYING 1,000 AND OVER

(In the broad sense, *i.e.*, including commerce, transportation and communications, etc.)

	1907	1925	1933[1]
Number of establishments	586	1,122	639
Number employed (millions)	1.38	2.50	1.22

Proportion of above establishments to entire industry:

	1907	1925	1933
a) according to no. of establishments	0.017	0.032	0.018
b) " " " " employed (%)	9.6	13.4	8.4
c) " " total motive power (%)	32.0	41.2	32.4
d) " " electric motors (%)	32.0	41.6	31.7

[1] *Cf.* footnote to page 13.

SOURCES: The figures for 1907 are quoted from Lenin; Lenin gives the figure 9.6 in round numbers as "one-tenth." The figures for 1925 and 1933 are quoted from the industrial censuses published in *Statistik des Deutschen Reichs*, Bd. 413, I. Teil, S. 252, 276-79 and Bd. 462, H. 2, S. 5, 58-61.

In another advanced country of modern capitalism, the United States, the growth of the concentration of production is still greater. Here statistics single out industry in the narrow sense of the word and group enterprises according to the value of their annual output. In 1904 large-scale enterprises with an annual output of one million dollars and over numbered 1,900 (out of 216,180, i.e., 0.9 per cent). These employed 1,400,000 workers (out of 5,500,000, i.e., 25.6 per cent) and their combined annual output was valued at $5,600,000,000 (out of $14,800,000,000, i.e., 38 per cent). Five years later, in 1909, the corresponding figures were : large-scale enterprises: 3,060 out of 268,491, i.e., 1.1 per cent; employing: 2,000,000 workers out of 6,600,-000, i.e., 30.5 per cent; output: $9,000,000,000 out of $20,700,000,000, i.e., 43.8 per cent.[1]

Almost half the total production of all the enterprises of the country was carried on by a *hundredth part* of those enterprises!

---

[1] *Statistical Abstract of the United States*, 1912, p. 202.

CONCENTRATION OF PRODUCTION IN UNITED STATES MANUFACTURING INDUSTRY

	1904	1909	1914	1914	1923	1929
	(Establishments with total value of products of over $500 per annum)			(Establishments with total value of products of over $5,000 per annum)		
Entire manufacturing industry						
Number of establishments	216,180	268,491	272,518	177,110	196,309	210,959
Number of workers in all establishments (millions)	5.5	6.6	7.0	6.9	8.6	8.8
Products, total value (billion dollars)	14.8	20.7	24.2	24.0	60.6	70.4
Big establishments with an annual output of over 1 million dollars:						
Number of establishments	1,900	3,060	3,819	3,819	10,327	11,763
Number of workers (mill.)	1.4	2.0	2.5	2.5	5.0	5.1
Products, total value (billion dollars)	5.6	9.0	11.8	11.8	40.2	48.8
Proportion of establishments with an annual output over 1 million dollars to total (%):						
According to number of establishments	0.9	1.1	1.4	2.2	5.3	5.6
According to number of workers	25.6	30.5	35.7	36.2	56.8	58.0
According to total value of products	38.0	43.8	48.8	49.2	66.3	69.3

Unlike pre-war censuses, post-war censuses do not take into account very small establishments having an output of 500 to 5,000 dollars per annum. In order to show the significance of this change in the system of computation, the table contains two columns of figures for 1914: the first row includes all establishments having an output of over 500 dollars per annum, while the other includes establishments having an output of over 5,000 dollars per annum. As can be seen from these columns, the exclusion of the very small establishments hardly affects the share of the several groups of establishments of the total number of workers employed and of gross output; but it does materially affect them in regard to their proportion to the total number of establishments.

SOURCES: The figures for 1904 and 1909 are quoted from Lenin. Except for the total number of establishments, the figures for 1914, 1923 and 1929 are taken from the *Statistical Abstract of the United States*, 1932, pp. 730-31. The figures of the total number of establishments for 1914 are taken from the *Biennial Census of Manufactures*, 1923, p. 12; and for the years 1923 and 1929 from the *Fifteenth Census of the United States*, Vol. I, p. 16.

These 3,000 giant enterprises embrace 268 branches of industry. From this it can be seen that, at a certain stage of its development, concentration itself, as it were, leads right to monopoly; for a score or so of giant enterprises can easily arrive at an agreement, while on the other hand, the difficulty of competition and the tendency towards monopoly arise from the very dimensions of the enterprises. This transformation of competition into monopoly is one of the most important—if not the most important—phenomena of modern capitalist economy, and we must deal with it in greater detail. But first we must clear up one possible misunderstanding.

CONCENTRATION OF PRODUCTION IN UNITED STATES MANUFACTURING INDUSTRY

Year	Entire Industry (enterprises with an output over $5,00 per annum)	Establishments employing:			
		Up to 5 workers	From 6 to 50 workers	Over 50 workers	
				Total	Employing over 1,000 workers
Number of establishments					
1909	175,142	70,652	80,742	23,748	540
1914	177,110	75,638	76,833	24,639	648
1929	210,959	103,193	78,546	29,220	996
1933	141,769	61,670	58,752	21,347	—
Number of workers employed (thousands)					
1909	6,473	170	1,405	4,898	1,013
1914	6,896	183	1,344	5,369	1,255
1929	8,839	280	1,410	7,149	2,160
1933	6,056	158	1,046	4,852	—
Mechanical power (thousands h.p.)					
1929	42,931	1,694	5,903	35,334	11,582
PROPORTION TO ENTIRE INDUSTRY (%)					
(According to number of establishments)					
1909	100	40.3	46.1	13.6	0.3
1914	100	42.7	43.4	13.9	0.4
1929	100	48.9	37.2	13.9	0.5
1933	100	43.5	41.4	15.1	—
(According to number of workers employed)					
1909	100	2.6	21.7	75.7	15.6
1914	100	2.7	19.5	77.8	18.2
1929	100	3.2	16.0	80.8	24.4
1933	100	2.6	17.3	80.1	—
(According to motive power)					
1929	100	3.9	13.8	82.3	27,0

SOURCES: *Thirteenth Census of the United States*, 1910, Vol. VIII, pp. 180, 206, 207; *Biennial Census of Manufactures*, 1923, pp. 1180, 1181; *Fifteenth Census of United States Manufactures*, 1929, Vol. I: General Report, pp. 62, 63, 147; *Statistical Abstract of the U.S.*, 1935, p. 716.

CONCENTRATION OF PRODUCTION IN BRITISH INDUSTRY (1930)

Industries	Number of establishments				Number of persons employed (thousands)				Proportion according to number employed (%)			
	from 11 to 49 persons	from 50 to 299 persons	from 300 to 999 persons	1000 persons and over	from 11 to 49 persons	from 50 to 299 persons	from 300 to 999 persons	1000 persons and over	from 11 to 49 persons	from 50 to 299 persons	from 300 to 999 persons	1000 persons and over
Iron and Steel (total)	1,651	1,339	319	68	43	161	163	126	8.7	32.7	33.0	25.6
a) Blast furnaces	67	121	76	39	2	17	42	76	1.5	12.4	30.6	55.5
b) Smelting and rolling	1,506	1,020	239	73	39	122	126	158	8.8	27.4	28.3	35.5
Mechanical engineering	304	230	82	37	8	28	46	110	4.2	14.6	23.9	57.3
Electrical engineering	156	151	63	31	4	19	34	67	3.2	15.3	27.4	54.1
Shipbuilding	420	268	83	39	11	32	47	106	5.6	15.9	24.1	54.4
Motor and cycle												
Aircraft	9			8	0.2		10	12	1.1		44.8	54.1
Non-ferrous metals	794	470	64	5	20	52	31	6	18.3	47.8	28.4	5.5
Textiles (total)	2,244	3,349	662	92	61	443	317	174	6.1	44.5	31.9	17.5
a) cotton spinning	174	560	169	8	5	86	79	20	2.6	45.3	41.6	10.5
b) cotton weaving	230	795	144	13	7	109	64	18	3.4	55.0	32.4	9.2
c) woolen and worsted	415	736	157	28	12	99	77	41	5.2	43.2	33.6	18.0
d) silk & artificial silk	69	94	18	14	2	12	10	36	3.3	20.0	16.7	60.0
Clothing, shoes, headwear & millinery	3,886	1,931	253	32	94	217	118	48	19.7	45.5	24.7	10.1

This table has been compiled on the basis of the first two volumes of the Fourth Census of British Production, as published in 1934, which gives combined statistical data on the concentration of British industry. The accuracy of the figures is diminished by the fact that individual establishments forming part of combines are regarded as independent production units, which lowers the level of concentration. On the other hand, in a number of cases, firms owning several production units of an analogous kind in one locality gave information concerning them as of a single establishment.

The table does not take into account establishments employing less than 11 persons. The proportion of persons employed in these small establishments to the *total* number employed according to industry is as follows:

Iron and steel 6.5%; general engineering 5.3%; electrical engineering 3%; shipbuilding 1.9%; smelting and refining of non-ferrous metals 11%; textiles 1.5%; wool manufacture 1.4%; silk and artificial silk 0.6%; clothing, footwear, headwear and millinery 20.1%.

SOURCE: *Final Report on the Fourth Census of Production* (1930), London, 1934, Vol. I, II.

CONCENTRATION OF PRODUCTION IN FRENCH INDUSTRY

	Without Alsace-Lorraine		Including Alsace-Lorraine	
	1906	1926	1921	1926
Total number of establishments ...	2,335,114	1,515,382	1,721,212	1,560,918
No. of establishments employing over 50 persons	9,091	13,909	12,394	14,737
Proportion of these establishments to total (%)	0.38	0.91	0.72	0.94
No. of persons employed (millions): in all establishments	6.2	6.7	6.3	7.1
in establishments employing over 50 persons	1.9	3.0	2.6	3.2
Proportion of these establishments to total (%)	30.6	44.8	41.3	45.1
Giant establishments employing over 1000 persons: Number of establishments	207	362	311	397
Number of persons employed (millions)	0.5	0.9	0.7	1.0
Proportion of these establishments to all industry (%) According to number of establishments ...	0.008	0.02	0.02	0.03
According to number of persons employed	8.1	13.4	11.1	14.1

SOURCE: *Bulletin de la Statistique Générale de la France*, Avril-Juin, 1933, pp. 404, 406.

DEVELOPMENT OF CONCENTRATION IN JAPAN

	1909	1913	1918	1923	1927	1933
Total number of companies	11,549	15,406	23,028	32,089	38,516	71,196
No. of big companies (with capital over 5 million yen)	38	59	293	589	687	713
Proportion of big companies to total (%)	0.3	0.4	1.3	1.8	1.8	1.0
Paid-up capital of all companies (million yen)	1,367	1,983	4,707	10,194	12,634	14,547
Paid-up capital of big companies with capital of over 5 million yen (million yen).........	495	755	2,523	6,227	8,113	9,264
Proportion of capital of big companies to total capital (%) ..	36.2	38.1	53.6	61.1	64.2	63.7

SOURCES: *Résumé Statistique de l'Empire du Japon*, Tokyo, 1912, p. 108; 1924, p. 72; 1930, p. 46; 1934, p. 4; 1936, pp. 46-47.

CONCENTRATION OF PRODUCTION IN JAPANESE INDUSTRY

Year	All Industry	Establishments employing:		
		from 5 to 50 workers	from 50 to 1000 workers	over 1000 workers
Number of establishments				
1914	31,717	28,550	3,082	85
1926	51,906	46,719	4,939	248
1931	65,026	59,531	5,335	160
1933	72,605	66,596	5,830	179
Number of workers employed (thousands)				
1914	948	366	421	161
1926	1,875	581	782	512
1931	1,766	631	837	298
1933	2,010	732	912	366
PROPORTION TO WHOLE OF INDUSTRY (%) *(According to number of establishments)*				
1914	100	90.0	9.7	0.3
1926	100	90.0	9.5	0.5
1931	100	91.5	8.2	0.3
1933	100	91.7	8.1	0.2
(According to number of workers employed)				
1914	100	38.6	44.4	17.0
1926	100	31.0	41.7	27.3
1931	100	35.7	47.4	16.9
1933	100	36.4	45.4	18.2

The above table shows a reduction in 1931 of the number of giant establishments employing over 1,000 workers, a reduction in the proportion of workers there employed to the total number of workers employed and a slight increase in the number of small establishments.

This is accounted for by the following:

1. The factory statistics on which this table is based do not take into account temporarily employed workers, whose proportion in the large-scale establishments greatly increased during the crisis. For this reason many of the big establishments, actually employing over 1,000 workers, have been classified with smaller establishments inasmuch as the number of workers permanently employed in them was less than 1,000.

2. The factory statistics did not take into account a large number of big establishments engaged in the manufacture of war materials. Thus, in 1931, 35 government establishments (17 engineering works, 6 chemical works, 7 food manufacturing establishments, etc.) and in 1933, 36 establishments were not included in the figures.

3. Owing to the curtailment of production during the crisis, a number of establishments which formerly employed over 1,000 workers reduced their staffs below 1,000 and were therefore classified with the smaller establishments. The staffs of these establishments were still further reduced as a result of rationalisation, which, by speeding up labour to an intense degree, brought about a sharp increase in the output per worker. (In the cotton industry the output of cloth per worker was raised from 26,500 yards per annum in 1926 to 61,300 yards in 1932. In the coal industry the annual output per worker was raised from 149 tons in 1929 to 193 tons in 1932.)

For all these reasons, the figures showing the changes in the number of establishments employing over 1,000 workers do not accurately reflect the actual concentration of production that took place during the period of 1926-31.

The increase in the number of small establishments is due to the fact that, in view of the specific economic conditions in Japan, a number of large establishments consider it more profitable to have parts of the articles they manufacture produced by smaller outside establishments, which are dependent on the larger ones and are severely exploited by them.

SOURCES: *Rodo Tokey Yoran*, 1926-35.

American statistics say: 3,000 giant enterprises in 250 branches of industry, as if there were only a dozen large-scale enterprises for each branch of industry.

But this is not the case. Not in every branch of industry are there large-scale enterprises;

UNEVEN CONCENTRATION OF PRODUCTION

The uneven concentration of production in different industries, which Lenin emphasises, is of decisive importance in explaining the uneven degree to which monopolies embrace different spheres of production.

The following figures indicate how uneven the concentration of production has been in post-war industry. (See table on p. 31.)

PROPORTION OF GIANT ESTABLISHMENTS EMPLOYING OVER 1,000 WORKERS[1]

UNITED STATES INDUSTRY IN 1929[2]

Groups of Industries	Number of giant establishments	Proportion of workers employed to total workers (%)
Transportation equipment	131	66.0
Rubber products	33	65.2
Iron and steel and their products	160	41.7
Products of petroleum and coal	26	37.3
Machinery, not incl. transportation equipment	144	34.8
Railroad repair shops	63	28.5
Non-ferrous metals and their products	40	23.0
Chemicals and allied products	31	22.5
Textiles and their products	192	18.5
Leather and its manufactures	23	12.5
Food and kindred products	48	11.2
Stone, clay and glass products	16	7.2
Forest products	34	6.1
Paper and allied products	9	5.9
Printing, publishing and allied industries	11	5.8

GERMAN INDUSTRY IN 1925

Groups of Industries	Number of giant establishments	Proportion of workers employed to total workers (%)
Mining	210	69.8
Rubber & asbestos	10	51.8
Metallurgy	55	41.6
Electrical machinery	74	39.4
Chemical	35	34.4
Machinery (not incl. electrical)	176	32.6
Textile	99	13.4
Leather	6	8.2
Paper & printing	26	8.1
Metal-working	26	5.4
Stone, clay and glass products	20	3.9
Food and kindred products	30	3.4
Musical instruments & toys	3	3.2
Clothing	14	1.6
Forest products and woodworking	4	0.6

[1] German statistics include wage earners and salaried employees.

[2] In speaking of 3,000 giant enterprises in the United States, Lenin had in mind establishments with an output of over 1 million dollars per annum. Of such establishments there were in United States manufacturing industry 3,060 in 1909 and 11,763 in 1929 (*cf.* table on p. 17). For our table, however, we have taken still larger establishments, *i.e.*, those employing over 1,000 workers. Of such establishments there were in United States manufacturing industry 540 in 1909 and 996 in 1929.

SOURCES: *Fifteenth Census of United States Manufactures*, 1930, Vol. I, p. 63; *Statistik des Deutschen Reichs*, Bd. 413, I. Teil, S. 278-79.

and, moreover, a very important feature of capitalism in its highest stage of development is so-called "combined production," that is to say, the grouping in a single enterprise of different branches of industry, which either represent the consecutive stages in the working up of raw materials (for example, the smelting of iron ore into pig iron, the conversion of pig iron into steel, and then, perhaps, the manufacture of steel goods)—or are auxiliary to one another (for example, the utilisation of waste or of by-products, the manufacture of packing materials, etc.).

"Combination," writes Hilferding, "levels out the fluctuations of trade and therefore assures to the combined enterprises a more stable rate of profit. Secondly, combination has the effect of eliminating trading. Thirdly, it has the effect of rendering possible technical improvements, and, consequently, the acquisition of superprofits over and above those obtained by the 'pure' (i.q., non-combined) enterprises. Fourthly, it strengthens the position of the combined enterprises compared with that of 'pure' enterprises in the competitive struggle in periods of serious depression, when the fall in prices of raw materials does not keep pace with the fall in prices of manufactured articles."[1]

The German bourgeois economist, Heymann, who has written a book especially on "mixed," that is, combined, enterprises in the German iron industry, says: "Pure enterprises perish, crushed between the high price of raw material and the low price of the finished product." Thus we get the following picture:

"There remain, on the one hand, the great coal companies, producing millions of tons yearly, strongly organised in their coal syndicate, and on the other, the great steel works, closely allied to the coal mines, having their own steel syndicate. These giant enterprises, producing 400,000 tons of steel per annum, with correspondingly extensive coal, ore and blast furnace plants, as well as the manufacturing of finished goods, employing 10,000 workers quartered in company houses, sometimes owning their own ports and railroads, are today the standard type of German iron and steel plant. And concentration still continues. Individual enterprises are becoming larger and larger. An ever increasing number of enterprises in one given industry, or in several different industries, join together in giant combines, backed up and controlled by half a dozen Berlin banks. In the German mining industry, the truth of the teachings of Karl Marx on concentration is definitely proved, at any rate in a country like ours where it is protected by tariffs and freight rates. The German mining industry is ripe for expropriation."[2]

Such is the conclusion which a conscientious bourgeois economist, and such are exceptional, had to arrive at. It must be noted that he

---

[1] Rudolf Hilferding, Das Finanzkapital (Finance Capital), Vienna, 1910, p. 239.
[2] Hans Gideon Heymann, Die gemischten Werke im deutschen Grosseisengewerbe (Combined Plants in the German Big Iron Industry), Stuttgart, 1904, pp. 256 and 278.

GROWTH OF COMBINED PLANTS IN INDUSTRY

The process of formation of combined plants in capitalist industry has been very intense during the last two decades. Its main trends have been as follows:

1. *The enormous increase in the size of combined plants.* The size of present-day combined plants can be judged from the following examples:

In the U.S.A.—The United States Steel Corporation has attained unprecedented dimensions (a description of this trust is given on page 51). This trust has embraced every stage of metallurgical production from the mining of iron ore and coal to the gigantic blast furnaces, steel furnaces, rolling mills and plants for coke by-products, etc. The output capacity of the Gary Mills alone, which is an affiliate of the Steel Trust, is 3.1 million tons[1] of pig iron, 5.3 million tons of steel, and 3.4 million tons of rolled metal. This plant has 12 blast furnaces, 49 open-hearth furnaces, 18 rolling mills (including the largest rail-rolling mill in the world, with an output capacity of about 1 million tons), about one thousand coke ovens with apparatus for obtaining by-products, a cement factory with an output capacity of 900,000 tons and a briquette factory. It also has its own electric power plant with a capacity of 160,000 kilowatts, etc.

In Germany.—The Steel Trust (Vereinigte Stahlwerke), which was organised in 1926, is a huge combine, incomparably more powerful than the largest combines in the German pre-war iron and steel industry (a description of this trust is given on pp. 49-51). Besides the Steel Trust, post-war Germany has the following gigantic metallurgical combines: Krupp, Hösch, Klöckner, Gutehoffnungshütte, Mitteldeutsche Stahlwerke and Lincke-Hoffmann-Basch. The Krupp combine alone, whose principal enterprises are situated in Essen and Rheinhausen, by 1929 had an output capacity of 2 million tons of pig iron and 2.3 million tons of steel. In 1929 it employed a total of 89,800 workers. The combine embraces: 35 coal mines with numerous coking plants, 9 open-hearth furnaces, Thomas, crucible and electric smelting departments, 7 rolling departments in Essen, 12 rolling mills in Rheinhausen, a forge and press department, foundry and machine shops, general engineering shops and departments for the manufacture of railway equipment, an iron construction shop and a wheel shop, a cement and brick factory, and numerous armament factories.

2. *The expansion of the sphere of combined production, particularly owing to the intense development of the chemical industry during the war and post-war period.* This is expressed in the following:

---

[1] Metric tons, when not otherwise specified (1 m.ton = 2,204.62 lbs.).

seems to place Germany in a special category because her industries are protected by high tariffs. But the concentration of industry and the formation of monopolist manufacturers' combines, cartels, syndicates, etc.. could only be accelerated by these circumstances.

a) *New industrial branches* joining already existing combines of the old type. Thus, the majority of metallurgical works have now developed the coke by-products industry (Gary, most of the works of the Bethlehem Steel Corp., Krupp in Rheinhausen, etc.), while nitrogen plants are as a rule located in the vicinity. The new Bronn-Linde method of obtaining synthetic nitrogen direct from coke gas has greatly extended the possibilities of combining the chemical industry with the iron and steel industry. Germany now has several such plants with an aggregate capacity of several hundred thousand tons; all of these are under the control of the monopolist coal companies. Besides this we more and more frequently find the combination of iron and steel works with engineering enterprises (Krupp in Essen and Rheinhausen, most of the plants of the Bethlehem Steel Corp., etc.).

b) The creation of special *combined chemical plants* of enormous dimensions, unknown in pre-war times. Such, for instance, is the Leunawerke (I. G. Farbenindustrie), which combines: plants producing synthetic ammonia through the conversion of water gas (capacity: about 300,000 tons of pure nitrogen per annum); a plant for the conversion of ammonia into ammonia-sulphate; a plant for the manufacture of Norwegian nitrates; a plant for the manufacture of mixed fertilisers and a liquefaction of coal plant with an output capacity of 350,000 tons.

In addition, the *complex utilisation of raw materials* is assuming increasing importance: the utilisation of waste gases from copper smelting plants in the sulphuric acid industry (Tennessee plant, U.S.A.), the combining of the caustic soda industry with chloride products (Montecatini, Italy), the combining of the manufacture of plastic materials with coke by-products, the complex utilisation of carnallite for the production of potassium, magnesium chloride, bromide, hydrochloric acid, etc.

c) The creation of combined *power and metallurgical* and *power and chemical* plants. An example of the combination of power and metallurgy is the utilisation of coke gas which is obtained as a by-product in the iron and steel plants in the Ruhr. This gas is transmitted over the long distance pipe lines of the Ruhr Gas Company to a number of towns and works in the Ruhr; and the share of this gas taken by industrial enterprises for power purposes is steadily increasing. From 1928 to 1936 the Ruhr Gas Company increased its sales of gas from 122,000,000 cubic metres to 2,027,000,000 cubic metres. An example of the combination of power, metallurgy and chemicals is the Inn Works in Bavaria, where the hydroelectric power station supplies power to the aluminium works as well as to the nitrogen works.

It is extremely important to note that in free-trade England, concentration *also* leads to monopoly, although somewhat later and perhaps in another form. Professor Hermann Levy, in his special work of research entitled *Monopolies, Cartels and Trusts*, based on data on British economic development, writes as follows:

"In Great Britain it is the size of the enterprise and its capacity which harbour a monopolist tendency. This, for one thing, is due to the fact that the great investment of capital per enterprise, once the concentration movement has commenced, gives rise to increasing demands for new capital for the new enterprises and thereby renders their launching more difficult. Moreover (and this seems to us to be the more important point) every new enterprise that wants to keep pace with the gigantic enterprises that have arisen on the basis of the process of concentration would produce such an enormous quantity of surplus goods that it could only dispose of them either by being able to sell them profitably as a result of an enormous increase in demand or by immediately forcing down prices to a level that would be unprofitable both for itself and for the monopoly combines."

d) The creation of powerful combined plants in certain branches of *light industry.* Here are some examples:

1. The meat packing trust of Swift and Co. (U.S.A.), which combines the manufacture of meat products with the diverse utilisation of waste (bones, bristle, hides, blood, etc.) and its conversion into flour, glue, soap, washing powder, albumen, etc.

2. The Bata Shoe Combine in Zlyn (Czechoslovakia). The output capacity of this factory is from 26 to 30 million pairs of boots and shoes per annum. The combine owns a tannery, an electric power station, a last factory, engineering works with its own foundry, a printing plant, a factory for rubber footwear, a paper and cardboard factory, forests, oil refineries, etc.

3. The Unilever Margarine Trust of Great Britain combines in one gigantic trust palm and other plantations for oil seed, dairy farms, whale-hunting companies, a great number of margarine, soap and glycerine factories, as well as a number of factories for the conversion of by-products. This trust owns its own enterprises for the transportation of raw materials and finished products as well as commercial companies.

In noting the tremendous successes of combines, however, it must be emphasised that under capitalism combined production is handicapped by private ownership, by the narrowness and restriction of markets, by fierce competition, etc.

SOURCES: Marquand, *The Dynamics of Industrial Combinations,* London, 1931, pp. 52-53; Marcus, *Die grossen Chemiekonzerne,* Leipzig, 1929; Marcus, *Die grossen Eisen- und Metallkonzerne,* Leipzig, 1929, S. 46, 91-92, 165; *Iron Age,* 1929-1934; *Berliner Börsenzeitung,* 3, II, 1936; *Steel,* 13, IV, 1936, p. 15.

MONOPOLIES IN GREAT BRITAIN

To illustrate the thesis that "in free-trade England, concentration *also* leads to monopoly," we cite a few outstanding examples showing the rapid growth of monopolies in Great Britain during the last two decades, and particularly in the years of the world economic crisis.

IRON AND STEEL

a) Vickers Limited. This armament firm expanded considerably as a result of the war, and in 1928 it amalgamated its war materials and shipbuilding works with the corresponding plants of the Armstrong concern. In 1929 Vickers-Armstrongs together with Cammel Laird formed the English Steel Corporation, which is now the largest iron and steel concern in the country. Vickers embraces in England and abroad a large number of enterprises producing armaments and war materials, metals, ships.

In England, unlike other countries where protective tariffs facilitate the formation of cartels, monopolist alliances of *entrepreneurs*, cartels and trusts, arise in the majority of cases only when the number of competing enterprises is reduced to "a couple of dozen or so." "Here the influence of the concentration movement on the formation of large industrial monopolies in a whole sphere of industry stands out with crystal clarity." [1]

Fifty years ago, when Marx was writing *Capital*, free competition appeared to most economists to be a "natural law." Official science tried, by a conspiracy of silence, to kill the works of Marx, which by a theoretical and historical analysis of capitalism showed that free competition gives rise to the concentration of production, which, in turn, at a certain stage of development, leads to monopoly. Today, monopoly has become a fact. The economists are writing mountains of books in which they describe the diverse manifestations of monopoly, and continue to declare in chorus that "Marxism is refuted." But facts are stubborn things, as the English proverb says, and they have to be reckoned with, whether we like it or not. The facts show that differences between capitalist countries, *e.g.*, in the matter of protection or free trade, only give rise to insignificant variations in the form of monopolies or in the moment of their appearance; and that the rise of monopolies, as the result of the concentration of production, is a general and fundamental law of the present stage of development of capitalism.

For Europe, the time when the new capitalism *definitely* superseded the old can be established with fair precision: it was the beginning of the twentieth century. In one of the latest compilations on the history of the "formation of monopolies," we read:

"A few isolated examples of capitalist monopoly could be cited from the period preceding 1860; in these could be discerned the embryo of the forms that are common today; but all this undoubtedly represent pre-history. The real beginning of modern monopoly goes back, at the earliest, to the 'sixties. The first important period of development of monopoly commenced with the international industrial depression of the 'seventies and lasted until the beginning of the 'nineties. . . . If we examine the question on a European scale, we will find that the development of free competition reached its apex in the 'sixties and 'seventies. Then it was that England completed the construction of its old style capitalist organisation. In Germany, this organisation had entered into a fierce struggle with handicraft and domestic industry, and had begun to create for itself its own forms of existence. . . ."

---

[1] Hermann Levy, *Monopole, Kartelle und Trusts* (*Monopolies, Cartels and Trusts*), Jena, 1909, pp. 286, 290, 298.

aeroplanes, machines, electrical equipment, etc. It is known to have close connections with Barclays Bank, the Midland Bank and with Glynn, Mills & Co. It owns shares in 12 other big companies (1933). It has enterprises in Canada, Australia, Spain, Rumania, Jugoslavia, Japan, etc. It owns steel mills in 11 districts in the United Kingdom. The total capital (shares and debentures) of the leading companies of this concern, *i.e.*, Vickers-Limited, Vickers-Armstrongs, English Steel Corporation, Cammel Laird and Metro-Vickers (Associated Electrical Industries), amounts to £46,500,000 (1933).

b) United Steel Companies was founded in 1930 through the merger of two companies. It produces 16 per cent of the entire steel output in the United Kingdom, more than 2 million tons of coal, a large quantity of coke and pig iron. In 1932 this concern concluded an agreement with the big firm of Stewarts & Lloyds for the purpose of maintaining a uniform policy in regard to production and sales.

c) In 1929 Dorman, Long & Co. after merging with Bolckow, Vaughan & Co. increased its output capacity to 1.7 million tons of steel, 1.5 million tons of pig iron, 3.5 million tons of coal, 2.5 million tons of iron ore. It owns 7 companies abroad. Total capital, £11,000,000 (1933).

d) British (Guest, Keen & Baldwins) Iron & Steel Company was founded in 1930 by the amalgamation of the interests of Guest, Keen & Nettlefolds with the firm of Baldwin. They employ a total of 60,000 workers. Total capital, £24,700,000 (1933).

e) The Lancashire Steel Corporation was formed in 1930 through the merger of three iron and steel manufacturing firms with the aid of the Bank of England, which obtained the right to appoint a director of the company. This corporation has 4 blast furnaces, 9 open-hearth furnaces, coke ovens, engineering works in Warrington, works in Kirkless, a dock on the Manchester Ship Canal and 13 coal mines which are managed through a special subsidiary company. The capital of the corporation (including the capital of the subsidiary coal company) is £6,000,000 (1933).

THE COAL INDUSTRY

a) The Amalgamated Anthracite Collieries, formed in 1923. In 1931 its coal output amounted to 4 million tons. It now controls 80 per cent of the Welsh and 71 per cent of the entire British output of anthracite. Capital, £8,600,000.

b) The Yorkshire Amalgamated Collieries, formed in 1927. Its output is 3.5 million tons of coal per annum. Capital, £3,700,000.

c) Manchester Collieries Limited, formed in 1929 through the merger

"The great revolutionisation commenced with the crash of 1873, or rather, the depression which followed it and which, with hardly discernible interruptions in the early 'eighties, and the unusually violent, but short-lived boom about 1889, marks twenty-two years of European economic history. . . . During the short boom of 1889-90, the system of cartels was widely resorted to in order to take advantage of the favourable business conditions. An ill-considered policy drove prices still higher than would have been the case otherwise and nearly all these cartels perished ingloriously in the smash. Another five-year period of bad trade and low prices followed, but a new spirit reigned in industry; the depression was no longer regarded as something to be taken for granted: it was regarded as nothing more than a pause before another boom.

"The cartel movement entered its second epoch: instead of being a transitory phenomenon, the cartels became one of the foundations of economic life. They are winning one field after another, primarily, the raw materials industry. At the beginning of the 'nineties the cartel system had already acquired—in the organisation of the coke syndicate on the model of which the coal syndicate was later formed—a cartel technique which could hardly be improved. For the first time the great boom at the close of the nineteenth century and the crisis of 1900-03 occurred entirely—in the mining and iron industries at least—under the *ægis* of the cartels. And while at that time it appeared to be something novel, now the general public takes it for granted that large spheres of economic life have been, as a general rule, systematically removed from the realm of free competition." [1]

Thus, the principal stages in the history of monopolies are the following: 1) 1860-70, the highest stage, the apex of development of free competition; monopoly is in the barely discernible, embryonic stage. 2) After the crisis of 1873, a wide zone of development of cartels; but they are still the exception. They are not yet durable. They are still a transitory phenomenon. 3) The boom at the end of the nineteenth century and the crisis of 1900-03. Cartels become one of the foundations of the whole of economic life. Capitalism has been transformed into imperialism.

Cartels come to an agreement on the conditions of sale, terms of payment, etc. They divide the markets among themselves. They fix the quantity of goods to be produced. They fix prices. They divide the profits among the various enterprises, etc.

---

[1] Th. Vogelstein: *Die finanzielle Organisation der kapitalistischen Industrie und die Monopolbildungen* (*Financial Organisation of Capitalist Industry and the Formation of Monopolies*) in *Grundriss der Sozialökonomik* (*Outline of Social Economics*). 1914, Tüb., Sec. VI, pp. 222 *et seq*. See also by the same author: *Organisationsformen des Eisenindustrie und der Textilindustrie in England und Amerika*, Bd. I., Lpz. 1910 (*The Organisational Forms of the Iron and Textile Industries of England and America*, Vol. I, Leipzig, 1910).

of 10 coal firms in Lancashire. This company has 20 mines with docks and warehouses, with coke ovens and plants for different by-products. It employs 19,000 workers. Capital, £5,500,000.

d) Welsh Associated Collieries, formed in 1930. Annual output capacity, 9 million tons of coal. Capital, £8,200,000.

In accordance with the Coal Mines Acts passed in 1930 and 1932 a number of regional combines have been organised in the United Kingdom for the control of production and prices as well as for the rationalisation of the industry. In the beginning of 1934 there were 17 such regional combines.

THE CHEMICAL INDUSTRY

Imperial Chemical Industries, formed in 1926. Capital, £77,000,000 (1934). (*Cf.* description on page 57.)

THE TEXTILE INDUSTRY

a) The Lancashire Cotton Corporation formed in 1929 with the assistance of the Bank of England. It amalgamated 139 mills working on American cotton. Fifty-three of these mills of an aggregate value of £3,000,000 were totally scrapped. The company now owns 6.25 million spindles comprising 13 per cent of all the spindles in the United Kingdom. Capital, £11,035,000.

b) Fine Cotton Spinners' and Doublers' Association Ltd.; owns over 5,000,000 spindles, *i.e.*, about 28 per cent of all spindles of the Egyptian section (1927); capital, £8,350,000.

c) Combined Egyptian Mills formed in 1929 by the amalgamation of mills working on Egyptian cotton; owns a total of 3.2 million spindles, *i.e.*, 19.6 per cent of all the spindles in the Egyptian section. Capital, £2,882,000.

d) Courtaulds, Ltd., artificial silk manufacturers, controls 80 per cent of the entire output of artificial silk in Great Britain. It is closely connected with artificial silk trusts in other countries. Capital, £32,000,000.

THE FOOD INDUSTRY

Unilever, Ltd. was organised in 1927-30 by the amalgamation of three margarine concerns, Jurgens (Great Britain), Van den Berghs (Holland), and the British margarine concern, Lever Brothers. During the crisis this combine acquired control of a number of other companies. It now controls the greater part of the margarine industry in Europe. It also has interests in oil presses, oil refineries and allied enterprises. It represents

The number of cartels in Germany was estimated at about 250 in 1896 and at 385 in 1905, with about 12,000 firms participating.[1] But

---

[1] Dr. Riesser, *Die deutschen Grossbanken und ihre Konzentration im Zusammenhang mit der Entwicklung der Gesamtwirtschaft in Deutschland* (*The German Big Banks and their Concentration in Connection with the Development of the General Economy in Germany*), fourth ed., 1912, p. 149; cf. also Robert Liefmann, *Kartelle und Trusts und die Weiterbildung der volkswirtschaftlichen Organisation* (*Cartels and Trusts and the Further Development of Economic Organisation*), second ed., 1910, p. 25.

a combine of 400 companies; it owns and controls plants and distributing organisations in 51 countries. The aggregate capital of only 38 of the largest companies of this trust amounts to £204,000,000.

THE AUTOMOBILE INDUSTRY

Morris Motors Limited, formed in 1919. In 1926 it merged with Hollick & Pratt, Morris Engines and Osberton Radiators. It owns automobile plants in Cowley, Oxford and Coventry. It turns out about one half of the automobiles manufactured in Great Britain and employs 10,000 workers. Capital, £5,000,000.

TRANSPORTATION

By the Railway Act of 1921, 121 railroad companies were compelled to merge into 4 monopolist companies, which in 1935 had a capital of £1,103,000,000. These operate 19,266 miles of railways, steamships (77,417 net register tons), docks, ports, wharves and hotels. In 1933 three of these companies entered into a financial and operating agreement.

In 1933 all the city and suburban passenger transportation systems of London combined under the London Passenger Transport Board.

In addition to the above, a number of the old monopolies have greatly expanded during the post-war period, e.g., the Royal-Dutch Shell in the oil industry, the White Star Line and Cunard Line in the shipping trade and the Coates sewing-cotton trust.

SOURCES: *The Stock Exchange Official Yearbook*, 1934; Fox, *The Food Combines*, 1931, p. 5; *Der Deutsche Volkswirt*, Nos. 16, 36, 39, 41,. 1934; *Automotive Industry and Trade of Great Britain and Ireland*, 1928, pp. 9-10; Neumann, *Economic Organisation of the British Coal Industry*, 1934, pp. 92, 151, 153, 154; P. Fitzgerald, *Industrial Combinations in England*, 1927, p. 12; Ministry of Transport, Returns of the Railway Companies of Great Britain for the year 1935.

NUMBER OF CARTELS IN GERMANY[1]

1865	1887	1896	1905	1911	1922	1925	1930
4	70	250	385	550—600	1,000	1,500	2,100

The statistics on cartels also take into account various kinds of trade agreements, conventions and price agreements. These agreements are frequently of a temporary and unstable nature. It is quite evident that the leading role in monopolist capital is enjoyed by a score or more of

[1] Figures for 1865 estimated by Sombart; 1887, Phillipovich; 1896 and 1905, quoted from Lenin; 1911, Tschierschky; 1922, Liefmann; 1925, Metzner; 1930, Wagenführ.

it is generally recognised that these figures are underestimations. From the statistics of German industry for 1907 we quoted above, it is evident that even 12,000 large enterprises control certainly more than half the steam and electric power used in the country. In the United States, the number of trusts in 1900 was 185, and in 1907, 250.

American statistics divide all industrial enterprises into three categories, according to whether they belong to individuals, to private firms or to corporations. These latter in 1904 comprised 23.6 per cent, and in 1909, 25.9 per cent (*i.e.*, more than one-fourth of the total industrial enterprises in the country). These employed in 1904, 70.6 per cent, and in 1909, 75.6 per cent (*i.e.*, more than three-fourths) of the total wage earners. Their output amounted at these two dates to $10,900,000,000 and to $16,300,000,000, *i.e.* to 73.7 per cent and 79 per cent of the total respectively.

Not infrequently cartels and trusts concentrate in their hands seven or eight tenths of the total output of a given branch of industry. The Rhine-Westphalian Coal Syndicate, at its foundation in 1893, controlled 86.7 per cent of the total coal output of the area. In 1910, it controlled 95.4 per cent.[1] The monopoly so created assures enormous profits, and leads to the formation of technical productive units of formidable magnitude.

---

[1] Dr. Fritz Kestner, *Der Organisationszwang. Eine Untersuchung über die Kämpfe zwischen Kartellen und Aussenseitern* (*The Compulsion to Organise. An Investigation of the Struggles between Cartels and Outsiders*), Berlin, 1912, p. 11.

the largest national cartels of the type of the Rhine-Westphalian Coal Syndicate, the German Steel Cartel, cement combines, etc.

For a number of other countries the following estimates are available concerning the number of cartels for the year 1931: Great Britain 170; France 80; Austria 100; Czechoslovakia 120; Hungary 70; Switzerland 85. According to the figures published by the German Institute for Business Research, cartels control about 50 per cent of industrial production in Germany, 50 per cent in Austria, 37 per cent in Poland.

SOURCES: *Allgemeines Statistisches Archiv*, 1932, B. 22, H. 2, S. 243, 249.

GROWTH OF CORPORATIONS IN THE U.S.A.[1]

	1904	1909	1919	1929
Gross value of products of establishments belonging to corporations (in billion dollars)	10.9	16.3	54.7	64.9
Share of corporations in entire industry (%)				
According to number of establishments	23.6	25.9	31.5	48.3
According to number of workers employed	70.6	75.6	86.6	89.9
According to gross value of products	73.7	79.0	87.7	92.2

[1] Post-war censuses do not include establishments with products valued at from $500 to $5000 per annum.

SOURCES: The figures for 1904 and 1909 are quoted from Lenin. The figures for 1919 and 1929 are taken from the *Fifteenth Census of United States Manufactures*, 1929, Vol. I, p. 95.

THE RHINE-WESTPHALIAN COAL SYNDICATE

Changes in the syndicate's share:

	1893	1910	1913	1920	1925	1930
In production of the Rhine-Westphalian district	86.7	95.4	—	98.2	99.0	99.6
In the total production of Germany	45.4	55.4	—	66.7	77.9	74.5
In the production of coke	—	—	61.3	—	—	90.0
In Germany's coal exports	—	—	—	—	—	82.0

SOURCES: The figures for 1893 and 1910 are quoted from Lenin. The figures for other years are taken from the *Bericht des Rheinisch-Westfälischen Kohlensyndikats*, 1931-32.

The famous Standard Oil Company in the United States was founded in 1900:

"It has an authorised capital of $150,000,000. It issued $100,000,000 common and $106,000,000 preferred stock. From 1900 to 1907 the following dividends were paid on this stock: 48, 48, 45, 44, 36, 40, 40, 40 per cent, in the respective years, *i.e.*, in all, $367,000,000. From 1882 to 1907, out of a total net profits to the amount of $889,000,000, $606,000,000 were distributed in dividends, and the rest went to reserve capital.[1] . . . In 1907 the various works of the United States Steel Corporation employed no less than 210,180 workers and other employees. The largest enterprise in the German mining industry, the Gelsenkirchen Mining Company (*Gelsenkirchner Bergwerksgesellschaft*) employed in 1908 46,048 persons." [2]

---

[1] Robert Liefmann, *Beteiligungs- und Finanzierungsgesellschaften. Eine Studie über den modernen Kapitalismus und das Effektenwesen (Holding and Finance Companies—A Study in Modern Capitalism and Securities)*, first ed., Jena, 1909, p. 212.

[2] *Ibid.*, p. 218.

THE STANDARD OIL COMPANY GROUP

Owing to the so-called Anti-Trust Act, the Standard Oil Company was split up in 1911 and formed 34 subsidiary companies. Officially these are "independent" companies but it is known that they are unified under single control. The largest of them and the one that plays the leading role is the Standard Oil Company (New Jersey).

The changes in capital and dividends of the Standard Oil Companies are as follows:

CAPITAL (million dollars)

1900	1913	1920	1925	1931
Entire Standard Oil Group		*Standard Oil Co. (New Jersey)*		
150	100	310	825	750

CASH DIVIDENDS (million dollars)

Entire Standard Oil Group		*All companies of Standard Oil Group*	*Standard Oil Co. (New Jersey)*
1882-1907	1900-07	1912-30	1913-34
606	367	2,684	735

In addition to this, from 1911 to the middle of 1928, all the companies in the Standard Oil group paid dividends in the form of new stock amounting to $1,450,000,000.

The stock dividends paid in addition to cash dividends were so great that the rate, compared with the original share capital, amounted during the period of 1912-22 to the following: Standard Oil (N. J.) 400%; Standard Oil of N.Y. 600%; Atlantic Refining Co. 900%; Continental Oil Co. 1,100%; Standard Oil of Indiana 3,150%.

CASH DIVIDENDS (%)

Entire Standard Oil Group

1900-01	1902	1903	1904	1905-07
48	45	44	36	40

Standard Oil Company (N. J.) only

1913	1914-22	1923-25	1929	1930-32
60	20	4	7.5	8

It must be borne in mind that the rate of dividends had been artificially reduced during the post-war years, especially during 1923-25, owing to the watering of the total share capital and, in particular, owing to the payment of dividends in the form of stock and to the placing of large sums to reserve, as can be seen from the following table:

RESERVE CAPITAL (million dollars)

Entire Standard Oil group	Standard Oil Co. (N. J.) only		
1882-1907	1913	1929	1931
283	151.7	628.0	688.9

Concerning the power of the entire Standard Oil group, *Die Wirtschaftskurve* for 1926 says the following: "The market value of the shares of the companies which became 'independent' in 1912 and which, therefore, belong to the Standard Oil group in the narrow sense of the word, reached approximately 20 billion marks in 1925. This does not include the value of the shares of the subsidiaries of these companies."

SOURCES: *Annuaire du Pétrole*, 1929, pp. 592-3; *Moody's Industrials*, 1930, p. 3021, 1932, p. 3878, 1935, p. 3042-46; *Handbuch der Internationalen Petroleumindustrie*, 1931-32, S. 847; *Wirtschaftskurve*, 1926, H. II, S. 195; Laidler, *Concentration in American Industry*, 1931, p. 25.

THE GERMAN STEEL TRUST (VEREINIGTE STAHLWERKE)

The largest enterprise in the mining and metal industry in Germany today is the gigantic trust, Vereinigte Stahlwerke, which was formed in 1926 with a share capital of 800 million marks, and which absorbed the largest iron and steel trusts in Germany, including the Gelsenkirchen Mining Company (exclusive of its coal mines) referred to by Lenin.

In 1929 the trust employed 177,000 workers and salaried employees. In 1933 this trust's share of the country's production was as follows: coal 20%; pig iron 50%; steel 40%.

Vereinigte Stahlwerke constitutes at present the largest combined plant in the German iron and steel industry. It controls every link in the production process from the extraction of raw materials to the finished product.

THE TRUST'S ASSETS AT THE BEGINNING OF 1933

Coal fields	360 mill. m²
Iron ore fields	2,700 " "
Railways	1,300 km.
Locomotives	421
Cars	11,500
Docks	14
Electric power stations	481,000 kw.

OUTPUT CAPACITY OF THE TRUST'S ENTERPRISES (1931-32)

(million tons)

Coal mines	36.0	Blast furnaces	9.7
Coking plants	10.0	Steel foundries	9.3

In 1902, the United States Steel Corporation had already produced 9,000,000 tons of steel.[1] Its output constituted in 1901, 66.3 per cent, and in 1908, 56.1 per cent of the total output of steel in the United States.[2] The output of mineral ore was 43.9 per cent and 46.3 per cent respectively.

[1] Dr. S. Tschierschky, *Kartelle und Trusts*, Göttingen, 1903, p. 13.
[2] Vogelstein, *Organisationsformen* (*Forms of Organisation*), p. 275.

In the autumn of 1933 the steel trust was reorganised and its share capital was reduced to 560 million marks. The effect of the reorganisation was to strengthen the trust's financial control over all its component enterprises, while technical and production concentration was relaxed. The trust is now split up into 13 formally "independent" companies; actually, however, they are the component parts of a single monopoly. Business connected with finance, investments and the purchase of raw materials continues to be transacted by the trust. It is noteworthy that the actual head of the trust, Thyssen, is on the directorates of all the companies.

SOURCES: *Die Bank*, 8, XI, 1933, S. 1611; *Deutsche Bergwerkszeitung*, 29, XI, 1933; *Grünbuch der Aktiengesellschaften*, 1933, Bd. II, S. 1781, 1783-85, 1797.

U. S. STEEL CORPORATION

Subsequent development led to an immense expansion of the output capacity of this trust: in 1929 its steel production amounted to 21.9 million long tons. It then employed 237,000 workers. From 1901 (the year of its foundation) to 1930 it produced 462 million long tons of steel and made 4,482 million dollars profit. Its fixed capital in 1932 was estimated at 1,651 million dollars. The drop in the corporation's share of the total steel output of the country, which Lenin notes, continued also in subsequent years; in 1931 its share of the total iron ore output was 43.3 per cent and steel—38.9 per cent. This drop is due to the rise in importance of a number of other iron and steel monopolies, such as the Bethlehem Steel Corporation, Republic Steel Corporation, etc.

The U. S. Steel Corporation is the most perfect type of "combined production," of a "technical productive unit of formidable magnitude" of which Lenin speaks. The trust owns 143 establishments embracing every link of the production process from the extraction of raw materials to the finished product. They include rail and water transportation for carrying raw materials and finished products, and establishments for the storage and sale of the products.

SOURCES: *Annual Report of the American Iron and Steel Institute*, 1931; *Metal Statistics*, 1931, pp. 177-78, and the annual reports of the Steel Corporation; *Tabulated History of U.S. Steel Corporation*, 1901-33; *The Wall Street Journal*, June 2, 1934.

The report of the American Government Commission on Trusts states:

"The superiority of the trust over competitors is due to the magnitude of its enterprises and their excellent technical equipment. Since its inception, the Tobacco Trust has devoted all its efforts to the substitution of mechanical for manual labour on an extensive scale. With this end in view, it bought up all patents that had anything to do with the manufacture of tobacco and spent enormous sums for this purpose. Many of these patents at first proved to be of no use, and had to be modified by the engineers employed by the trust. At the end of 1906, two subsidiary companies were formed solely to acquire patents. With the same object in view, the trust built its own foundries, machine shops and repair shops. One of these establishments, that in Brooklyn, employs on the average 300 workers; here experiments are carried out on inventions concerning the manufacture of cigarettes, cheroots, snuff, tinfoil for packing, boxes, etc. Here, also, inventions are perfected." [1]

"Other trusts also employ so-called developing engineers whose business it is to devise new methods of production and to test technical improvements. The United States Steel Corporation grants big bonuses to its workers and engineers for all inventions suitable for raising technical efficiency, or for reducing cost of production." [2]

---

[1] *Report of the Commission of Corporations on the Tobacco Industry*, Washington, 1909, p. 266, cited according to Dr. Paul Tafel, *Die nordamerikanischen Trusts und ihre Wirkungen auf den Fortschritt der Technik* (*North American Trusts and their Effect on Technical Progress*), Stuttgart, 1913, p. 48.

[2] Dr. P. Tafel, *ibid.*, pp. 48-49.

MONOPOLISATION OF INVENTION

The degree to which inventions and technical progress are monopolised under post-war capitalism may be judged from the following facts concerning American trusts:

1. The American Telephone & Telegraph Co. (capital 2 billion dollars), which controls 99 per cent of the telephone stations in the U.S.A., maintains a staff of about 4,000 research workers and spends annually 15 million dollars on research work. The company owns or controls over 9,000 different patents.

2. The Westinghouse Electric & Mfg. Co. (capital 200 million dollars), in whose hands are concentrated over 25 per cent of the output of American electrical generators, transformers, etc., spends annually 2.3 million dollars on scientific research.

3. Du Pont de Nemours & Co. (total assets of all units 600 million dollars in 1933) has been spending in recent years an average of 3.5 million dollars annually for the same purpose; and in 1933 the amount spent was almost 6 million dollars.

4. The General Electric Co. (capital 225 million dollars) employs in its scientific research laboratory in Schenectady approximately 3,000 engineers; the annual expenditure for this purpose ranges from 10 to 15 million dollars. Men like Edison, Steinmetz and other scientists of world-wide reputation have been employed in its laboratories.

The famous Edison Institute in Menlo Park and, later, in Orange, N. J., while formally independent, actually serves only a few monopolist firms in the electrical industry.

Edison's patents, which in his early years he transferred to the Western Electric Co., subsequently fell into the hands of the American Telephone & Telegraph Co. In his later years Edison was closely connected with the General Electric Co., and partially also with Ford. In the Edison Institute specialisation has been carried to extreme limits: each member of the staff is given a small assignment in one special subject and the results of his work are summarised by the director. In this manner, Edison succeeded in amassing 1,200 patents during the 84 years of his life.

SOURCES: *Die Chemische Industrie*, 1932-34; *Chemical and Metallurgical Engineering*, 1932-34; *Stock Exchange Official Yearbook*, 1933, p. 1403; *Wirtschaftsdienst*, 1929, No. 19, S. 797.

In German large-scale industry, *e.g.*, in the chemical industry, which has developed so enormously during these last few decades, the promotion of technical improvement is organised in the same way. By 1908, the process of concentration production had already given rise to two main groups which, in their way, were in the nature of monopolies. First these groups represented "dual alliances" of two pairs of big factories, each having a capital of from twenty to twenty-one million marks: on the one hand, the former Meister Factory at Höchst and the Cassella Factory at Frankfort-on-Main; and on the other hand, the aniline and soda factory at Ludwigshafen and the former Bayer Factory at Elberfeld. In 1905, one of these groups, and in 1908 the other group, each concluded a separate agreement with yet another big factory. The result was the formation of two "triple alliances," each with a capital of from forty to fifty million marks. And these "alliances" began to come "close" to one another, to reach "an understanding" about prices, etc.[1]

Competition becomes transformed into monopoly. The result is immense progress in the socialisation of production. In particular, the process of technical invention and improvement becomes socialised.

---

[1] Riesser, *op. cit.*, third ed., pp. 547-48. The newspapers (June 1916) report the formation of a new gigantic trust which is to combine the chemical industry of Germany.

THE GERMAN CHEMICAL TRUST (I. G. FARBENINDUSTRIE)

The concentration of the German chemical industry proceeded at a great rate during the imperialist war and after. This brought about the formation of the German chemical trust. In 1916 a pact was concluded on the "community of interests" (*Interessen-Gemeinschaft*) between the two "triple alliances" of which Lenin speaks. The pact dealt mainly with the regulation of prices, sales, etc. In this manner the foundation was laid for the "gigantic trust" which actually monopolised the chemical industry of Germany. The I. G. Farbenindustrie has been in existence in its present form since the autumn of 1925. It controls the whole of the basic chemical industry: over 80 per cent of synthetic nitrogen, nearly 100 per cent of synthetic gasoline and dyes, 40 per cent of pharmaceutical products, 25 per cent of artificial silk, etc. The productive capacity of the two biggest nitrogen plants of the I.G. (Merseburg and Oppau) in 1931 was estimated at from 900,000 to one million tons, while the productive capacity of the entire nitrogen industry in Germany is now more than 1.3 million tons in 1932-33.

The I. G. also owns the largest plant in the world producing synthetic gasoline, the Leunawerke (capacity 350,000 tons). The share capital of I. G. in 1933 amounted to one million marks; in 1935 its fixed assets amounted to 423 million marks. On January 1, 1936, the chemical plants of the trust employed 98,000 workers and office employees, and if the auxiliary enterprises (coal mines, etc.) are added the number employed will be 148,000. Notwithstanding the crisis, I. G. in 1932 and 1933 paid fairly high dividends—7 per cent (compared with 12 per cent in 1929.)

The comparatively favourable financial position of the trust is to be explained, of course, by the large war orders it receives. Its power extends far beyond the borders of Germany. It is closely connected with the Kuhlmann Chemical Trust in France and with the Swiss, Austrian and Norwegian chemical industries. It owns subsidiaries in the U.S.A. In the United States I. G. is connected by agreements with the Standard Oil Co. (synthetic oil) and with Ford (synthetic rubber). It is also connected with the Imperial Chemical Industries in Great Britain (dyes), etc.

SOURCES: Dorothy Woodman, *Hitler Rearms*, London. 1934, pp. 223, 225; *Die Chemische Industrie*, 13, VI. 1936, S. 509, 511; *Moody's Industrials*, 1932, pp. 1919-21; A. Marcus, *Die Grossen Chemiekonzerne*, Leipzig, 1929, S. 29, 58; *Berliner Börsenzeitung*, 8, VI, 1936; Chekin, *Present State of the World Nitrogen Industry*, Magazine of the Chemical Industry (in Russian), 1931, No. 21/22, pp. 38-39.

This is no longer the old type of free competition between manufacturers, scattered and out of touch with one another, and producing for an unknown market. Concentration has reached the point at which it is possible to make an approximate estimate of all sources of raw materials (for example, the iron ore deposits) of a country and even, as we shall see, of several countries, or of the whole world. Not only are such estimates made, but these sources are captured by gigantic monopolist combines. An approximate estimate of the capacity of markets is also made, and the combines divide them up amongst themselves by agreement. Skilled labour is monopolised, the best engineers are engaged; the means of transport are captured: railways in America, shipping companies in Europe and America. Capitalism in its imperialist stage arrives at the threshold of the most complete socialisation of production. In spite of themselves, the capitalists are dragged, as it were, into a new social order, a transitional social order from complete free competition to complete socialisation.

Production becomes social, but appropriation remains private. The social means of production remain the private property of a few. The general framework of formally recognised free competition remains, but the yoke of a few monopolists on the rest of the population becomes a hundred times heavier, more burdensome and intolerable.

IMPERIAL CHEMICAL INDUSTRIES, LIMITED

The British chemical trust, the next largest trust in Europe after the German I. G. Farbenindustrie, was formed in 1926 as a result of the merger of a number of large companies. At the head of it up to 1931 stood Alfred Mond (Lord Melchett). After his death his position was taken by Harry McGowan. At present the trust is divided into the following 8 groups; 1) basic chemicals, 2) mineral fertilisers, 3) alkalis, 4) explosives 5) metals, 6) lime, 7) dyes, 8) rexin (leather substitute). All these groups are under the control of one financial organisation. The Imperial Chemical Industries Ltd. controls 95 per cent of the British output of basic chemicals, 95 to 100 per cent of nitrogen and 40 per cent of dyes. The nitrogen plant in Billingham—one of the largest in the world—has a productive capacity of 250,000 tons of pure nitrogen per annum. In addition a plant for the liquefaction of coal with an output capacity of 150,000 tons of synthetic gasoline per annum was started in 1935. On December 31, 1935, its paid-up share capital amounted to £77,000,000. In 1930 the trust employed approximately 50,000 workers. The following table shows the movement of I. C. I.'s profits:

	1928	1929	1930	1931	1932	1933	1934-36
Gross profit (£million)	5.99	6.50	5.13	4.67	6.42	7.66	—
Dividends (%)	8	8	6	4.5	6	7.5	8

In 1932 profits increased 37 per cent in comparison with the previous year, and in 1933 they increased an additional 20 per cent. This is to be accounted for primarily by increased war orders.

Imperial Chemical Industries is closely connected with the American Allied Chemical and Dye Corporation. In 1928 the Finance Company of Great Britain and America was organised with Alfred Mond at the head. In addition, the Nobel Dynamite Trust of Great Britain (now incorporated in I.C.I.) is closely connected with American and German explosives manufacturers.

In the beginning of 1932 this trust joined the European aniline dyes cartel; in other words, it established contact with the German chemical trust. This contact, however, does not hinder these two chemical giants from waging a fierce competitive struggle for markets and spheres of influence, particularly in Czechoslovakia, Rumania, in the Eastern markets, etc.

SOURCES: A. Marcus, *Die Grossen Chemiekonzerne*, Leipzig, 1929, p. 7; *Die wirtschaftlichen Kräfte der Welt* (Dresdner Bank), 1930, p. 40; Chekin, *op. cit.*, p. 41; *U.S. Department of Commerce Reports:* "British Chemical Development," 1932, p. 3; *Deutsche Bergwerkszeitung*, 17, X, 1935; *Manchester Guardian*, 15, IV, 1933; *Stock Exchange Official Yearbook*, 1934, p. 2003, 1936, p. 1346; *Moody's Industrials*, 1932, 1934; *Die Chemische Industrie*, 18, IV, 1936, S. 330; *The Economist*, 1, V, 1937, p. 302.

The German economist, Kestner, has written a book especially on the subject of "the struggle between the cartels and outsiders," *i.e.*, enterprises outside the cartels. He entitled his work *Compulsory Organisation*, although, in order to present capitalism in its true light, he should have given it the title: "Compulsory Submission to Monopolist Combines." This book is edifying if only for the list it gives of the modern and civilised methods that monopolist combines resort to in their striving towards "organisation."

They are as follows: 1. Stopping supplies of raw materials ("one of the most important methods of compelling adherence to the cartel"); 2. Stopping the supply of labour by means of "alliances" (*i.e.*, of agreements between employers and the trade unions by which the latter permit their members to work only in cartelised enterprises); 3. Cutting off deliveries; 4. Closing of trade outlets; 5. Agreements with the buyers, by which the latter undertake to trade only with the cartels; 6. Systematic price cutting (to ruin "outside" firms, *i.e.*, those which refuse to submit to the monopolists. Millions are spent in order to sell goods for a certain time below their cost price; there were instances when the price of benzine was thus lowered from 40 to 22 marks, *i.e.*, reduced almost by half!); 7. Stopping credits; 8. Boycott.

This is no longer competition between small and large-scale industry, or between technically developed and backward enterprises. We see here the monopolies throttling those which do not submit to them, to their yoke, to their dictation. This is how this process is reflected in the mind of a bourgeois economist:

"Even in the purely economic sphere," writes Kestner, "a certain change is taking place from commercial activity in the old sense of the word towards organisational-speculative activity. The greatest success no longer goes to the merchant whose technical and commercial experience enables him best of all to understand the needs of the buyer, and who is able to discover and effectively awake a latent demand; it goes to the speculative genius [?!] who knows how to estimate, or even only to sense in advance the organisational development and the possibilities of connections between individual enterprises and the banks." [1]

Translated into ordinary human language this means that the development of capitalism has arrived at a stage when, although commodity production still "reigns" and continues to be regarded as the basis of economic life, it has in reality been undermined and the big profits go to the "geniuses" of financial manipulation. At the basis of these swindles and manipulations lies socialised production; but the immense progress of humanity, which achieved this socialisation, goes to benefit the speculators. We shall see later how "on these grounds" reactionary, petty-

Kestner, *op. cit.*, p. 241.—*Ed.*

COMPULSORY CARTELISATION DURING THE YEARS OF THE WORLD ECONOMIC CRISIS

One of the most important features of the process of growth of monopolies during the world economic crisis is the widespread application by a number of governments of measures for compulsory cartelisation. Such direct state support of monopolies is most widely practised in fascist Germany. Preparations for war is one of the important motives for this.

Germany: On July 15, 1933, a law was promulgated providing for compulsory cartelisation. On the basis of this law the following measures were carried out in the industries enumerated:

Watchmaking .... The erection of new factories prohibited.   March 1934

Cigarettes and tobacco.. All manufacturers compelled to form cartel. Erection of new factories and extension of old ones prohibited.   April and June 1934

Paper and cardboard... Temporary compulsory cartel formed. Regulation of sales introduced. Erection of new factories and extension of old ones prohibited.   August-October 1933, May 1934

Soap industry.......... Compulsory cartel formed.   Jan. and May 1934

Glass industry.......... Compulsory cartel formed. Sales and price regulations introduced. Acquisition and use of automatic machines prohibited. Control of investments introduced.   February 1934

Wire netting........... Existing cartel reorganised; all outsiders compelled to join.   January 1934

Drawn steel wire........ All outsiders compelled to join one of the two existing cartels while negotiations proceeded to amalgamate the two. Erection of new factories and the opening of those that had been closed temporarily prohibited.   October 1933

River shipping......... All companies operating on the Elbe and Oder compelled to form temporary cartel.   September 1933

Lime and solutions of lime .... All outsiders compelled to join the Berlin cartel. Erection of new plants prohibited.   August 1933, July 1934

Jute fabrics............ Erection of new mills and increase in number of looms prohibited.   November 1933

(Continued on p. 61)

bourgeois critics of capitalist imperialism dream of going *back* to "free," "peaceful," and "honest" competition.

"The prolonged raising of prices which results from the formation of cartels," says Kestner, "has hitherto been observed only in relation to the most important means of production, particularly coal, iron and potassium, but has never been observed for any length of time in relation to manufactured goods. Similarly, the increase in profits resulting from that has been limited only to the industries which produce means of production. To this observation we must add that the raw materials industry not only has secured advantages from the cartel formation in regard to the growth of income and profitableness, to the detriment of the finished goods industry, but that it has secured also a *dominating position* over the latter, which did not exist under free competition."[1]

The words which we have italicised reveal the essence of the case which the bourgeois economists admit so rarely and so unwillingly, and which the modern defenders of opportunism, led by K. Kautsky, so zealously try to evade and brush aside. Domination, and violence that is associated with it, such are the relationships that are most typical of the "latest phase of capitalist development"; this is what must inevitably result, and has resulted, from the formation of all-powerful economic monopolies.

We will give one more example of the methods employed by the cartels. It is particularly easy for cartels and monopolies to arise when it is possible to capture all the sources of raw materials, or at least, the most important of them. It would be wrong, however, to assume that monopolies do not arise in other industries in which it is impossible to corner the sources of raw materials.

---

[1] Kestner, *op. cit.*, p. 254.

Salt industry...........	New cartel formed for whole industry. Quotas introduced. Formation of new enterprises, erection of new plants and extension of old prohibited,	March 1934
Automobile tires........	Compulsory cartel formed for all enterprises of the industry. Erection of new plants prohibited.	July 1934
Dairy products.........	Compulsory cartel formed..............	October 1933
Fish canning	Government control established over erection of new plants and the opening of closed plants. The regulation of sales and prices introduced.	February 1934

Mention should be made of a number of other compulsory measures introduced in other branches of industry on the basis of the same law, such as the prohibition of new construction and extension of plants in the production of rolled zinc and lead, synthetic nitrogen, superphosphate, arsenic, various kinds of dyes, electric cables, electric bulbs, crockery, buttons, cigarette boxes, radios, horseshoes, stockings, gloves, building stone, fibre, cotton yarn, etc.

The process of compulsory cartelisation and the reinforcement of existing cartels continued during the period 1934-36. As a result, by the end of 1936 (according to the estimates of the Berlin Institute for Business Research) cartels embraced no less than two-thirds of the total German industry (the whole of the raw materials and semi-manufactures industries and 50 per cent of the finished goods industries) as against 40 per cent at the end of 1933.

Great Britain: By the Coal Mines Acts of 1930 and 1932 seventeen regional syndicates were formed for the purpose of controlling production and prices as well as for the rationalisation of the industry. In addition, the production of electric power is being strictly regulated by the Central Electricity Board, which was created in 1926.

U.S.A.: Although compulsory cartelisation was not the direct purpose of Roosevelt's "codes of fair competition" (on the basis of the National Industrial Recovery Act of June 13, 1933) nevertheless, as was admitted by a Senate Committee on Investigation of Codes, these codes undoubtedly strengthened monopolist tendencies and facilitated the subjugation of small and medium size enterprises to the monopolies.

Italy: Since the passing of the compulsory cartels act on June 16, 1932, such cartels have been formed in the cotton, hemp, silk and dyes industries.

The cement industry, for instance, can find its raw materials everywhere. Yet in Germany it is strongly cartelised. The cement manufacturers have formed regional syndicates: South German, Rhine-Westphalian, etc. The prices fixed are monopoly prices: 230 to 280 marks a carload (at a cost price of 180 marks!). The enterprises pay a dividend of from 12 per cent to 16 per cent—and let us not forget that the "geniuses" of modern speculation know how to pocket big profits besides those they draw by way of dividends. Now, in order to prevent competition in such a profitable industry, the monopolists resort to sundry stratagems. For example, they spread disquieting rumours about the situation in their industry. Anonymous warnings are published in the newspapers, like the following: "Investors, don't place your capital in the cement industry!" They buy up "outsiders" (those outside the syndicates) and pay them "indemnities" of 60,000, 80,000 and even 150,000 marks.[1] Monopoly everywhere hews a path for itself without scruple as to the means, from "modestly" buying off competitors to the American device of "employing" dynamite against them.

The statement that cartels can abolish crises is a fable spread by bourgeois economists who at all costs desire to place capitalism in a favourable light. On the contrary, when monopoly appears in *certain* branches of industry, it increases and intensifies the anarchy inherent in capitalist production *as a whole*. The disparity between the development of agriculture and that of industry, which is characteristic of capitalism, is increased. The privileged position of the most highly cartelised industry, so-called *heavy* industry, especially coal and iron, causes "a still greater lack of concerted organisation" in other branches

---

[1] Ludwig Eschwege, *Zement* in *Die Bank*, 1909, Vol. I, p. 115 *et seq.*

Switzerland: New erection, expansion and reconstruction of watch factories have been prohibited.

Laws for compulsory cartelisation of certain branches of industry have been enacted in Poland.

SOURCES: *Kartellrundschau* for 1933-34, various issues; *Commercial and Financial Chronicle*, 24, III, 1934, p. 2016; *Weekly Report of the German Institute for Business Research*, 22. VIII, 1934, p. 1; *Wochenbericht des Instituts für Konjunkturforschung*, 9, XII, 1936, S. 197-98.

CEMENT SYNDICATES IN GERMANY

The cement industry in Germany today is even more highly monopolised. In 1929, four syndicates, which are united by agreements, shared about 85 to 90 per cent of the country's cement output. During the years of crisis, as a result of the intense competition between the syndicates and outside concerns the share of outsiders, among which there are big establishments, increased to 20-25 per cent. In October 1933, members of the cartel were prohibited from withdrawing from it. In March 1934 new construction and extension of plants fell under the ban. Simultaneously, an attempt was made to compel outsiders to join the cartel by prohibiting sales at prices below those of the cartel. This attempt failed, however, and towards the end of 1934 the prohibition was withdrawn and the war between the cartel and the outsiders became more acute than ever.

DIVIDENDS OF FOUR LARGE ENTERPRISES OF THE NORTH GERMAN SYNDICATE IN 1929

Alsen	Hemmoor	Germania	Teutonia
14%	15%	14%	12%

Net Profits of These Enterprises in 1929
(thousand marks)

780	1,194	923	408

Sums Transferred to Reserve
(thousand marks)

1,730	758	851	1,025

Syndicate price for cement in 1929 — 500 marks per carload (10 tons).

SOURCES: *Kartellrundschau*, No. 10, 1933; *Der Deutsche Volkswirt*, 10, XI, 1933; *Frankfurter Zeitung*, 28, IV, 1933.

of production—as Jeidels, the author of one of the best works on the relationship of the German big banks to industry, puts it.[1]

"The more developed an economic system is," writes Liefmann, one of the most unblushing apologists of capitalism, "the more it resorts to risky enterprises, or enterprises abroad, to those which need a great deal of time to develop, or finally, to those which are only of local importance." [2]

The increased risk is connected in the long run with the prodigious increase of capital, which overflows the brim, as it were, flows abroad, etc. At the same time the extremely rapid rate of technical progress gives rise more and more to disturbances in the co-ordination between the various spheres of national economy, to anarchy and crisis. Liefmann is obliged to admit that:

"In all probability mankind will see further important technical revolutions in the near future which will also affect the organisation of the economic system. . . ." (For example, electricity and aviation.) "As a general rule, in such periods of radical economic change, speculation develops on a large scale." [3]

Crises of every kind—economic crises more frequently, but not only these—in their turn increase very considerably the tendency towards concentration and monopoly. In this connection, the following reflections of Jeidels on the significance of the crisis of 1900, which, as we have already seen, marked the turning point in the history of modern monopoly, are exceedingly instructive.

"Side by side with the giant plants in the basic industries, the crisis of 1900 found many plants organised on lines that today would be considered obsolete, the 'pure' [non-combined] plants, which had arisen on the crest of the industrial boom. The fall in prices and the falling off in demand put these 'pure' enterprises into a precarious position, which did not affect the big combined enterprises at all, or only affected them for a very short time. As a consequence of this the crisis of 1900 resulted in a far greater concentration of industry than former crises, like that of 1873. The latter crisis also produced a sort of selection of the best equipped enterprises, but owing to the level of technical development at that time, this selection could not place the firms which successfully emerged from the crisis in a position of monopoly. Such a durable monopoly exists to a high degree in the gigantic enterprises in the modern iron and steel and electrical industries, and to a lesser degree, in the engineering industry and certain metal, transport and other

---

[1] Otto Jeidels, *Das Verhältnis der deutschen Grossbanken zur Industrie, mit besonderer Berücksichtigung der Eisenindustrie* (*The Relationship of the German Big Banks to Industry, with Special Reference to the Iron Industry*), Leipzig, 1905, p. 271.

[2] Robert Liefmann, *Beteiligungs- und Finanzierungsgesellschaften.* (*Holding and Finance Companies*), p. 434.

[3] *Ibid.,* pp. 465-6.

MONOPOLIES IN JAPAN

The Japanese writer, Inomata Tsuneo, in his book *Japanese Monopolist Capitalism*, points out that in Japan all basic industries are controlled by cartels, in which the predominant role is played by companies owned by a few big financial magnates (Mitsui, Mitsubishi, Sumitomo, Yasuda, Okura, Furukawa, Kuhara, etc.). He describes the position of some of the industries as follows:

Coal. Out of a total of 25.3 million tons of coal produced in Japan in 1930, 24.2 million tons were produced by the companies affiliated to the Sekitan Kogyo Rengokai coal cartel. The predominant role is played by Mitsui and Mitsubishi, whose share amounts to 50 per cent of the total coal output of Japan.

Iron and Steel. The predominant role in this industry is played by government-owned enterprises (which produce approximately 50 per cent of the total output of the country). The other plants are in the hands of Mitsui, Mitsubishi and Okura. In July 1933 the Japanese Diet passed an act providing for the amalgamation of the state and principal private iron and steel enterprises of the country. As a result of this merger, which was consummated in February 1934, the new combine embraces 90 per cent of pig iron and 65 per cent of steel production in Japan.

Copper Smelting. Ninety-four per cent of the total copper output of the country is controlled by the copper cartel "Suiyokai," to which the Sumitomo, Kuhara, Mitsubishi, Furukawa and Fujita interests are affiliated.

Cement. Almost the entire output of the country is controlled by the cartel Nippon Cemento Rengokai. The leading role is played by Onoda Cemento, a Mitsui concern, which controls 20 per cent of the entire output, and Asano Cemento, controlled by Yasuda, which is responsible for 50 per cent of the entire output.

Shipbuilding. Here the dominant role is played by the Mitsubishi concern.

Electrical Engineering. The predominant role in this industry is played by four concerns: Mitsui, Mitsubishi, Furukawa and Kuhara.

Artificial Silk. Ninety per cent of the entire output capacity is in the hands of five companies headed by Mitsui and Mitsubishi.

Paper. Ninety-seven per cent of the total output is supplied by enterprises belonging to the cartel. This cartel is dominated by three companies controlled by Mitsui and Mitsubishi. In 1932 these merged into one company controlled by Mitsui.

Cotton Yarn. Of a total of 7,064,000 spindles in the country (1928),

branches in consequence of their complicated technique, their extensive organisation and the magnitude of their capital." [1]

Monopoly! This is the last word in the "latest phase of capitalist development." But we shall only have a very insufficient, incomplete, and poor notion of the real power and the significance of modern monopolies if we do not take into consideration the part played by the banks.

---

[1] Jeidels, *op. cit.*, p. 108.

6,902,000 belong to companies affiliated to the Dai Nippon Boseki Rengokai. This cotton cartel is dominated by nine companies belonging to Kikuto Abe, Mitsui and Mitsubishi, which control 70 per cent of the total spindles in Japan.

Sugar. The entire sugar industry of Japan is controlled by a sugar cartel in which the predominating role is played by three companies belonging to Mitsui and Mitsubishi, which produce 82 per cent of the total output.

PAID-UP CAPITAL OF COMPANIES CONTROLLED BY THE BIGGEST JAPANESE CONCERNS

Name of concern	Capital of controlled companies (million yen)	Percentage of total capital of all companies in Japan
Mitsui	1,906	15
Mitsubishi..............	2,045	16
Sumitomo	1,207	9
Yasuda	1,844	14

It must be borne in mind that several concerns are interested in a number of the same companies and the capital of these concerns is represented in the table two and three times. Hence, the total capital of the companies controlled by the four concerns is somewhat less than that given in the above table. The total capital of all Japanese companies in 1928 amounted to 12,634,000,000 yen.

SOURCES: Inomata Tsuneo, *Japanese Monopolist Capitalism*, 1931, and Takahashi Kamekiti, *Financial Description of Concerns*, a series of articles in the Japanese magazine *Chuokoron*, 1930; *Kaijo Nenkan*, 1935.

MONOPOLY PRICES

Below, we cite several examples of price raising in the post-war period under the influence of monopolies:

I. After the formation of two organisations in the copper industry in America, the Copper Institute and Copper Exporters, Inc., which began to function in 1927, the price of copper began to rise as follows: in 1927 the average price was 13.17 cents per pound; in January 1928 it was 14.09 cents; in October 1928—16 cents, and finally, in March 1929 the price of copper rose to 24 cents per pound. Later on, the crisis brought about a sharp fall in price.

II. In 1925 and the beginning of 1926, the Polish iron syndicate encountered the competition of a powerful outsider, the Sosnowicer Röhren- und Eisengesellschaft. In May 1926 the latter joined the syndicate, after which prices were raised 22 to 25 per cent.

III. After the formation of a wire rope syndicate in Germany, the price was raised 20 to 40 per cent.

IV. As a result of the formation of the European Steel Cartel (E.R.G.) in 1926 the price of assorted iron was raised on the world market from 96 marks per ton in August 1926 to 118.5 marks towards the end of 1926.

V. In 1922 the so-called Stevenson scheme was introduced in the rubber market with the object of raising the price of rubber by restricting exports. As a result, the price of rubber in the New York market was practically doubled: it rose from 14 cents per pound in August 1922 to 27.4 cents per pound towards the end of that year. In the beginning of 1925 the price of rubber in New York reached the peak of 1.03 dollars per pound. Subsequently, the competition of outsiders drove the price down.

VI. The formation of the International Zinc Syndicate in December 1928 caused a rise in the price of zinc, and even in the United States, which did not join the syndicate, the price of zinc went up from 5.9 cents per pound in February 1928, to 7.15 cents in July and August 1929.

Monopolist organisations, while forcing up prices during periods of industrial boom, retard the dropping of prices in times of crisis. The following table gives a comparison between the movements of monopoly and competitive prices in the period 1928-36.

INDICES OF MONOPOLY AND FREE MARKET PRICES
(of raw materials and semi-manufactures)

Years	Germany: 1928=100		Poland: 1928=100		Austria: 1923-31=100	
	Monopoly prices	Free market prices	Monopoly prices	Free market prices	Monopoly prices	Free market prices
1928	100.0	100.0	100.0	100.0	97	110
1929	103.6	91.2	107.5	93.6	98	100
1933	78.4	45.4	91.9	49.1	104	73
1934	78.3	54.3 [1]	87.6	49.1	105	76
1935	78.3	—	81.7	47.3	105	76
1936	78.6	—	75.4	50.9	105	78

[1] November 1934

Years	Monopolised commodities			Non-monopolised commodities	
	Coal: Rhine-Westphalian (marks per t.)	Pig iron: Pittsburgh ($ per long t.)	U.S.A. cement ($ per barrel)	Wheat: Manitoba No. 1 Canada ($ per 100 bushels)	Cotton: New Orleans ($ per 100 lbs.)
1929.....	16.87	19.99	1.60	134.30	18.60
1933.....	14.21	17.79	1.51	61.00	8.50
Percentage of drop	—15.8	—11.0	—5.6	—54.6	—54.3

The above tables show: 1) that monopoly prices continued to rise even in 1929 when free market prices already began to drop; 2) that on the whole, the drop in monopoly prices was immeasurably slower and that their level remained higher than that of the free market prices. It must be borne in mind, however, that during the crisis the monopolists gave their customers large rebates, so that the actual drop in the monopoly prices is considerably greater than is shown in the tables.

The operation of the monopoly price policy during the "depression of a special kind" (Stalin) can be illustrated by the following facts: the European Steel Cartel, which was re-established in the summer of 1933, managed to raise prices 30 to 50 per cent. As a result of the restriction of rubber production and the establishment of the International Rubber Committee, from the spring of 1934 to the autumn of the same year rubber prices rose 40 per cent. The restrictions on tea imposed in 1933 caused a rise in tea prices of 50 per cent.

SOURCES: U.S.A.—*The Masquerade of Monopoly*, by Frank A. Fetter, p. 197; *Record Book of Business Statistics*, Dept. of Commerce, Part III, p. 50; *Survey of Current Business, Annual Supplement*, 1936, pp. 116, 138; *The Iron Age*, 5, I, 1933, p. 92; Poland—Gustav Lucae, *Ausseinseiter von Kartellen*, 1929; *Konjunktura Gospodarcza*, 1937, No. 4, p. 2; Germany—W. Boje, *Der internationale Eisenpakt*, 1932, S. 93; *Vierteljahrshefte zur Konjunkturforschung*, 1936-37, Teil B; Austria—*Monatsberichte des Österreichischen Instituts für Konjunkturforschung*, 1935, No. 12, p. 278; 1937, No. 1, p. 15; *International Yearbook of Agricultural Statistics*, 1933-34, pp. 596, 639; *Jahresbericht des Reichskohlenverbandes*, 1934-35, S. 20.

CHAPTER II

THE BANKS AND THEIR NEW ROLE

THE principal and primary function of banks is to serve as an intermediary in the making of payments. In doing so they transform inactive money capital into active capital, that is, into capital producing a profit; they collect all kinds of money revenues and place them at the disposal of the capitalist class.

As banking develops and becomes concentrated in a small number of establishments the banks become transformed, and instead of being modest intermediaries they become powerful monopolies having at their command almost the whole of the money capital of all the capitalists and small business men and also a large part of the means of production and of the sources of raw materials of the given country and in a number of countries. The transformation of numerous modest intermediaries into a handful of monopolists represents one of the fundamental processes in the transformation of capitalism into capitalist imperialism. For this reason we must first of all deal with the concentration of banking.

In 1907-08, the combined deposits of the German joint stock banks, each having a capital of more than a million marks, amounted to 7,000,000,000 marks, while in 1912-13, they amounted to 9,800,000,000 marks. Thus, in five years their deposits increased by 40 per cent. Of the 2,800,000,000 increase, 2,750,000,000 was divided amongst 57 banks, each having a capital of more than 10,000,000 marks.

CONCENTRATION OF BANKS IN GERMANY
DEPOSITS IN GERMAN JOINT STOCK BANKS POSSESSING CAPITAL OF OVER ONE MILLION MARKS EACH [1]
(billion marks)

1907-08	1912-13	1924 [2]	1927	1929	1930 [3]	1934 [3]
7	9.8	1.9	13.5	16.9	16.0	9.1

The drop in deposits in 1924 as compared with 1912-13 is due to the consequences of the inflation period which brought about a tremendous devaluation of deposits expressed in terms of gold currency. The table shows an increase of deposits compared with the pre-war period, which indicates a considerable increase in the power of finance capital.

In computing the deposits for 1929-34, we have conditionally taken the proportion of the deposits of banks with a capital of less than one

[1] Excluding the Reichskreditgesellschaft and other "public credit" institutions.
[2] As of January 1st.
[3] The diminution of deposits in the period 1930-34 is due to withdrawals during the crisis.

The·distribution of the deposits between big and small banks was as follows: [1]

PERCENTAGE OF TOTAL DEPOSITS

Year	In 9 big Berlin banks	In the other 48 banks with a capital of more than 10 million marks	In 115 banks with a capital of 1 to 10 million marks	In the small banks with a capital of less than 1 million marks
1907-08........	47	32.5	16.5	4
1912-13........	49	36	12	3

The small banks are being pushed aside by the big banks, of which nine concentrate in their hands almost half the total deposits. But we have left out of account many important details, for instance, the transformation of numerous small banks practically into branches of big banks, etc. Of this we shall speak later on.

At the end of 1913, Schulze-Gaevernitz estimated the deposits in the nine big Berlin banks at 5,100,000,000 marks, out of a total of about 10,000,000,000 marks. Taking into account not only the deposits, but the total resources of these banks, this author wrote:

"At the end of 1909, the nine big Berlin banks, *together* with their *affiliated banks* controlled 11,276,000,000 marks . . . that is, about 83 per cent of the total German bank capital. The Deutsche Bank, *which together with its affiliated banks* controls nearly 3,000,000,000 marks, represents, parallel with the Prussian State Railway Administration, the biggest and also the most decentralised accumulation of capital in the old world." [2]

---

[1] Alfred Lansburgh, *Fünf Jahre deutsches Bankwesen* (*Five Years of German Banking*) in *Die Bank*, No. 8, 1913, S. 728.

[2] Schulze-Gaevernitz. *Die deutsche Kreditbank, Grundriss der Sozialökonomik* (*The German Credit Bank* in *Outline of Social Economics*), Sec. V, Part II, Tübingen, 1915, pp. 12 and 137.

million marks to total bank deposits at three per cent. Any error that may have crept into this calculation will not exceed one per cent and, therefore, will not affect the result to any material degree.

SOURCES: Figures for the pre-war period are quoted from Lenin. For subsequent years the figures are taken from: *Die Deutsche Banken 1924 bis 1926*, and *Statistisches Jahrbuch für das Deutsche Reich*, 1929, S. 318; 1931, S. 335; 1932, S. 331; 1936, S. 369; *Die Bank*, 12, IV, 1931; 6, II, 1935 and 24, II, 1937.

PERCENTAGE OF TOTAL DEPOSITS [1]

Year	In big Berlin banks	In the other 48 banks with a capital of more than 10 million marks	In 115 banks with a capital of 1 to 10 million marks	In the small banks with a capital of less than 1 million marks
1907-08.....	47	32.5	16.5	4
1912-13.....	49	36	12	3
1924[2].......	54.6	39.3		6.1
1927........	59.6	37.0		3.4
1929........	67.5		32.5	
1934[3]	65.5		34.5	

[1] Excluding deposits of the Reichskreditgesellschaft, other "public credit" institutions and mortgage banks.

[2] As of January 1st.

[3] The diminution of the share of the big banks is due to the withdrawal of foreign deposits during the crisis.

SOURCES: Figures for the pre-war period quoted from Lenin. For subsequent years the figures are taken from: *Die Deutschen Banken im Jahre 1924*, S. 26; *Die Deutschen Banken 1924 bis 1926* and *Statistisches Jahrbuch für das Deutsche Reich*, 1929, S. 318, 1931, S. 334-35, 1936, S. 368-69; *Die Bank*, 12, IV, 1930, S. 566, 6, II, 1935, S. 135.

DEPOSITS IN GERMAN BANKS [1]
(billion marks)

Year	Total deposits	In 9 big Berlin banks
1913..............	10	5.1
1927..............	14.0	8.0
1929..............	17.5	11.4
1934 [2]	9.4	5.8

Owing to the absorption of some banks by others, the number of big banks dropped from the 9 indicated by Lenin to 7 in 1924 and 1927, 5 in 1929 and 4 in 1934.

[1] *Cf.* footnote 1 on p. 73.

[2] *Cf.* footnote 3 on p. 73.

SOURCES: *Statistisches Jahrbuch für das Deutsche Reich*, and *Die Bank*, issues and pages as above.

We have emphasised the reference to the "affiliated" banks because this is one of the most important features of modern capitalist con-centration. Large-scale enterprises, especially the banks, not only completely absorb small ones, but also "join" them to themselves, sub-ordinate them, bring them into their "own" group or *concern* (to use the technical term) by having "holdings" in their capital, by purchasing or exchanging shares, by controlling them through a system of credits, etc., etc. Professor Liefmann has written a voluminous "work" of about 500 pages describing modern "holding and finance companies,"[1] unfortun-ately adding "theoretical" reflections of a very poor quality to what is frequently partly digested raw material. To what results this "holding" system leads in regard to concentration is best illustrated in the book written on the big German banks by the banker Riesser. But before examining his data, we will quote an example of the "holding" system.

The Deutsche Bank group is one of the biggest, if not the biggest banking group. In order to trace the main threads which connect all the banks in this group, it is necessary to distinguish between holdings of the first, second and third degree, or what amounts to the same thing, be-tween dependence (of the lesser establishments on the Deutsche Bank) in the first, second, and third degree. We then obtain the following pic-ture:[2]

THE DEUTSCHE BANK PARTICIPATES:

	Permanently	For an indefinite period	Occasionally	Total
1st degree · · · ·	in 17 banks	in 5 banks	in 8 banks	in 30 banks
2nd degree · ·	of which 9 participate in 34 others		of which 5 participate in 14 others	of which 14 participate in 48 others
3rd degree · ·	of which 4 participate in 7 others		of which 2 participate in 2 others	of which 6 participate in 9 others

Included in the eight banks dependent on the Deutsche Bank in the "first degree," "occasionally," there are three foreign banks: one Aus-trian, the Wiener Bankverein, and two Russian, the Siberian Commercial

---

[1] Robert Liefmann, *Beteiligungs- und Finanzierungsgesellschaften. Eine Studie über den modernen Kapitalismus und das Effektenwesen* (*Holding and Finance Companies—A Study in Modern Capitalism and Securities*), first ed., Jena, 1909, p. 212.

[2] A. Lansburgh, *Das Beteiligungssystem im deutschen Bankwesen* (*The Holding System in German Banking*), in *Die Bank*, 1910, I, p. 500 *et seq.*

CONCENTRATION OF BANKS IN UNITED KINGDOM[1]

The following may serve as an illustration to Lenin's thesis on the concentration of banks.

NUMBER OF ENGLISH JOINT STOCK BANKS

Year	With capital of £1,000,000 and over	With capital from £500,000 to £1,000,000	Small banks with capital up to £500,000	All banks
1900	24	17	57	98
1908	26	16	28	70
1913	27	14	20	61
1924	20	6	3	29
1929	20	5	2	27
1932	20	5	2	27
1936	20	4	2	26

PERCENTAGE OF DEPOSITS IN U. K. JOINT STOCK BANKS

Year	With capital of £1,000,000 and over		With capital of £500,000 to £1,000,000	Small banks with capital up to £500,000
	All banks	The "Big Five" London banks		
1900	68.2	27.0	15.3	16.5
1908	79.3	32.4	13.9	6.8
1913	85.7	39.7	9.3	5.0
1924	95.7	72.4	4.2	0.1
1929	96.8	73.5	3.1	0.1
1932	96.8	74.1	3.1	0.1
1936	98.1	74.6	1.7	0.2

[1] Not including the Bank of England (nor the Irish Free State banks for post-war years).

SOURCES: This table is compiled from figures given in *The Economist,* Banking Supplement, May issue for 1901, 1909, 1914, 1925, 1930, 1933, 1937.

CONCENTRATION OF BANKS IN U.S.A.

NUMBER OF NATIONAL BANKS

Year	With capital over $5,000,000	With capital from $1,000,000 to $5,000,000	With capital less than $1,000,000
1923	21	100	8,063
1930	39	177	6,822
1934	40	182	5,245

PERCENTAGE OF DEPOSITS IN NATIONAL BANKS

1923	22.1	20.1	57.8
1930	43.3	17.1	39.6
1934	47.8	20.6	31.6

SOURCES: This table is compiled from figures given in the *Report of the Comptroller of the Currency*: for 1924, p. 66, 1931, p. 80, 1935, p. 97.

TOTAL NUMBER OF BANKS IN U.S.A.

Year [1]		Year [1]	
1914	26,274	1929	25,110
1921	30,560	1936	15,752

[1] As of June 30.

SOURCES: *Annual Report of the Federal Reserve Board,* 1933, p. 159; *Federal Reserve Bulletin,* February 1937, p. 129.

Bank and the Russian Bank for Foreign Trade. Altogether, the Deutsche Bank group comprises, directly and indirectly, partially and totally, no less than 87 banks; and the capital—its own and others which it controls—is estimated at between two and three billion marks.

It is obvious that a bank which stands at the head of such a group, and which enters into agreement with a half dozen other banks only slightly smaller than itself for the purpose of conducting big and profitable operations like floating state loans, is no longer a mere "intermediary" but a combine of a handful of monopolists.

The rapidity with which the concentration of banking proceeded in Germany at the end of the nineteenth and the beginning of the twentieth centuries is shown by the following data which we quote in an abbreviated form from Riesser:

SIX BIG BERLIN BANKS

Year	Branches in Germany	Deposit banks and exchange offices	Constant holdings in German joint stock banks	Total establishments
1895	16	14	1	42
1900	21	40	8	80
1911	104	276	63	450

We see the rapid extension of a close network of canals which cover the whole country, centralising all capital and all revenues, transforming thousands and thousands of scattered economic enterprises into a single national, capitalist, and then into an international, capitalist, economic unit. The "decentralisation" that Schulze-Gaevernitz, as an exponent of modern bourgeois political economy, speaks of in the passage previously quoted, really means the subordination of an increasing number of formerly relatively "independent," or rather, strictly local economic units, to a single centre. In reality it is *centralisation*, the increase in the role, the importance and the power of monopolist giants.

CONCENTRATION OF BANKS IN JAPAN

THE FIVE BIGGEST BANKS

Year	Total deposits in 5 banks (million yen)	Per cent of total deposits in all private commercial banks
1926............	2,233	24.3
1929............	3,210	34.6
1936 [1]	4,585	41.9

TOTAL NUMBER OF BANKS IN JAPAN

Year		Year	
1914 2,155		1929..............1,001	
1921 2,009		1935.............. 563	

[1] If a new big bank, formed by a merger of 3 banks in December 1933, be included, the total deposits of the six big banks will rise to 5,783 million yen or 52.9% of deposits of all banks.

SOURCES: *Toyo Keizai Shimpo,* 17, IV, 1937, p. 50;*Financial and Economic Annual of Japan,* 1916, p. 120, 1928, p. 154, 1936, p. 164; Inomata Tsuneo, *Nippon no dokusen shihon Shugi,* 1931, pp. 61, 342.

GROWTH IN NUMBER OF BRANCHES OF BERLIN BANKS

DATA FOR THE SIX BIG BERLIN BANKS WHICH IN 1933 COMBINED INTO THREE

Year	Branches in Germany	Deposit and exchange offices	Constant holdings in German joint stock banks	Total establishments
1895............	16	14	1	42
1900............	21	40	8	80
1911............	104	276	63	450
1932............	449	365	23	844 [1]

The six big Berlin banks in Lenin's table (for 1911) are as follows: 1) Darmstädter Bank, 2) Berliner Handelsgesellschaft, 3) Deutsche Bank, 4) Disconto-Gesellschaft, 5) Dresdner Bank, 6) Schaffhausenscher Bankverein.

In the process of concentration the number of these banks by 1932 had been reduced to three. Mergers have taken place among the following banks:

---

[1] This table does not include figures of the branches of the Berlin Commerz und Privatbank which in 1933 had 395 branches. In recent times there has been a reduction in the number of branches owing to bank mergers and rationalisation. From 1929 to the middle of 1933 the number of branches of the big Berlin banks was reduced from 792 to 687.

In the older capitalist countries this "banking network" is still more close. In Great Britain (including Ireland), in 1910, there were in all 7,151 branches of banks. Four big banks had more than 400 branches each (from 447 to 689); four had more than 200 branches each, and eleven more than 100 each.

a) In 1931, the Darmstädter Bank, which in 1922 had absorbed another big bank (Nationalbank), merged with the Dresdner Bank.

b) In 1929 the Deutsche Bank merged with the Disconto-Gesellschaft; the latter, as far back as 1914, had merged with Schaffhausenscher Bankverein.

The reduction in the number of holdings is explained by the fact that the giant banks have absorbed the weaker banks which formerly had been nominally independent.

SOURCES: The figures for 1895, 1900 and 1911 are quoted from Lenin. The figures for 1932 are taken from the reports of the banks and *Grünbuch der Aktiengesellschaften*, 1932; figures for 1933—from *Untersuchung des Bankwesens*, 1933, Teil I.

GROWTH IN NUMBER OF BRANCHES OF BRITISH BANKS

NUMBER OF BRANCHES OF ALL BANKS IN GREAT BRITAIN AND IRELAND [1]

1910	1913	1929	1936
7,151	7,730	11,730	12,182

NUMBER OF BANKS HAVING BRANCHES

Year	Over 400	Over 200	Over 100
1910	4 (from 447 to 689 branches)	4	11
1913	3 (from 570 to 867 branches)	8	18
1924	5 (from 704 to 1,778 branches)	4	11
1932	6 (from 553 to 2,103 branches)	7	6
1936	7 (from 555 to 2,136 branches)	6	5

[1] Not including the Bank of England (nor the Irish Free State banks for postwar years).

SOURCES: Figures for 1910 are quoted from Lenin. For subsequent years the figures are taken from *The Economist*, Banking Supplement, May issue for 1914, 1925, 1933, 1937.

In France, *three* big banks (Crédit Lyonnais, the Comptoir National d'Escompte and the Société Générale) extended their operations and their network of branches in the following manner: [1]

	Number of branches and offices			Capital in million francs	
Year	In the provinces	In Paris	Total	Own capital	Borrowed capital
1870........	47	17	64	200	427
1890........	192	66	258	265	1,245
1909........	1,033	196	1,229	887	4,363

In order to show the "connections" of a big modern bank, Riesser gives the following figures of the number of letters dispatched and received by the Disconto-Gesellschaft, one of the biggest banks in Germany and in the world, the capital of which amounted to 300,000,000 marks in 1914:

Year	Letters received	Letters dispatched
1852.............................	6,135	6,292
1870.............................	85,800	87,513
1900.............................	533,102	626,043

In 1875, the big Paris bank, the Crédit Lyonnais, had 28,535 accounts. In 1912 it had 633,539.[2]

These simple figures show perhaps better than long explanations how the concentration of capital and the growth of their turnover is radically changing the significance of the banks. Scattered capitalists are transformed into a single collective capitalist. When carrying the current accounts of a few capitalists, the banks, as it were, transact a purely technical and exclusively auxiliary operation. When, however, these operations grow to enormous dimensions we find that a handful of monopolists control all the operations, both commercial and industrial, of the whole of capitalist society. They can, by means of their banking connections, by running current accounts and transacting other financial operations, first *ascertain exactly* the position of the various capitalists, then *control* them, influence them by restricting or enlarging, facilitating or hindering their credits, and finally they can *entirely determine* their fate, determine their income, deprive them of capital, or, on the other hand,

---

[1] Eugen Kaufmann, *Das französische Bankwesen*, (*French Banking*), Tübingen, 1911, pp. 356 and 362.
[2] Jean Lescure, *L'épargne en France* (*Savings in France*), Paris, 1914, p. 52.

GROWTH IN NUMBER OF BRANCHES OF FRENCH BANKS

Year	Number of branches and offices			Capital in million francs	
	In the provinces	In Paris	Total	Own capital	Borrowed capital
1870........	47	17	64	200	427
1890........	192	66	258	265	1,245
1909........	1,033	196	1,229	887	4,363
1930........	3,035	281	3,316	561 [1]	7,215 [2]
1935........	3,152	278	3,430	561 [1]	5,349 [2, 3]

[1] Reduced to francs of pre-war parity. According to balance sheet figures of 1930 and 1935 own capital remained at 2,760,000,000 francs (1928 parity).

[2] Reduced to francs of pre-war parity. According to balance sheet figures borrowed capital amounted in 1930 to 35,500,000,000 and in 1935 to 26,345,000,000 francs (1928 parity).

[3] The diminution of borrowed capital due to deposit withdrawals during the crisis.

SOURCES: Figures for pre-war years are quoted from Lenin. For 1930 and 1935 the figures are taken from *The Statist*, 1930, 1933, 1936, International Banking Section; *Bankers' Almanac and Yearbook*, 1930-31, 1935-36; Maurice Gougne, Tendances d'après-guerre des Banques Françaises de Dépot, Paris, 1934, pp. 235-36.

permit them to increase their capital rapidly and to enormous dimensions, etc.

We have just mentioned the 300,000,000 marks' capital of the Disconto-Gesellschaft of Berlin. The increase of the capital of this bank was one of the incidents in the struggle for hegemony between two of the biggest Berlin banks—the Deutsche Bank and the Disconto.

In 1870, the Deutsche Bank, a new enterprise, had a capital of only 15,000,000 marks, while that of the Disconto was 30,000,000 marks. In 1908, the first had a capital of 200,000,000, while the second had 170,000,000. In 1914, the Deutsche Bank increased its capital to 250,000,000 and the Disconto, by merging with a very important bank, the Schaffhausenscher Bankverein, increased its capital to 300,000,000. And, of course, while this struggle for hegemony goes on the two banks more and more frequently conclude "agreements" of an increasingly durable character with each other. This development of banking compels specialists in the study of banking questions—who regard economic questions from a standpoint which does not in the least exceed the bounds of the most moderate and cautious bourgeois reformism—to arrive at the following conclusions:

The German review, *Die Bank,* commenting on the increase of the capital of the Disconto-Gesellschaft to 300,000,000 marks, writes:

"Other banks will follow this same path and in time the three hundred men, who today govern Germany economically, will gradually be reduced to fifty, twenty-five or still fewer. It cannot be expected that this new move towards concentration will be confined to banking. The close relations that exist between certain banks naturally involve the bringing together of the manufacturing concerns which they favour. . . . One fine morning we shall wake up in surprise to see nothing but trusts before our eyes, and to find ourselves faced with the necessity of substituting state monopolies for private monopolies. However, we have nothing to reproach ourselves with, except with us having allowed things to follow their own course, slightly accelerated by the manipulation of stocks." [1]

This is an example of the impotence of bourgeois journalism which differs from bourgeois science only in that the latter is less sincere and strives to obscure essential things, to conceal the wood by trees. To be "surprised" at the results of concentration, to "reproach" the government of capitalist Germany, or capitalist "society" ("us"), to fear that the introduction of stocks and shares might "accelerate" concentration in the same way as the German "cartel specialist" Tschierschky fears the American trusts and "prefers" the German cartels on the

---

[1] A. Lansburgh, *Die Bank mit den 300 Millionen* (*The 300 Million Mark Bank*), in *Die Bank,* 1914, I, p. 426.

OUTCOME OF STRUGGLE BETWEEN DEUTSCHE BANK AND DISCONTO-GESELLSCHAFT

After the inflation in the beginning of 1924, preponderance was attained by the Deutsche Bank whose capital on January 1, 1924, amounted to 150 million marks, against that of 100 million marks of the Disconto-Gesellschaft. In 1926, however, the Disconto-Gesellschaft again increased its capital to 135 million marks, almost to the size of that of the Deutsche Bank. Finally, this protracted struggle for hegemony between these two biggest banks, which in the process became interlocked as a result of agreements of increasing frequency and durability concluded between them, was brought to an end by their amalgamation in 1929.

SOURCES: *Grünbuch der Aktiengesellschaften*, 1933; *Geschäftsbericht der Deutschen Bank- und Disconto-Gesellschaft*, 1933.

CONCENTRATION OF BANKS AND COMPETITION AMONG BANKS

From the beginning of 1914 to the middle of 1933 six big German banks absorbed 191 banks having 1,699 main offices and branches (including agencies, deposit offices, etc.). Three of these six, the largest Berlin banks, absorbed 100 banks having 1,357 branches.[1] Of the total number of absorbed branches 1,303 remained as branches of the parent institutions, while 396 were closed in the process of rationalisation. This enormous growth of bank monopolies was accompanied by increased competition among the big banks. The following table illustrates the growing competition:

NUMBER OF CENTRES OF POPULATION WHERE THE BIG BANKS HAVE BRANCHES

Year	Total	do not compete	Centres where the banks:			
			compete			
			Total number of centres where competition takes place	competition between		
				2 banks	3 banks	4-5 banks
1929	521	324	197	114	39	44
1933	482	268	214	139	69	6

[1] If the number of previous absorptions among the absorbed banks is taken into account, the total number of direct and indirect bank absorptions for the period under consideration will be far greater: 416, of which 285 banks were absorbed by the 3 big Berlin banks.

grounds that they may not, like the trusts, "accelerate technical and economic progress to an excessive degree"[1]—is not this impotence?

But facts remain facts. There are no trusts in Germany; there are "only" cartels—but Germany is *governed* by not more than three hundred magnates of capital, and the number of these is constantly diminishing. At all events, banks in all capitalist countries, no matter what the law in regard to them may be, greatly intensify and accelerate the process of concentration of capital and the formation of monopolies.

The banking system, Marx wrote half a century ago in *Capital*, "presents indeed the form of common bookkeeping and distribution of means of production on a social scale, but only the form." The figures we have quoted on the growth of bank capital, on the increase in the number of the branches and offices of the biggest banks, the increase in the number of their accounts, etc., present a concrete picture of this "common bookkeeping" of the *whole* capitalist class; and not only of the capitalists, for the banks collect, even though temporarily, all kinds of financial revenues of small businessmen, office clerks, and of a small upper stratum of the working class. It is "common distribution of means of production" that, from the formal point of view, grows out of the development of modern banks, the most important of which, numbering from three to six in France, and from six to eight in Germany, control billions and billions.

---

[1] Tschierschky, *op. cit.*, p. 128.

The table shows that as a result of the crisis the number of centres where the big banks have branches has been reduced by 39, whereas the number of centres where competition takes place has *increased* by 17.

SOURCES: *Untersuchung des Bankwesens*, 1933, I. Teil, S. 179; *Materialien zur Vorbereitung der Bankenenquete*, S. 104-06.

REDUCTION IN THE NUMBER OF MAGNATES OF CAPITAL

F. Fried, in his book, notes in reference to Germany that in the basic raw materials industries (coal, potassium, iron and steel) 19 persons, or families, own wealth to the amount of 810 million marks, in the manufacturing industries—11 persons, or families, own wealth to the amount of 230 million marks, and in the chemical industry—12 persons, or families, own wealth to the amount of 210 million marks. Altogether, 42 persons, or families, own wealth to the amount of 1.25 billion marks. The same author points out that in the sphere of finance capital in Germany, 110 persons, or families, own wealth to the amount of about 3.4 billion marks.

James W. Gerard, former U.S. Ambassador to Germany, has stated that 64 men control the national wealth of the U.S.A. Gerard said that these men are too busy to occupy political posts, but they decide who are to occupy these posts.

The following is a list of names of United States magnates classified according to the branches of economy they control:

Bankers

J. P. Morgan

George F. Baker, Chairman of Board of First National Bank of New York

William H. Crocker, Pres. and director of First National Bank of San Francisco, and officer and director of many large railroad, mining and lumber organisations in the West

Edward J. Berwind, financier and director of many large corporations

Thomas W. Lamont, member of J. P. Morgan and Co., director of Guaranty Trust Co.

Albert Chase Wiggin, Chairman of Board of Chase National Bank

Charles E. Mitchell, Chairman of Board of National City Bank

Daniel Guggenheim and William Loeb, financiers and directors of mining and utility companies

Charles Hayden (financier)

Oil

John D. Rockefeller, Jr.

Walter C. Teagle, Pres., Standard Oil Co. (N. J.)

R. C. Holmes, Pres., Texas Corp.

Iron and Steel

Myron C. Taylor, Chairman of the Finance Committee, U.S. Steel Corp.

James A. Farrell, Pres., U.S. Steel Corp.

Charles M. Schwab, Chairman, Bethlehem Steel Corp.

Eugene G. Grace, Pres., Bethlehem Steel Corp.

Copper

John D. Ryan, Pres., Anaconda Mining Co.

Daniel C. Jackling, Pres., Utah Copper Co.

Aluminum

Andrew W. Mellon, former Secretary of the Treasury, Aluminum Co. of
America

Arthur V. Davis, Pres., Aluminum Co. of America

Automobiles

Henry Ford

John J. Raskob, General Motors

Fisher Bros.

Chemicals

The Dupont Family, officers and directors of the E. I. duPont de Nemours
& Co.

Electrical Supplies

Owen D. Young, Chairman, General Electric Co.

Gerard Swope, Pres., Gen. Elec. Co.

Walter G. Gifford, Chairman, American Tel. & Tel.

Sosthenes Behn, Chairman, International Tel. & Tel.

Samuel Insull

P. G. Gossler, Pres., Columbia Gas & Electric Co.

Railways

Van Sweringen Bros.

W. W. Atterbury, Pres., Pennsylvania R.R.

Daniel Willard, Pres., Baltimore & Ohio R.R.

Arthur Curtiss James

Lumber Mills

Frederick Weyerhaeuser, millionaire lumber king, Tacoma, Wash.

Tobacco

G. W. Hill (President of American Tobacco Co.)

Commerce

Julius Rosenwald, Pres., Sears Roebuck & Co.

SOURCES: F. Fried, *Das Ende des Kapitalismus.* 1931, pp. 72, 80; *Commercial and Financial Chronicle,* 30, VIII, 1930, p. 1315.

In point of fact, however, the distribution of means of production is by no means "common," but private, i.e., it conforms to the interests of big capital, and primarily, of very big monopoly capital, which operates in conditions in which the masses of the population live in want, in which the whole development of agriculture hopelessly lags behind the development of industry, and within industry itself the "heavy industries" exact tribute from all other branches of industry.

The savings banks and post offices are beginning to compete with the banks in the matter of socialising capitalist economy; they are more "decentralised," i.e., their influence extends to a greater number of localities, to more remote places, to wider sections of the population. An American commission has collected the following data on the comparative growth of deposits in banks and savings banks:[1]

---

[1] Cf. Statistics of the National Monetary Commission, quoted in Die Bank, 1910, I, p. 1200.

MONOPOLIST EXPLOITATION OF BANK RESOURCES

Lenin's thesis that "in point of fact the distribution of means of production is by no means 'universal,' but private, *i.e.*, it conforms to the interests of big capital, and primarily, of very big monopoly capital ..." can be illustrated by the following figures showing the exploitation of funds which are concentrated in present-day banks.

DISTRIBUTION OF LOANS IN FOUR BIG BERLIN BANKS INCLUDING THEIR BRANCHES (OCTOBER 1931)

Dimension of loan (marks)	Number of loans	%	Total (mill. marks)	%	Average dimension of loan (marks)
Up to 20,000..........	158,730	84.6	501.8	7.9	3,161
From 20,000 to 100,000.	20,568	10.9	908.0	14.2	44,145
Total of small and medium loans	179,298	95.5	1,409.8	22.1	7,863
From 100,000 to 500,000	6,516	3.5	1,408.9	22.0	216,217
From 500,000 to 2 million	1,496	0.8	1,445.1	22.5	966,007
Over 2 million	390	0.2	2,137.0	33.4	5,479,341
Total	187,700	100.0	6,400.8	100.0	34,101

The table shows that the total sum of money advanced on 390 of the largest loans represents 2,137,000,000 marks, whereas 158,730 small loans amount to only 501,000,000 marks.

From the above figures it can be seen that the number of loans over 500,000 marks represents only one per cent of the total number of loans, although these loans absorbed 56 per cent of the total sum advanced by the banks. In this connection it must be borne in mind that a considerable portion of the smaller loans were also received by the biggest companies. It is highly significant, too, that the biggest monopolies have the biggest percentage of loan capital (including bond issues and long and short term loans). The following figures taken from a sample investigation prove this point very clearly.

OWN AND BORROWED CAPITAL OF JOINT STOCK COMPANIES IN GERMANY, 1933

Capital of each company (million marks)	Number of companies taken in each sample group	Own capital	Borrowed capital (million marks)	Per cent borrowed capital to own capital
Up to 10	6	31.4	6.6	21.0
10 to 20	6	93.7	27.6	29.5
20 to 30	5	117.7	47.0	39.9
30 to 50	9	342.5	173.0	50.5
50 to 100	4	233.8	149.3	63.9
100 to 1000	3	1,446.3	1,244.3	86.1

SOURCES: *Materialien zur Vorbereitung der Bankenenquete*, 1933, S. 139; *Wirtschaftsdienst*, 10, XI, 1933, S. 1547.

DEPOSITS (in billions of marks)

Year	England		France		Germany		
	Banks	Savings Banks	Banks	Savings Banks	Banks	Credit Societies	Savings Banks
1880	8.4	1.6	?	0.9	0.5	0.4	2.6
1888	12.4	2.0	1.5	2.1	1.1	0.4	4.5
1908	23.2	4.2	3.7	4.2	7.1	2.2	13.9

As they pay interest at the rate of 4 per cent and $4\frac{1}{4}$ per cent on deposits, the savings banks must seek "profitable" investments for their capital, they must deal in bills, mortgages, etc. The boundaries between the banks and the savings banks "become more and more obliterated." The Chambers of Commerce at Bochum and Erfurt, for example, demand that savings banks be prohibited from engaging in "purely" banking business, such as discounting bills. They demand the limitation of the "banking" operations of the post office.[1] The banking magnates seem to be afraid that state monopoly will steal upon them from an unexpected quarter. It goes without saying, however, that this fear is no more than the expression, as it were, of the rivalry between two department managers in the same office; for, on the one hand, the billions entrusted to the savings banks are in the final analysis actually controlled by *these very same* bank magnates, while, on the other hand, state monopoly in capitalist society is nothing more than a means of increasing and guaranteeing the income of millionaires on the verge of bankruptcy in one branch of industry or another.

The change from the old type of capitalism, in which free competition predominated, to the new capitalism, in which monopoly reigns, is expressed, among other things, by a decrease in the importance of the Stock Exchange. The German review, *Die Bank*, wrote:

"For a long time now, the Stock Exchange has ceased to be the indispensable intermediary of circulation that it was formerly when the banks were not yet able to place the bulk of new issues with their clients."[2]
"Every bank is a Stock Exchange, and the bigger the bank, and the more successful the concentration of banking, the truer does this proverb become."[3]

"While formerly, in the 'seventies, the Stock Exchange, flushed with

---

[1] *Die Bank*, 1913, I, 811, 1022; 1914, p. 743.
[2] *Die Bank*, 1914. I, p. 316.
[3] Oskar Stillich, *Geld und Bankwesen* (*Money and Banking*), Berlin, 1907, p. 169.

COMPARATIVE CHANGES IN DEPOSITS IN BANKS AND SAVINGS BANKS

DEPOSITS (in billions of marks)

Year	England		France		Germany			United States	
	Banks[1]	Savings Banks	Banks[2]	Savings Banks	Banks[10]	Credit Societies	Savings Banks	Banks	Savings Banks
1880	8.4	1.6	?	0.9	0.5	0.4	2.6	5.5	3.4
1888	12.4	2.0	1.5	2.1	1.1	0.4	4.5	8.6	5.7
1908	23.2	4.2	3.7	4.2	7.1	2.2	13.9	39.1	14.6
1913	30.9	5.2	5.5[2]	4.7	10.1	4.0	19.7	52.6	19.8
1928	72.0	8.4	7.8[2]	4.5	16.6	—	7.2[3]	180.6	43.0
1936 [4]	78.9[6]	13.2	6.4[7,9]	9.7	9.4[7]	—	14.3[8]	124.0[7,9]	44.5[7]
1936 [5]	47.2[6]	8.0	—	9.0	—	—	—	74.0[7]	26.6[7]

[1] Including (as in Lenin) the Bank of England, private banks and Dominion and colonial joint-stock banks with London offices.

[2] In six deposit and four investment banks (1913); the latter were subsequently reduced to 3 in 1928 and 2 in 1934. The data given by Lenin apply to a larger number of banks, but we have been unable to deal with these owing to lack of data.

[3] With the introduction of the gold mark in 1924, after inflation, the total savings deposits dropped to 595 million marks. Subsequently a considerable increase in these deposits took place.

[4] Calculated in marks, no allowance being made for depreciation of respective currencies.

[5] Calculated in marks, allowance being made for depreciation of respective currencies.

[6] 1935.   [7] 1934.   [8] Including savings banks in the Saar.

[9] Withdrawal of deposits due to crisis.   [10] See footnote 1 on p. 73.

SOURCES: Data on England, France and Germany for 1880, 1888 and 1908 are quoted from Lenin. For subsequent years the figures are taken as follows: for England, *The Economist*, Banking Supplement, May and October issues, 1913, 1914, 1929, 1936; for France, *Banques Commerciales*, 1913-29, pp. 144-45; *Annuaire Statistique* S.d.N. 1935-36, p. 271; for Germany from *Die Deutschen Banken 1924 bis 1926 S. 36, 135* and *Statistisches Jahrbuch für das Deutsche Reich*, 1930, S. 355. Figures on saving banks in the first three countries are taken from *Annuaire Statistique*, S.d.N. 1927 and 1933-34 and *Monthly Bulletin of Stat. L. of N.*, 1937. Figures for the U.S.A. are taken from the *Statistical Abstract of the United States*, 1912-35.

PARTICIPATION OF BANKS ON SUPERVISORY BOARDS OF JOINT STOCK COMPANIES IN GERMANY

Data gleaned from an investigation of the German banks made in 1933 presents the following picture of the participation of representatives of banks on the supervisory boards of commercial and industrial joint stock companies.

Of a total of 9,634 joint stock companies in Germany (end of 1932) 2,656 companies, the total membership of whose boards was 18,171, gave information as to the composition of their supervisory boards. According to these incomplete figures joint stock and private banks were rep-

the exuberance of youth" (a "subtle" allusion to the crash of 1873, and to the company promotion scandals), "opened the era of the industrialisation of Germany, nowadays the banks and industry are able to 'do it alone.' The domination of our big banks over the Stock Exchange . . . is nothing else than the expression of the completely organised German industrial state. If the domain of the automatically functioning economic laws is thus restricted, and if the domain consciously regulated by the banks is considerably increased, the national economic responsibility of a very small number of guiding heads is infinitely increased,"[1] so wrote Professor Schulze-Gaevernitz, an apologist of German imperialism, who is regarded as an authority by the imperialists of all countries, and who tries to gloss over a "detail," *viz.*, that the "conscious regulation" of economic life by the banks consists in the fleecing of the public by a handful of "completely organised" monopolists. For the task of a bourgeois professor is not to lay bare the mechanism of the financial system, or to divulge all the machinations of the finance monopolists, but, rather, to present them in a favourable light.

In the same way, Riesser, a still more authoritative economist and himself a bank man, makes shift with meaningless phrases in order to explain away undeniable facts. He writes:

". . .The Stock Exchange is steadily losing the feature which is absolutely essential for national economy as a whole and for the circulation of securities in particular—that of being an exact measuring-rod and an almost automatic regulator of the economic movements which converge on it." [2]

In other words, the old capitalism, the capitalism of free competition, and its indispensable regulator, the Stock Exchange, are passing away. A new capitalism has come to take its place, which bears obvious features of something transitory, which is a mixture of free competition and monopoly. The question naturally arises: to *what* is this new, "transitory" capitalism leading? But the bourgeois scholars are afraid to raise this question.

"Thirty years ago, employers, freely competing against one another, performed nine-tenths of the work connected with their businesses other than manual labour. At the present time, nine-tenths of this business 'brain work' is performed by *officials*. Banking is in the forefront of this evolution." [3]

---

[1] Schulze-Gaevernitz, *Die deutsche Kreditbank, Grundriss der Sozialökonomik* (*German Credit Bank* in *Outline of Social Economics*), Tübingen, 1915, Schulze-Gaevernitz, *ibid.*, p. 151.

[2] Riesser, *op. cit.*, fourth ed., p. 629.

[3] *Die Bank*, 1912, p. 435.

resented on the boards of 1,541 joint stock companies which had a total of 11,948 supervisory board members.

The following table shows the manner in which the bank representatives were distributed among the various groups of joint stock companies investigated.

Groups of joint stock companies according to percentage of bank representatives on their supervisory boards	Joint stock companies in each group		Number of members on supervisory board in each group	Number of bank representatives in these groups	Average per cent of bank representatives in each group
	Number	% of total			
Over 50%	159	10.3	1,138	773	68
25 to 50%	583	38.1	4,150	1,535	37
10 to 25%	700	45.7	5,293	985	19
Up to 10%	99	5.9	1,367	104	8
Total	1,541	100.0	11,948	3,397	28

SOURCE: *Untersuchung des Bankwesens,* 1933, II. Teil, "Statistiken," S. 167.

THE GROWTH OF "PERSONAL UNION" OR INTERLOCKING DIRECTORATES

The extent to which the "personal union" has advanced in modern capitalism is well brought out in the following examples:

In 1934 a report was submitted to the United States Congress giving interesting data concerning the personal union existing between the public utilities and the finance companies which finance them.

At the head of the list of names occupying the largest number of seats on the boards and supervisory boards of the public utilities companies we find the following:

Number
of seats

E. P. Sommerson, Electric Bond & Share 240
A. I. Koch, American Utilities Co. 212
J. F. McKenna, American Utilities Co. 190
C. A. Dougherty, Associated Gas & Electric Co. 180
Arthur S. Ray, Electric Bond & Share 179
I. T. Edmonds, American Utilities Co. 155
W. W. Bell, Altoona and Logan Valley Electric Railway Co. . 127
I. Weinberger, American Utilities Co. 114
I. W. Hill, Electric Bond & Share 112
Wm. H. Wilds, Alabama Utilities Service Co. 102
R. B. Small, Alabama Utilities Service Co. 102
W. M. MacFarland, Alabama Utilities Service Co. 102
Luke S. Bradley, Alabama Utilities Service Co. 101
L. L. Fenton, Alabama Utilities Service Co. 101
M. S. O'Keefe, American Utilities Co. 100

This admission by Schulze-Gaevernitz brings us once again to the question as to what this new capitalism, capitalism in its imperialist stage, is leading to.

Among the few banks which remain at the head of all capitalist economy as a result of the process of concentration, there is naturally to be observed an increasingly marked tendency towards monopolist agreements, towards a *bank trust*. In America, there are not nine, but *two* big banks, those of the billionaires Rockefeller and Morgan, which control a capital of eleven billion marks.[1] In Germany, the absorption of the Schaffhausenscher Bankverein by the Disconto-Gesellschaft, to which we referred above, was commented on in the following terms by the *Frankfurter Zeitung*, one of the organs of the Stock Exchange interests:

"The concentration movement of the banks is narrowing the circle of establishments from which it is possible to obtain large credits, and is consequently increasing the dependence of big industry upon a small number of banking groups. In view of the internal links between industry and finance, the freedom of movement of manufacturing companies in need of bank capital is restricted. For this reason, big industry is watching the growing trustification of the banks with mixed feelings. Indeed, we have repeatedly seen the beginnings of certain agreements between the individual big banking concerns, which aim at limiting competition." [2]

Again, the final word in the development of the banks is monopoly.

The close ties that exist between the banks and industry are the very things that bring out most strikingly the new role of the banks. When a bank discounts a bill for an industrial firm, opens a current account for it, etc., these operations, taken separately, do not in the least diminish the independence of the industrial firm, and the bank plays no other part than that of a modest intermediary. But when such operations are multiplied and become an established practice, when the bank "collects" in its own hands enormous amounts of capital, when the running of a current account for the firm in question enables the bank—and this is what happens—to become better informed of the economic position of the client, then the result is that the industrial capitalist becomes more completely dependent on the bank.

At the same time a very close personal union is established between the banks and the biggest industrial and commercial enterprises, the merging of one with another through the acquisition of shares, through the appointment of bank directors to the Supervisory Boards

---

[1] *Die Bank*, 1912, p. 435.
[2] Quoted by Schulze-Gaevernitz, *ibid.*, p. 155.

THE HOUSE OF MORGAN
SYSTEM OF FINANCIAL CONTROL (1929)

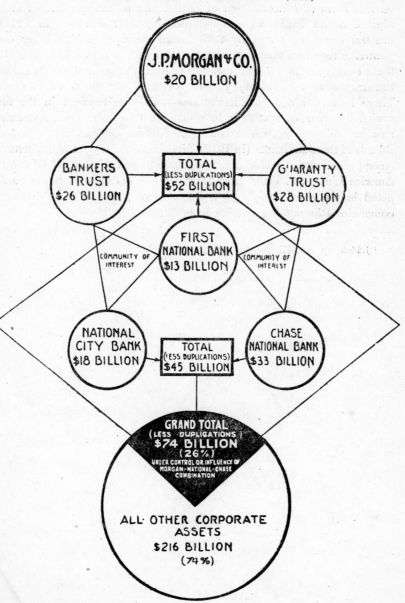

SOURCE: Lewis Corey, *The House of Morgan.*

(or Boards of Directors) of industrial and commercial enterprises, and *vice versa*. The German economist, Jeidels, has compiled very complete data on this form of concentration of capital and of enterprises. Six of the biggest Berlin banks were represented by their directors in 344 industrial companies; and by their board members in 407 other companies. Altogether, they supervised a total of 751 companies. In 289 of these companies they either had two of their representatives on each of the respective Supervisory Boards, or held the posts of chairmen. These industrial and commercial companies are engaged in the most varied branches of industry: in insurance, transport, restaurants, theatres, art industry, etc. On the other hand, there were on the Supervisory Boards of these six banks (in 1910) fifty-one of the biggest manufacturers, among whom were director of Krupp, of the powerful "Hapag" (Hamburg-America Line), etc. From 1895 to 1910, each of these six banks participated in the share and bond issues of several hundreds of industrial companies (the number ranging from 281 to 419).[1]

---

[1] Jeidels, *op. cit.*; Riesser, *op. cit.*—*Ed.*

Fourteen persons occupy leading positions in 75 to 100 companies each; while 61 persons are members of boards and supervisory boards of 50 to 75 companies each.

Albert Aymé-Martin, in his well-known book, *Nos grands financiers contre la nation*, cites a number of striking examples of personal union in French monopolist capital (1930):

Octave Homberg is a member of the board of 52 companies. Of fourteen of these companies he is either president or vice-president. The most important of these are Société Financière française et coloniale; Société Franco-Belge de matériel de chemins de fer; Banque de l'Indochine; The Central Mining Co., and others.

Gabriel Cordier is president or member of the board of 23 companies. The most important of these are: Compagnie des chemins de fer Paris-Lyon-Méditerranée; Compagnie du Canal de Suez, and others.

Théodore Laurent is a member of the board of 21 companies, of seven of which he is president. The most important of these are: Société Lorraine des Aciéries de Rombas; Les Forges et Aciéries de la Marne et d'Homécourt and Ateliers et Chantiers de France.

André Lebon is a member of the board of 15 companies, of four of which he is president. The most important of these are: Crédit Foncier d'Algérie et de Tunisie; Messageries maritimes; Compagnie générale des Colonies, and others.

Edmond Philippar is president or vice-president of six companies and member of the board of 18 more. Marcel Trélat is on 11 companies. The three Mirabaud brothers (Albert, Eugène and Pierre) occupy leading posts in 21 companies, and their partner, Henri Puerari, is president or member of the board of nine other companies, etc.

SOURCES: *Neue Züricher Zeitung*, 11, V, 1934, No. 838; Albert Aymé-Martin, *Nos grands financiers contre la nation*, Paris, 1931, pp. 113-42.

The *Lenin Miscellany,* Vol. XXII, p. 277, Russ. ed. contains a reproduction of the following table found in Lenin's notebooks on imperialism:

At the end of 1903 the big banks were represented on the *Supervisory Boards* of industrial companies as follows:

	Deutsche Bank	Disconto-Gesellschaft	Darmstädter Bank	Dresdner Bank	Schaffhausen-scher Bank-verein	Handelsge-sellschaft	Total (mine) for six big banks
By directors	101	31	51	53	68	40	344
By their members on Supervisory Boards.	120	61	50	80	62	34	407
Total....	221	92	101	133	130	74	751
By Chairman or by more than 2 persons	98	43	36	41	38	33	289

751 ⎫
      ⎬ 1,040
289 ⎭

NUMBER OF PLACES OCCUPIED BY BANK REPRESENTATIVES IN INDUSTRIAL COMPANIES IN GERMANY

The big banks were represented on the supervisory boards of industrial companies as follows:

Represented by:	Deutsche Bank and Disconto-Gesellschaft [1]		Dresdner Bank [2]		Berliner Handels-gesellschaft		Total for big banks	
	1903	1932	1903	1932	1903	1932	1903	1932
Directors [4]	200	—	104	—	40	—	344	—
Bank directors............	—	73	—	— [3]	—	4	—	77
Directors of bank branches	—	478	—	— [3]	—	—	—	478
Members of boards of directors of banks..........	—	141	—	86	—	85	—	312
Members of supervisory boards of banks (or administrative council)........	243	204	130	195	34	218	407	617
Total	443	896	234	281	74	307	751 ⎱ 1,040	1484 ⎱ 1,712
By Chairman or by more than 2 persons..........	179	158	77	31	33	39	289 ⎰	228 ⎰

[1] In 1929 the Deutsche Bank merged with the Disconto-Gesellschaft, while in 1914 the Disconto-Gesellschaft had merged with Schaffhausenscher Bankverein. In 1903 each of these banks carried on its operations independently.

[2] In 1931 the Dresdner Bank merged with the Darmstädter Bank. In 1903 each of them carried on operations independently.

[3] Data not available.

[4] Lenin puts this item under the heading: "by directors"; we have divided it under two headings: "by bank directors" and "by directors of bank branches."

SOURCES: The figures for 1903 are quoted from Lenin. The figures for 1932 are compiled from those in the *Handbuch der Deutschen Aktiengesellschaften, Die Berliner Börse, Adressbuch der Angestelltenräte.*

PARTICIPATION OF INDUSTRIAL MONOPOLIES IN THE MANAGEMENT OF BANKS

The following data illustrate how strongly in their turn the biggest industrial companies are represented on the boards of banks.

In 1932 seventy big industrialists were members of the supervisory boards of the three biggest Berlin banks, the Deutsche Bank and Disconto-Gesellschaft, the Dresdner Bank and the Berliner Handelsge-

The "personal union" between the banks and industry is completed by the "personal union" between both and the state.

"Seats on the Supervisory Board," writes Jeidels, "are freely offered to persons of title, also to ex-civil servants, who are able to do a great deal to facilitate" (!!) "relations with the authorities.". . . "Usually on the Supervisory Board of a big bank there is a member of parliament or a Berlin city councillor." [1]

The building, so to speak, of the great capitalist monopolies is therefore going on full steam ahead in all "natural" and "supernatural" ways. A sort of division of labour amongst some hundreds of kings of finance who reign over modern capitalist society is being systematically developed.

"Simultaneously with this widening of the sphere of activity of certain big industrialists" (sharing in the management of banks, etc.) "and together with the allocation of provincial bank managers to definite industrial regions, there is a growth of specialisation among the managers of the big banks. . . . Generally speaking, this specialisation is only conceivable when banking is conducted on a large scale, and particularly when it has widespread connections with industry. This division of labour proceeds along two lines: on the one hand, the relations with industry as a whole are entrusted to one manager, as his special function; on the other, each

---

[1] Jeidels, *op. cit.*, pp. 149, 152.—*Ed.*

sellschaft. Among these were directors of Krupp, the Hapag Steamship Company, the I. G. Farbenindustrie, the two electrical trusts, A.E.G. and Siemens, the German Steel Trust, representatives of all the biggest iron and steel enterprises, etc.

The big French concern, Schneider-Creusot, besides participating in the management of the Banque de l'Union parisienne—which had a capital of 300 million francs until May 1934—and partly controlling it,[1] also participated in the management of the following banks and finance companies: Banque des Pays du Nord, the Niederoesterreichische Escompte Bank,[2] Credit Anstalt, the Ungarische Allgemeine Credit-Bank, Framerican Industrial Development Co., etc., having a total capital of 1.4 billion francs.

The well-known Belgian Solvay chemical trust participates in the management of two of the biggest banks in Belgium which have a total capital of 1.6 billion francs. In addition, it owns three finance companies: one in Belgium, with a capital of 300 million francs, and two in the U.S.A., the largest of which has a capital of 74.5 million dollars.

SOURCES: Liefmann, *Beteiligungs- und Finanzierungsgesellschaften*, 1931, S. 386; *Berliner Börsenzeitung*, 3 and 11, XII, 1933; *Grünbuch der Aktiengesellschaften*, 1932, 1933; Augustin Hamon et X. Y. Z., *Les Maîtres de la France*, Paris, 1936, pp. 107-08. Banker's Almanac, 1934-35, p. 1138.

THE PERSONAL UNION BETWEEN MONOPOLIES AND GOVERNMENTS

The following are a few examples illustrating the personal union between monopolies and governments in recent years.

GERMANY

In 1932-33 the following were represented on the boards of directors and supervisory boards of the concerns indicated:

German Chemical Trust—1 Prussian Minister, 1 retired Provincial President, 1 Secretary of State (Vice Minister), 7 Privy Councillors, 1 ex-Police President, 1 Councillor of Ministry, etc.

Dresdner Bank—2 ex-Secretaries of State (of whom one was Chairman of the Board of Directors), 1 envoy, 1 private secretary of a Minister, etc.

Hapag-Lloyd—6 ex-Ministers, 1 ex-Secretary of State, 2 Councillors of State, etc.

---

[1] During the reorganisation of the bank in 1934, a new group, that of the banker G. de Lubersac, connected with British capital, acquired interests in it.

[2] In 1934 was absorbed by Credit Anstalt.

manager assumes the supervision of several isolated enterprises, or enterprises with allied interests, or in the same branch of industry, sitting on their Boards of Directors" (capitalism has reached the stage of organised *control* of individual enterprises). "One specialises in German industry, sometimes even in West German industry alone" (the West is the most industrialised part of Germany). "Others specialise in relations with foreign states and foreign industry, in information about manufacturers, in Stock Exchange questions, etc. Besides, each bank manager is often assigned a special industry or locality, where he has a say as a member of the Board of Directors; one works mainly on the Board of Directors of electric companies, another in the chemical, brewing or sugar beet industry; a third in a few isolated industrial enterprises but at the same time in non-industrial, *i.e.*, insurance companies. . . . It is certain that, as the extent and diversification of the big banks' operations increase, the division of labour among their directors also spreads, with the object and result of lifting them somewhat out of pure banking and making them better experts, better judges of the general problems of industry and the special problems of each branch of industry, thus making them more capable of action within the respective bank's industrial sphere of influence. This system is supplemented by the banks' endeavours to have elected to their own Board of Directors, or to those of their subsidiary banks, men who are experts in industrial affairs, such as manufacturers, former officials, especially those formerly in the railway service or in mining," etc.[1]

We find the same system, with only slight difference, in French banking. For instance, one of the three biggest French banks, the Crédit Lyonnais, has organised a financial research service (Service des études financières), which permanently employs over fifty engineers, statisticians, economists, lawyers, etc., at a cost of six or seven hundred thousand francs annually. The service is in turn divided into eight sections, of which one deals with industrial establishments, another with general statistics, a third with railway and steamship companies, a fourth with securities, a fifth with financial reports, etc.[2]

The result is twofold: on the one hand the merging, to an ever greater extent, or, as N. Bukharin aptly calls it, the coalescence of bank and industrial capital; and on the other hand, a transformation of the banks into institutions of a truly "universal character." On this question we think it necessary to quote the exact terms used by Jeidels, who has best studied the subject:

"An examination of the sum total of industrial relationships reveals the *universal character* of the financial establishments working on behalf of industry. Unlike other kinds of banks and contrary to the requirements often laid down in literature—according to which banks ought to specialise in one kind of business or in one branch of industry in order to maintain a firm footing—the big banks are striving to make their industrial connections as varied and far-reaching as possible, according to locality and branch of business, and are striving to do away with the inequali-

[1] Jeidels, *op. cit.*, pp. 156-57.
[2] Eugen Kaufmann, *Die Organisation der französischen Depositen-Grossbanken* (*Organisation of the Big French Deposit Banks*), in *Die Bank*, 1909, II, pp. 851, *et seq.*

GREAT BRITAIN (1933)

Reginald McKenna, Chairman of the Board of Directors of Midland Bank, ex-First Lord of the Admiralty and ex-Chancellor of the Exchequer.

Stanley Baldwin, leader of the Conservative Party, ex-Prime Minister, partner in Baldwins, Ltd., iron and steel manufacturers.

The late Viscount Grey of Fallodon, former Secretary of State for Foreign Affairs, Director of London and North Eastern Railway Co. (died in 1933).

Sir J. Stamp, Chairman of the Board and Director of the London Midland and Scottish Railway, Director of the Bank of England, member of the Economic Advisory Council, former British representative on the Dawes and Young Commissions. From 1896 to 1919 occupied leading posts in the Civil Service.

Sir Philip Cunliffe-Lister (Lloyd-Greame), Secretary of State for the Colonies, ex-President of the Board of Trade; was chairman of the tin syndicate.

U.S.A. (1933)

Andrew W. Mellon, former Ambassador to England, Secretary of the Treasury in the Hoover Cabinet, billionaire, head and ex-President of the Mellon National Bank and of numerous finance and industrial corporations, owner of the Aluminum Co. of America.

Owen D. Young, Chairman of the General Electric Company, Chairman of the Board of Directors and Director of numerous corporations, former Reparations Agent in Germany, Chairman of the Second Commission of Experts on Reparations (the Young Plan), formerly Acting Governor of the New York Federal Reserve Bank.

JAPAN

All the big monopolist concerns maintain very close personal contacts with the Court, the high bureaucracy, the high nobility, government circles, and with the leaders of the two big political parties (the Seyukai and the Minseito).

Thus, the Japanese Emperor is personally interested in the Mitsubishi concern. One of the daughters of Iwasaki (head of the concern) married the late leader of the Minseito Party, Kato; another married the Minister of Foreign Affairs in the last Minseito government, Shidehara; and a third married the Minister of Finance in the same government, Inouye, who was assassinated in 1932. One of the principals of the Mitsui concern, Fujiwara Ginjiro, is a member of the House of Peers;

ties in the distribution among localities and branches of business resulting from the historical development of individual banking houses. . . . One tendency is to make the ties with industry general; another tendency is to make these ties durable and close. In the six big banks both these tendencies are realised, not in full, but to a considerable extent and to an equal degree." [1]

Quite often industrial and commercial circles complain of the "terrorism" of the banks. And it is not surprising that such complaints are heard, for the big banks "command," as will be seen from the following example: on November 19, 1901, one of the big Berlin "D" bank (such is the name given to the four biggest banks whose names begin with the letter D[2]) wrote to the Board of Directors of the German Central Northwest Cement Syndicate in the following terms:

"As we learn from the notice you published in the *Reichsanzeiger* of the 18th instant, we must reckon with the possibility that the next general meeting of your company, fixed for the 30th of this month, may decide on measures which are likely to effect changes in your undertakings which are unacceptable to us. We deeply regret that, for these reasons, we are obliged henceforth to withdraw the credit which has been hitherto allowed you. . . . But if the said next general meeting does not decide upon measures which are unacceptable to us and if we receive suitable guarantees on this matter for the future, we shall be quite willing to open negotiations with you on the grant of a new credit." [3]

As a matter of fact, this is small capital's old complaint about being oppressed by big capital, but in this case it was a whole syndicate that fell into the category of "small" capital! The old struggle between big and small capital is being resumed on a new and higher stage of development. It stands to reason that undertakings, financed by big banks handling billions, can accelerate technical progress in a way that cannot possibly be compared with the past. The banks, for example, set up special technical research societies, and only "friendly" industrial enterprises benefit from their work. To this category belong the Electric Railway Research Association and the Central Bureau of Scientific and Technical Research.

The directors of the big banks themselves cannot fail to see that new conditions of national economy are being created. But they are powerless in the face of these phenomena.

"Anyone who has watched, in recent years, the changes of incumbents of directorships and seats on the Supervisory Boards of the big banks, cannot fail to have

---

[1] Jeidels, *op cit.*, p. 180.
[2] *I.e.*, Deutsche Bank, Disconto-Gesellschaft, Dresdner Bank and Darmstädter Bank.—*Ed.*
[3] Oskar Stillich, *Geld und Bankwesen*, Berlin, 1907, p. 147.

another, Yamamoto Jotaro, is a prominent leader of the Seyukai Party.

One of the most prominent feudal aristocrats, Prince Saionji (the last member of the Genro), is a brother of the founder of the Sumitomo concern, and an uncle of its present owner.

Of the Yasuda concern, Takahashi Korekiyo is one of the leaders of the Seyukai; Mori Hirozo is chairman of the Government Bank of Taiwan and Shijo Takahide was formerly Minister of Commerce and Industry.

FRANCE

Albert Aymé-Martin, in his book *Nos grands financiers contre la nation*, gives a list of 50 senators and deputies who in 1931 held leading posts on the boards of directors and supervisory boards of 96 of the biggest banks, insurance, industrial and transport joint stock companies. Tardieu, Dalimier, François Albert, Paul Doumer (President of the Republic, assassinated by Gorgouloff), Caillaux, François Piétri, Loucheur—all of these, either present or former ministers, senators, deputies of the Right and of the "Left," held, or still hold, leading posts in joint stock enterprises.

The *Deutsche Bergwerkszeitung*, the organ of German heavy industry, in its issue of June 14, 1934, published an article showing that behind the official government of France there stands an unofficial government composed of leaders of finance capital. The article contains a list of the names of this financial oligarchy and the roles they play. Below we reproduce the list with the newspaper's comments:

"*Presidency and Foreign Affairs*: Horace Finaly, managing director of the Banque de Paris et des Pays-Bas and François de Wendel, member of the Board of Governors of the Banque de France.

"*Industry and Commerce*: Duchemin, President of the Confederation de la Production Française, member of the Board of Governors of the Banque de France.

"*Foreign Trade*: Etienne Fougère, President of the National Association of Economic Expansion.

"*Agriculture*: Marquis de Vogüé, President of the United Farmers of France, President of the Suez Canal Co., member of the Board of Governors of the Banque de France.

"*General Insurance*: Mallet, President of the biggest insurance companies and member of the Board of Governors of the Banque de France.

"*Transport*: Rothschild, banker, President of the Northern Railway and member of the Board of Governors of the Banque de France.

noticed that power is gradually passing into the hands of men who consider the active intervention of the big banks in the general development of industry to be indispensable and of increasing importance. Between these new men and the old bank directors, disagreements of a business and often of a personal nature are growing on this subject. The question that is in dispute is whether or not the banks, as credit institutions, will suffer from this intervention in industry, whether they are sacrificing tried principles and an assured profit to engage in a field of activity which has nothing in common with their role as intermediaries in providing credit, and which is leading the banks into a field where they are more than ever before exposed to the blind forces of trade fluctuations. This is the opinion of many of the older bank directors, while most of the young men consider active intervention in industry to be a necessity as great as that which gave rise, simultaneously with big modern industry, to the big banks and modern industrial banking. The two parties to this discussion are agreed only on one point: and that is, that as yet there are neither firm principles nor a concrete aim in the new activities of the big banks." [1]

The old capitalism has had its day. The new capitalism represents a transition towards something. It is hopeless, of course, to seek for "firm principles and a concrete aim" for the purpose of "reconciling" monopoly with free competition. The admission of the practical men has quite a different ring from the official praises of the charms of "organised" capitalism sung by its apologists, Schulze-Gaevernitz, Liefmann and similar "theoreticians."

At precisely what period were the "new activities" of the big banks finally established? Jeidels gives us a fairly exact answer to this important question:

"The ties between the banks and industrial enterprises, with their new content, their new forms and their new organs, namely, the big banks which are organised on both a centralised and a decentralised basis, were scarcely a characteristic economic phenomenon before the 'nineties; in one sense, indeed, this initial date may be advanced to the year 1897, when the important 'mergers' took place and when, for the first time, the new form of decentralised organisation was introduced to suit the industrial policy of the banks. This starting point could perhaps be placed at an even later date, for it was the crisis [of 1900] that enormously accelerated and intensified the process of concentration of industry and banking, consolidated that process, for the first time transformed the connection with industry into the monopoly of the big banks, and made this connection much closer and more active." [2]

Thus, the beginning of the twentieth century marks the turning point from the old capitalism to the new, from the domination of capital in general to the domination of finance capital.

---

[1] Jeidels, op. cit., pp. 183-84.
[2] Ibid., p. 181.

"*Armaments*: Schneider, of Schneider & Co. (Creusot), Managing
Director of the Paris-Lyons & Mediterranean Railway, Managing Director of the Banque des Pays du Nord and of the Crédit Lyonnais, President of the European Industrial and Financial Union.

"*The Press*: Pierre Guimier, Managing Director of the Havas Agency.

"*Internal Affairs and Propaganda*: Ernest Mercier, President of the
Redressement Français, Managing Director and member of the auditing
committees of twenty electric companies.

"*Culture*: Fouret, President of Messageries Hachette.

"*Colonies*: Emile Moreau, President of the Banque de Paris et des
Pays-Bas (to which the Madagascar Bank is subordinated), Managing
Director of the Banque de l'Indochine, President of the Compagnie Géné-
rale du Maroc and of the Compagnie Générale des Colonies.

"The industrial might of France is embodied in the General Confederation of French Industries and the National Association of Economic
Expansion. With the aid of these two centres of power, the Comité des
Forges, headed by de Wendel and Lambert-Ribot, and the Coal Committee, headed by de Peyerimhoff, control large insurance, electric, wool-
len and silk companies, the whole of commerce and industry.

"Five thousand men are at the head of the most important joint stock
companies.

"One hundred men rule this oligarchy.

"Twenty magnates, heads of industrial, commercial and agricultural
organisations, control the Banque de France, and consequently, the credit of the French Republic.

"Two men stand at the head of this oligarchy: Horace Finaly, Managing Director of the Banque de Paris et des Pays-Bas, and François de
Wendel. These two men embody and unite big capital in industry and
finance."

SOURCES: For Germany—*Grünbuch der Aktiengesellschaften*, 1932, 1933; for
England and U.S.A.—*Stock Exchange Yearbook, Who's Who in Finance, Bankers'
Almanac*, 1932; for France—A. Aymé-Martin, *Nos grands financiers contre la nation*,
1931, and *Deutsche Bergwerkszeitung*, 14, VI, 1934; for Japan—Takahashi, *Financial
Description of Concerns*, 1930 (in Japanese).

CHAPTER III

FINANCE CAPITAL AND FINANCIAL OLIGARCHY

"A steadily increasing proportion of capital in industry," Hilferding writes, "does not belong to the industrialists who employ it. They obtain the use of it only through the medium of the banks, which, in relation to them, represent the owners of the capital. On the other hand, the bank is forced to keep an increasing share of its funds engaged in industry. Thus, to an increasing degree the bank is being transformed into an industrial capitalist. This bank capital, *i.e.*, capital in money form which is thus really transformed into industrial capital, I call 'finance capital.' . . . Finance capital is capital controlled by banks and employed by industrialists." [1]

This definition is incomplete in so far as it is silent on one extremely important fact: the increase of concentration of production and of capital to such an extent that it leads, and has led, to monopoly. But throughout the whole of his work, and particularly in the two chapters which precede the one from which this definition is taken, Hilferding stresses the part played by *capitalist monopolies.*

The concentration of production; the monopoly arising therefrom; the merging or coalescence of banking with industry—this is the history of the rise of finance capital and what gives the term "finance capital" its content.

We now have to describe how, under the general conditions of commodity production and private property, the "domination" of capitalist monopolies inevitably becomes the domination of a financial oligarchy. It should be noted that the representatives of German bourgeois science —and not only of German science—like Riesser, Schulze-Gaevernitz, Liefmann and others are all apologists of imperialism and of finance capital. Instead of revealing the "mechanics" of the formation of an oligarchy, its methods, its revenues "innocent and sinful," its connections with parliaments, etc., they conceal, obscure and embellish them. They evade these "vexed questions" by a few vague and pompous phrases: appeals to the "sense of responsibility" of bank directors, praising "the sense of duty" of Prussian officials; by giving serious

---

[1] R. Hilferding, *Das Finanzkapital*, p. 283, 1912.

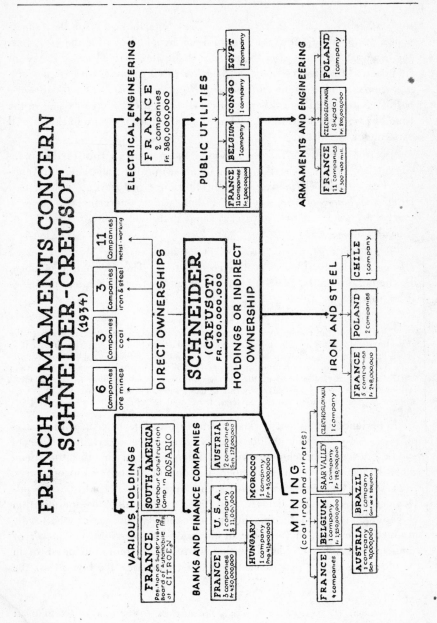

FRENCH ARMAMENTS CONCERN
SCHNEIDER-CREUSOT
(1934)

VARIOUS HOLDINGS

FRANCE
Position on supervising
Board of automobile firm
of CITROEN

SOUTH AMERICA
Harbour construction
Comp in ROSARIO

ELECTRICAL ENGINEERING

FRANCE
2 companies
Fr. 380,000,000

DIRECT OWNERSHIPS

| 6 Companies | 3 Companies | 3 Companies | 11 Companies |
| ore mines | coal | iron & steel | metal-working |

SCHNEIDER
(CREUSOT)
FR. 100,000,000

HOLDINGS OR INDIRECT
OWNERSHIP

PUBLIC UTILITIES

FRANCE
11 companies
Fr. 1,000,000,000

BELGIUM
1 company

CONGO
1 company

EGYPT
1 company

ARMAMENTS AND ENGINEERING

FRANCE
11 companies
Fr. 300-400 mill.

CZECHOSLOVAKIA
(Škoda)
Kr. 290,000,000

POLAND
1 company

BANKS AND FINANCE COMPANIES

FRANCE
3 companies
Fr. 450,000,000

U.S.A.
1 company
$1,100,000

AUSTRIA
2 companies
Sch 172,000,000

HUNGARY
1 company
Png. 41,000,000

MOROCCO
1 company
Fr. 45,000,000

MINING
(coal, iron and nitrates)

FRANCE
4 companies

AUSTRIA
1 company
Sch 10,000,000

BELGIUM
1 company
Fr. 1,250,000,000

BRAZIL
1 company
Gen reis 100,000

SAAR VALLEY
1 company
Fr. 190,000,000

CZECHOSLOVAKIA
1 company

IRON AND STEEL

FRANCE
5 companies
Fr. 248,000,000

POLAND
2 companies

CHILE
1 company

study to petty details, to ridiculous bills of parliament—for the "supervision" and "regulation" of monopolies; by playing with theories, like, for example, the following "scientific" definition, arrived at by Professor Liefmann: *"Commerce is an occupation having for its object: collecting goods, storing them and making them available."* (The Professor's bold-face italics.) From this it would follow that commerce existed in the time of primitive man, who knew nothing about exchange, and that it will exist under socialism!

But the monstrous facts concerning the monstrous rule of the financial oligarchy are so striking that in all capitalist countries, in America, France and Germany, a whole literature has sprung up, written from the *bourgeois* point of view, but which, nevertheless, gives a fairly accurate picture and criticism—petty-bourgeois, naturally—of this oligarchy.

The "holding system," to which we have already briefly referred above, should be placed at the corner-stone. The German economist, Heymann, probably the first to call attention to this matter, describes it in this way:

"The head of the concern controls the parent company; the latter reigns over the subsidiary companies which in their turn control still other subsidiaries. Thus, it is possible with a comparatively small capital to dominate immense spheres of production. As a matter of fact, if holding 50 per cent of the capital is always sufficient to control a company, the head of the concern needs only one million to control eight millions in the second subsidiaries. And if this "interlocking" is extended, it is possible with one million to control sixteen, thirty-two or more millions." [1]

Experience shows that it is sufficient to own 40 per cent of the shares of a company in order to direct its affairs,[2] since a certain number of small, scattered shareholders find it impossible, in practice, to attend general meetings, etc. The "democratisation" of the ownership of shares, from which the bourgeois sophists and opportunist "would-be" Social-Democrats expect (or declare that they expect) the "democratisation of capital," the strengthening of the role and significance of small-scale production, etc., is, in fact, one of the ways of increasing the power of financial oligarchy. Incidentally, this is why, in the more advanced, or in the older and more "experienced" capitalist countries, the law allows the

---

[1] Heymann, *Die gemischten Werke im deutschen Grosseisengewerbe*, Stuttgart 1904, pp. 268-69.

[2] R. Liefmann. *Beteiligungsgesellschaften*, p. 258.

THE HOLDING SYSTEM
GERMANY

A very characteristic example of how, with the aid of a comparatively small amount of capital, it is possible to control huge amounts of capital is provided by the holdings of the steel magnate Flick. As the owner of the majority of the stock of the Charlottenhütte iron and steel works, which has a capital of 20 million marks, he was able, up to 1932, by means of a complicated five-storey system of holdings, to control 82 companies, including the German Steel Trust, having a total capital of 1,706 million marks. Owing to financial difficulties, Flick lost control of the steel trust in 1932-33, and the dominating role passed to the Thyssen group.

UNITED STATES

The official investigation of the electrical industry conducted by the Federal Trade Commission revealed that by means of a "five-storey pyramid" of holdings, the Byllesby concern was able, with a capital investment of less than *one* million dollars, to acquire control over a productive capital exceeding 370 million dollars.

The Insull electric power concern, which went bankrupt during the crisis, controlled, through a "six-storey" system of holdings, 132 companies and had an interest in 248 other companies.

Professors Adolph A. Berle and Gardiner C. Means, of Columbia University, analysed the reports of 1929-30 of over 200 of the biggest companies and revealed the methods by which they were controlled. The

issue of shares of very small denomination. In Germany, it is not permitted by the law to issue shares of less value than one thousand marks, and the magnates of German finance look with an envious eye at England, where the issue of one-pound shares is permitted. Siemens, one of the biggest industrialists and "financial kings" in Germany, told the Reichstag on June 7, 1900, that "the one-pound share is the basis of British imperialism."[1] This merchant has a much deeper and more "Marxian" understanding of imperialism than a certain disreputable writer, generally held to be one of the founders of Russian Marxism, who believes that imperialism is a bad habit of a certain nation. . . .

But the "holding system" not only serves to increase enormously the power of the monopolists; it also enables them to resort with impunity to all sorts of shady tricks to cheat the public, for the directors of the parent company are not legally responsible for the subsidiary companies, which are supposed to be "independent," and *through the medium* of which they can "pull off" *anything*. Here is an example taken from the German review, *Die Bank*, for May 1914:

"The Spring Steel Company of Kassel was regarded some years ago as being one of the most profitable enterprises in Germany. Through bad management its dividends fell within the space of a few years from 15 per cent to nil. It appears that the Board, without consulting the shareholders, had loaned *six million marks* to one of the subsidiary companies, the Hassia, Ltd., which had a nominal capital of only some hundreds of thousands of marks. This commitment, amounting to nearly treble the capital of the parent company, was never mentioned in its balance sheets. This omission was quite legal, and could be kept up for two whole years because it did not violate any provision of company law. The chairman of the Supervisory Board, who as the responsible head had signed the false balance sheets, was, and still is, the president of the Kassel Chamber of Commerce. The shareholders only heard of the loan to the Hassia, Ltd., long afterwards, when it had long been proved to have been a mistake" (this word the writer should have put in quotation marks), "and when Spring Steel shares had dropped nearly 100 points, because those in the know had got rid of them. . . .

"*This typical example of balance-sheet jugglery, quite common in joint stock companies,* explains why their Boards of Directors are more willing to undertake risky transactions than individual dealers. Modern methods of drawing up balance sheets not only make it possible to conceal doubtful undertakings from the average shareholder, but also allow the people most concerned to escape the consequence of unsuccessful speculation by selling their shares in time while the individual dealer risks his own skin in everything he does.

"The balance sheets of many joint stock companies put us in mind of the palimpsests of the Middle Ages from which the visible inscription had first to be erased in order to discover beneath it another inscription giving the real meaning of the document." (Palimpsests are parchment documents from which the original inscription has been obliterated and another inscription imposed.)

---

[1] Schulze-Gaevernitz in "*Grdr. d. S.-Oek.*," V, 2, p. 110.

total combined assets of these companies amounted to 81 billion dollars, equal approximately to one-half of the entire corporate wealth of all industrial, railway and public utility concerns in the U.S.A. The results of this analysis are summarised in the following table:

Control was exercised by ownership of:	Number of companies	Assets (billion dollars)
Majority of capital stock	22	4.9
Minority of capital stock	176	75.9

Thus, $76,000,000,000, or 94 per cent of the total assets of the 200 companies, is controlled by a handful of monopolists owning a minority of the stock in each of them.

The authors mention the following methods by which control is exercised.

1. By owning a sufficiently large controlling block of stock, while the majority of the stock is distributed among a large number of disunited stockholders. For example, Baker and Vanderbilt control the Delaware, Lackawanna & Western R. R. Co., although they own only 18 per cent of the stock.

2. By an intricate series of pyramided holding companies. Pointing to the well-known case of the Van Sweringen brothers as a striking example of this, the authors say:

"In recent years the Van Sweringen brothers have been notably successful in using this device to create and retain control of a great railroad system. Through an intricate series of pyramided holding companies they gathered together vast railroad properties extending nearly from coast to coast. As the system was built up the structure of holding companies was simplified until at the beginning of 1930 it was not unduly complex. The major ramifications are shown in Chart III (see page 119 in this volume—*Ed.*). By this pyramid an investment of less than $20,000,000 has been able to control eight Class I railroads having combined assets of over $2,000,000,000. Less than 1 per cent of the total investment or hardly more than 2 per cent of the investment represented by stock has been sufficient to control this great system."[1]

---

[1] After the bankruptcy and reorganisation of the Van Sweringen concern in the autumn of 1935 and the death of both brothers in 1935-36 the United States Senate investigation in 1936 established: 1) That for an investment of $3,121,000 they controlled assets to the amount of $3,183,285,783, *i.e.*, control was concentrated not in one per cent but in one per thousand of total invested capital; 2) That, as Senator Wheeler, Chairman of the Investigation Commission, said, "the Van Sweringens were simply nominees of the Guaranty Trust," *i.e.*, of Morgan.

"The simplest and, therefore, most common procedure for making balance sheets indecipherable is to divide a single business into several parts by setting up subsidiary companies—or by annexing such. The advantages of this system for various objects—legal and illegal—are so evident that it is now quite unusual to find an important company in which it is not actually in use." [1]

As an example of an important monopolist company widely employing this system, the author quotes the famous General Electric Company (Allgemeine Elektrizitäts Gesellschaft—A.E.G.) to which we shall refer below. In 1912, it was calculated that this company held shares in from 175 to 200 other companies, controlling them, of course, and thus having control of a total capital of 1,500,000,000 marks! [2]

All rules of control, the publication of balance sheets, the drawing up of balance sheets according to a definite form, the public auditing of accounts, etc., the things about which well-intentioned professors and officials—that is, those imbued with the good intention of defending and embellishing capitalism—discourse to the public, are of no avail. For private property is sacred, and no one can be prohibited from buying, selling, exchanging or mortgaging shares, etc.

The extent to which this "holding system" has developed in the big Russian banks may be judged by the figures given by E. Agahd, who was for fifteen years an official of the Russo-Chinese Bank and who, in May 1914, published a book, not altogether correctly entitled Big Banks and the World Market. [3] The author divides the big Russian banks into two main categories: a) banks that come under a "holding system," and b) "independent" banks—"independence," however, being arbitrarily taken to mean independence of foreign banks. The author divides the first group into three sub-groups: 1) German participation, 2) British participation, and 3) French participation, having in view the "participation" and domination of the big foreign banks of the particular country mentioned. The author divides the capital of the banks into "productively" invested capital (in industrial and commercial undertakings), and "speculatively" invested capital (in Stock Exchange and financial operations),

---

[1] Ludwig Eschwege, Tochtergesellschaften (Subsidiary Companies) in Die Bank, 1914, I, pp. 544-46.

[2] Kurt Heinig, Der Weg des Elektrotrusts (The Path of the Electric Trust) in Die Neue Zeit, 1911-1912, Vol. II, p. 484.

[3] E. Agahd. Grossbanken und Weltmarkt. Die wirtschaftliche und politische Bedeutung der Grossbanken im Weltmarkt unter Berücksichtung ihres Einflusses auf Russlands Volkswirtschaft und die deutsch-russischen Beziehungen. Berl. ("Big Banks and the World Market. The economic and political significance of the big banks on the world market, with reference to their influence on Russia's national economy and German-Russian relations." Berlin, 1914, pp. 11-17.)

3. Control through various legal devices. The non-voting common stock of the Dodge Brothers, Inc. issued in 1925 can be quoted as an example. "In this case neither the preferred nor four-fifths of the common stock was entitled to vote in the election of directors. By owning 250,000 voting common shares representing an investment of less than two and one-quarter million dollars, Dillon, Read & Co. was able to exercise legal control over this hundred-and-thirty-million-dollar concern."

Another example is that of the Standard Gas & Electric Co. "Each share of $1 par preferred stock of that company had as much voting power as a $50 par common share. In 1929, the million shares of the cheap stock were able to cast 41 per cent of the votes outstanding. Here again a million dollar par value of stock presumably representing a million dollars of investment was able to exercise practical control over $1,000,000,000 of assets."

4. By securing the most important posts in the management, without owning a large block of stock. The authors, Berle and Means, assert that this is the method by which control is exercised over the biggest industrial and railroad concerns, such as the U. S. Steel Corp., the General Electric Co., the American Telephone & Telegraph Co., the Pennsylvania R.R., the New York Central R.R., etc.

SOURCES: *Grünbuch der Aktiengesellschaften,* 1933; C. D. Thompson, *The Confessions of the Power Trust,* 1933, pp. 234-41; A. A. Berle, Jr. and Gardiner C. Means, *The Modern Corppration and Private Property,* Macmillan, New York, 1933, pp. 19, 70-115; *Railway Age,* 12, 19 and 26, XII, 1936.

assuming, from his petty-bourgeois reformist point of view, that it is possible, under capitalism, to separate the first form of investment from the second and to abolish the second form.

Here are the figures he supplies:

BANK ASSETS

(According to reports for October-November, 1913, in millions of rubles)

Groups of Russian Banks	Capital Invested		
	Productive	Speculative	Total
A 1) Four banks: Siberian Commercial Bank, Russian Bank, International Bank, and Discount Bank	413.7	859.1	1,272.8
2) Two banks: Commercial and Industrial and Russo-British	239.3	169.1	408.4
3) Five banks: Russian-Asiatic, St. Petersburg Private, Azov-Don, Union Moscow, Russo-French Commercial	711.8	661.2	1,373.0
Total: (11 banks) ....A =	1,364.8	1,689.4	3,054.2
B Eight banks: Moscow Merchants, Volga-Kama, Junker and Co., St. Petersburg Commercial (formerly Wawelberg), Bank of Moscow (formerly Riabushinsky), Moscow Discount, Moscow Commercial, Private Bank of Moscow	504.2	391.1	895.3
Total: (19 banks)	1,869.0	2,080.5	3,949.5

According to these figures, of the approximately four billion rubles making up the "working" capital of the big banks, *more than three-fourths*, more than three billion, belonged to banks which in reality were only "subsidiary companies" of foreign banks, and chiefly of the Paris banks (the famous trio: Union Parisien, Paris et Pays-Bas and Société Générale), and of the Berlin banks (particularly the Deutsche Bank and Disconto-Gesellschaft). Two of the most important Russian banks, the Russian Bank for Foreign Trade and the St. Petersburg International Commercial, between 1906 and 1912 increased their capital from 44,000,000 to 98,000,000 rubles, and their reserve from 15,000,000 to 39,000,000 "employing three-fourths German capital." The first belongs to the Deutsche Bank group and the second to the Disconto-Gesellschaft. The worthy Agahd is indignant at the fact that the majority of the shares are held by the Berlin banks, and that, therefore, the Russian shareholders are powerless. Naturally, the country which exports capital skims the cream: for example, the Deutsche Bank, while introducing the shares of the Siberian Commercial Bank on the Berlin market,

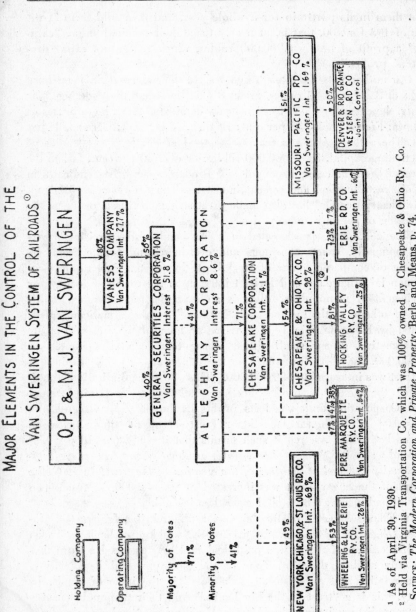

MAJOR ELEMENTS IN THE CONTROL OF THE
VAN SWERINGEN SYSTEM OF RAILROADS ©

O.P. & M.J. VAN SWERINGEN

VANESS COMPANY
Van Sweringen Int 27.7%

GENERAL SECURITIES CORPORATION
Van Sweringen Interest 51.8 %

ALLEGHANY CORPORATION
Van Sweringen Interest 8.6 %

MISSOURI PACIFIC RD. CO
Van Sweringen Int. 1.69 %

DENVER & RIO GRANDE
WESTERN RD CO
Joint Control

CHESAPEAKE CORPORATION
Van Sweringen Int. 4.1%

CHESAPEAKE & OHIO RY. CO.
Van Sweringen Int .98%

ERIE RD. CO.
Van Sweringen Int .60%

HOCKING VALLEY
RY.CO
Van Sweringen Int .25%

PERE MARQUETTE
RY.CO.
Van Sweringen Int. 64%

NEW YORK, CHICAGO & ST. LOUIS RD. CO.
Van Sweringen Int. .69 %

WHEELING & LAKE ERIE
RY.CO.
Van Sweringen Int. .26%

80%
56%
40%
41%
71%
51%
50%
54%
81%
23%
7%
17%
47%
38%
49%
53%

Holding Company

Operating Company

Majority of Votes 71%

Minority of Votes 41%

¹ As of April 30, 1930.
² Held via Virginia Transportation Co. which was 100% owned by Chesapeake & Ohio Ry. Co.
SOURCE: *The Modern Corporation and Private Property*, Berle and Means, p. 74.

kept them in its portfolio for a whole year, and then sold them at the rate of 193 for 100, that is, at nearly twice their nominal value, "earning" a profit of nearly 6,000,000 rubles, which Hilferding calls "promoters' profits."

Our author puts the total "resources" of the principal St. Petersburg banks at 8,235,000,000 rubles, about $8\frac{1}{4}$ billions, and the "holdings," or rather, the extent to which foreign banks dominated them, he estimates as follows: French banks, 55 per cent; English, 10 per cent; German, 35 per cent. The author calculates that of the total of 8,235,000,000 rubles of functioning capital, 3,687,000,000 rubles, or over 40 per cent, fall to the share of the syndicates, Produgol and Prodamet—and the syndicates in the oil, metallurgical and cement industries. Thus, the merging of bank and industrial capital has also made great strides in Russia owing to the formation of capitalist monopolies.

Finance capital, concentrated in a few hands and exercising a virtual monopoly, exacts enormous and ever-increasing profits from the floating of companies, issue of stock, state loans, etc., tightens the grip of financial oligarchies and levies tribute upon the whole of society for the benefit of monopolists. Here is an example, taken from a multitude of others, of the methods of "business" of the American trusts, quoted by Hilferding: in 1887, Havemeyer founded the Sugar Trust by amalgamating fifteen small firms, whose total capital amounted to $6,500,000. Suitably "watered," as the Americans say, the capital of the trust was increased to $50,000,000. This "over-capitalisation" anticipated the monopoly profits, in the same way as the United States Steel Corporation anticipated its profits by buying up as many iron fields as possible. In fact, the Sugar Trust set up monopoly prices on the market, which secured it such profits that it could pay 10 per cent dividend on capital "watered" *sevenfold, or about 70 per cent on the capital actually invested at the time of the creation of the trust!* In 1909, the capital of the Sugar Trust was increased to $90,000,000. In twenty-two years, it had increased its capital more than tenfold.

In France the role of the "financial oligarchy" (*Against the Financial Oligarchy in France*, the title of the well-known book by Lysis, the fifth edition of which was published in 1908) assumed a form that was only slightly different. Four of the most powerful banks enjoy, not a relative, but an "absolute monopoly" in the issue of bonds. In reality, this is a "trust of the big banks." And their monopoly ensures the monopolist profits from bond issues. Usually a country borrowing from France does not get more than 90 per cent of the total of the loan, the

THE INTERLOCKING OF INDUSTRIAL AND FINANCIAL JOINT STOCK COMPANIES IN GERMANY

(January 1, 1932)

	Number of companies	Total share capital (million marks)	Companies whose stock is owned by other companies						
			Number of joint stock companies	Total share capital	Share capital in the hands of other companies according to industry (million marks)				
					Total	Banks and Finance companies	Industrial companies	Water, Gas, Electricity	Transport
Banks and finance companies.............	986	4,478	346	2,993	823	495	227	47	38
Industrial companies ..	5,443	13,680	1,103	6,772	3,253	1,273	1,858	63	21
Water, gas, electricity.	286	2,885	203	2,138	1,013	521	48	437	8
Transport............	439	1,913	187	1,040	321	133	30	26	119
Total................	10,437	24,653	2,288	13,475	5,697	2,496	2,285	578	198

SOURCE: *Vierteljahrshefte zur Statistik d. Deutschen Reichs*, 1932, H. 2, S. 76, 78-80.

remaining 10 per cent goes to the banks and other middlemen. The profit made by the banks out of the Russo-Chinese loans of 400,000,000 francs amounted to 8 per cent; out of the Russian (1904) loan of 800,000,000 francs the profit amounted to 10 per cent; and out of the Moroccan (1904) loan of 62,500,000 francs, to 18.75 per cent. Capitalism, which began its development with petty usury capital, ends its development with gigantic usury capital. "The French," says Lysis, "are the usurers of Europe." All the conditions of economic life are being profoundly modified by this transformation of capitalism. With a stationary population, and stagnant industry, commerce and shipping, the "country" can grow rich by usury. "Fifty persons, representing a capital of 8,000,000 francs, can control *2,000,000,000* francs deposited in four banks." The "holding system," with which we are already familiar, leads to the same result. One of the biggest banks, the Société Générale, for instance, issues 64,000 bonds for one of its subsidiary companies, the Egyptian Sugar Refineries. The bonds are issued at 150 per cent, *i.e.*, the bank gaining 50 centimes on the franc. The dividends of the new company are then found to be fictitious. The "public" lost from 90 to 100 million francs. One of the directors of the Société Générale was a member of the board of directors of the Egyptian Sugar Refineries. Hence it is not surprising that the author is driven to the conclusion that "the French Republic is a financial monarchy"; "it is the complete domination of the financial oligarchy; the latter controls the press and the government." [1]

The extraordinarily high rate of profit obtained from the issue of securities, which is one of the principal functions of finance capital, plays a large part in the development and consolidation of the financial oligarchy.

"There is not within the country a single business of this type that brings in profits even approximately equal to those obtained from the flotation of foreign loans"[2] (says the German magazine, *Die Bank*).

---

[1] Lysis, *Contre l'oligarchie financiére en France* (*Against the Financial Oligarchy in France*), fifth ed., Paris, 1908, pp. 11, 12, 26, 39, 40, 47-48
[2] *Die Bank*, 1913, II, p. 630.

GERMAN GOVERNMENT[1] HOLDINGS IN JOINT STOCK COMPANIES
(January 1, 1932)

	All companies		Companies in which government owns stock		Government holdings		
	Number	Total Capital Stock (million marks)	Number	Total Capital Stock (million marks)	Total Holdings (million marks)	Per cent of total capital stock of all companies in given industry	Per cent of total capital of companies in which the government has interests
Banks and finance companies............	986	4,478	83	1,370	780	17.4	56.9
Industrial companies...	5,443	13,680	44	505	72	0.5	14.3
Water, gas, electricity	286	2,885	140	2,021	1,019	35.3	50.4
Transport............	439	1,913	199	1,285	813	42.5	63.3
Commerce	2,661	1,209	80	169	91	7.6	53.8
Total...............	10,437	24,653	583	5,374	2,789	11.3	51.9

During the world economic crisis government holdings in joint stock companies increased. The increase in government holdings was a form of subsidising joint stock companies, which, however, did not establish actual government control over them. Government holdings in joint stock companies are now being reduced by various financial manipulations.

[1] "Government" includes: The Reich Government, Land governments, Prussian provinces, municipalities, and other public bodies.

SOURCE: *Vierteljahrshefte zur Statistik d. Deutschen Reichs*, 1932, H. 2, S. 76, 84.

"No banking operation brings in profits comparable with those obtained from the issue of securities!"[1]

According to the *German Economist*, the average annual profits made on the issue of industrial securities were as follows: [2]

	Per cent		Per cent
1895	38.6	1898	67.7
1896	36.1	1899	66.9
1897	66.7	1900	55.2

"In the ten years from 1891 to 1900, *more than a billion* marks of profits were 'earned' by issuing German industrial securities."[3]

---

[1] Stillich, *op. cit.*, p. 143.—*Ed.*

[2] *Ibid.*—*Ed.*

[3] Stillich, *ibid.*, also Werner Sombart, *Die deutsche Volkswirtschaft im 19. Jahrhundert (German National Economy in the Nineteenth Century)*, second ed., Berlin, 1909, p. 526, Appendix.

MONOPOLY OF THE BANKS IN THE FLOTATION OF FOREIGN LOANS

The monopoly of a few very big banks in issuing securities is illustrated by the following figures of bond issues of the biggest banks in the U.S.A.

During the post-war period the following banks headed consortiums floating foreign loans to the amounts indicated:

	Year	Amount (million dollars)	Per cent of total foreign issues for period 1920-31
House of Morgan.........	1920-31	1,876	19.0
Dillon, Read & Co.	1919-31	1,491	15.1
Speyer & Co.	1920-30	276	2.8
Chase Securities Corp.	1921-30	1,023	10.4
Equitable Trust Co.	1921-30	479	4.9
Guaranty Trust Co. of N. Y.	1920-31	541	5.5
Total six banks		5,686	57.7

SOURCES: *Hearings of U.S. Senate Commission—Sale of Foreign Bonds in the United States,* 1932, Part 2.

BANK PROFITS FROM FLOTATION OF FOREIGN LOANS

An idea of the profits the banks rake in from bond issues can be obtained from the report of the U.S. Senate Commission which investigated the issue of foreign bonds on the American market during the post-war period. From a wealth of material we quote the following few examples:

Name of bank and date of issue	Title of loan	Nominal amount of issue (mill. dollars)	Per cent share received	
			by borrower	by banks and other agents
F. J. Lisman & Co. August 25, 1924	Lower Austria hydro-electric station ($6^{1}/_{2}\%$)...........	3	80.8	19.2
April 22, 1925	Tyrol hydro-electric station ($7^{1}/_{2}\%$)	3	84.4	15.6
January 20, 1925	Rima Steel Co. Hungary (7%)	3	81.7	18.3
Speyer & Co. December 17, 1924......	Greek State Loan (League of Nations) (7%)	11	91.0	9.0
July 15, 1925	Hungarian United Municipalities ($7^{1}/_{2}\%$)...............	10	91.6	8.4

(Continued on p. 127.)

While, during periods of industrial boom, the profits of finance capital are disproportionately large, during periods of depression, small and unsound businesses go out of existence, while the big banks take "holdings" in their shares, which are bought up cheaply or in profitable schemes for their "reconstruction" and "reorganisation." In the "reconstruction" of undertakings which have been running at a loss,

"the share capital is written down, that is, profits are distributed on a smaller capital and subsequently are calculated on this smaller basis. If the income has fallen to zero, new capital is called in, which, combined with the old and less remunerative capital, will bring in an adequate return."

"Incidentally," adds Hilferding, "these reorganisations and reconstructions have a twofold significance for the banks: first, as profitable transactions; and secondly, as opportunities for securing control of the companies in difficulties." [1]

Here is an instance. The Union Mining Company of Dortmund, founded in 1872, with a share capital of nearly 40,000,000 marks, saw the

---

[1] Hilferding, op, cit., pp. 142-143.

Name of bank and date of issue	Title of loan	Nominal amount of issue (mill. dollars)	Per cent share received	
			by borrower	by banks and other agents
Dillon, Read & Co.				
July 1924	Great United Power Co., Japan $(7^1/_2\%)$	15	87.4	12.6
August 1924	Sespedes Sugar Co., Cuba $(7^1/_2\%)$	3	90.9	9.1
September 1921	Brazilian State Loan (8%)	25	91.4	8.6
May 1926	Colombia Agricultural Mortgage Bank (7%)	3	90.4	9.6
February 1927	Bolivian State Loan (7%)	14	91.4	8.6
May 1928	St. Lawrence Paper Co., Canada (6%)	11	88.5	11.5
Chase Securities Corp.				
January 1, 1926	Buenos Aires Provincial Loan, Argentina (7%)	4.2	91.0	9.0
April 1, 1926	Buenos Aires Provincial Loan, Argentina (7%)	10.6	88.0	12.0
Harris Forbes & Co.				
March 1, 1925	General Electric Co., Germany $(6^1/_2\%)$	5	91.4	8.6

SOURCE: *Hearings of U.S. Senate Commission—Sale of Foreign Bonds in the United States*, 1932, Parts 1 and 2.

HOW THE BANKS TAKE ADVANTAGE OF THE CRISIS TO SUBORDINATE INDUSTRIAL ENTERPRISES

During the post-war period, and particularly during the world economic crisis, the banks very widely resorted to "reconstruction" as a means of subordinating weaker joint stock companies. The following are a few examples:

Dickerhoff and Wiedmann of Wiesbaden, one of the largest construction companies in Germany. After stabilisation of the mark, its share capital amounted to 7.3 million marks (1925). As a result of three "reconstructions" in 1927 and during the crisis, the capital of the company was reduced by 11.9 million marks; and the last "reconstruction" resulted in the control of the company passing from the Dickerhoff and Wiedmann families to the Dresdner Bank.

The Deschimag Company, the big shipbuilding firm, has had three "reconstructions" since the stabilisation of the mark—in 1926, 1930 and 1932. As a result, 30.84 million marks of the capital stock of the com-

market price of shares rise to 170 after it had paid a 12 per cent dividend
in its first year. Finance capital skimmed the cream and earned a "trifle"
of something like 28,000,000 marks. The principal sponsor of this company was that very big German Disconto-Gesellschaft which so successfully attained a capital of 300,000,000 marks. Later, the dividends of
the Union declined to nil: the shareholders had to consent to a "writing
down" of capital, that is, to losing some of it in order not to lose it all.
By a series of "reconstructions," more than 73,000,000 marks were
written off the books of the Union in the course of thirty years.

"At the present time, the original shareholders of this company possess only 5 per
cent of the nominal value of their shares." [1]

But the bank "made a profit" out of every "reconstruction."

Speculation in land situated in the suburbs of rapidly growing towns
is a particularly profitable operation for finance capital. The monopoly
of the banks merges here with the monopoly of ground rent and with
monopoly in the means of communication, since the increase in the value
of the land and the possibility of selling it profitably in allotments, etc.,
is mainly dependent on good means of communication with the centre
of the town; and these means of communication are in the hands of
large companies which are connected by means of the holding system and
by the distribution of positions on the directorates, with the interested
banks. As a result we get what the German writer, L. Eschwege, a contributor to *Die Bank*, who has made a special study of real estate business and
mortgages, etc., calls the formation of a "bog." Frantic speculation in suburban building lots: collapse of building enterprises (like that of the
Berlin firm of Boswau and Knauer, which grabbed 100,000,000 marks
with the help of the "sound and solid" Deutsche Bank—the latter acting,
of course, discreetly behind the scenes through the holding system and
getting out of it by losing "only" 12,000,000 marks), then the ruin of
small proprietors and of workers who get nothing from the fraudulent
building firms, underhand agreements with the "honest" Berlin police and
the Berlin administration for the purpose of getting control of the
issue of building sites, tenders, building licenses, etc. [2]

"American ethics," which the European professors and well-meaning
bourgeois so hypocritically deplore, have, in the age of finance capital,
become the ethics of literally every large city, no matter what country
it is in.

---

[1] Stillich, *op. cit.*, p. 138 and Liefmann, p. 51.
[2] Ludwig Eschwege, *Der Sumpf (The Bog)*, in *Die Bank*, 1913, II, p. 952, *et seq.*;
ibid., 1912, I, p. 223 *et seq.*

pany was written off. At the last "reconstruction" the capital of the company was reduced from 14 million marks to 700,000 marks. In 1933 the capital was again increased to 6.7 million marks. The new shares to the amount of 6 million marks were distributed among the creditors by the conversion of their credits into shares. More than half of the new shares went to the Norddeutsche Kredit Bank, which became the owner of the company; the rest was divided among six big banks.

In 1933, the Lothringen Coal Company while under "reconstruction" annulled its shares to the value of 4.4 million marks. The remaining capital of 45.6 million marks was reduced to 3.8 million marks. Later, it was raised to 20.9 million marks. Of the new 17.1 million marks of capital the banks (Deutsche Bank—Disconto-Gesellschaft and others) became holders of 12.7 million marks by the conversion of their credits into shares. In this manner the majority of the stock passed into the hands of the banks. After all this "reconstruction" the balance sheet of the company still shows huge bank credits to the extent of 14.2 million marks.

Even before its "reconstruction" the majority of the shares of the Karstadt Department Store belonged to the big Berlin banks. Its debts to banks amounted to 62.5 million marks. In the process of "reconstruction" its capital was reduced from 75 million marks to 7.7 million marks, which later was raised to 28.1 million. Of the new capital of 20.4 million marks, shares to the value of 15.9 million marks were allocated to the Dresdner Bank and the Kommerz- und Privatbank, and the rest to other banks by partial conversion of their credits into shares.

SOURCES: *Die Bank*, 16, VIII, 1933, S. 1192; *Grünbuch der Aktiengesellschaften*, 1933, S. 4684, 4885; *Der Deutsche Volkswirt*, 5, X, 1933.

RECENT EXAMPLES OF THE USE OF GOVERNMENT FUNDS FOR THE "RECONSTRUCTION" OF MONOPOLIES

Hapag-Lloyd, the biggest steamship concern in Germany, which was on the verge of bankruptcy in 1932, received a government subsidy of 40 million marks and guaranteed credits to the amount of 70 million marks. These funds enabled the company to avert bankruptcy.

In 1931, the Vereinigte Stahlwerke, the biggest steel trust in Europe, one of the actual owners of which was Flick, found itself in difficulties. The government "came to the aid" of Flick and granted him a large subvention by buying from him shares to the amount of 110 million marks at a price that was four times higher than the market price. The pre-

At the beginning of 1914, there was talk in Berlin of the proposed formation of a "transport trust," *i.e.*, of establishing "community of interests" between the three Berlin passenger transport undertakings: The Metropolitan electric railway, the tramway company and the omnibus company.[1]

"We know," wrote *Die Bank*, "that this plan has been contemplated since it became known that the majority of the shares in the bus company has been acquired by the other two transport companies. . . . We may believe those who are pursuing this aim when they say that by uniting the transport services, they will secure economies part of which will in time benefit the public. But the question is complicated by the fact that behind the transport trust that is being formed are the banks, which, if they desire, can subordinate the means of transportation, which they have monopolised, to the interests of their real estate business. To be convinced of the reasonableness of such a conjecture, we need only recall that at the very formation of the Elevated Railway Company the traffic interests became interlocked with the real estate interests of the big bank which financed it, and this interlocking even created the prerequisites for the formation of the transport enterprise. Its eastern line, in fact, was to run through land which, when it became certain the line was to be laid down, this bank sold to a real estate firm at an enormous profit for itself and for several partners in the transactions."[1]

A monopoly, once it is formed and controls thousands of millions, inevitably penetrates into *every* sphere of public life, regardless of the form of government and all other "details." In the economic literature of Germany one usually comes across the servile praise of the integrity of the Prussian bureaucracy, and allusions to the French Panama scandal and to political corruption in America. But the fact is that *even* the bourgeois literature devoted to German banking matters constantly has to go far beyond the field of purely banking operations and to speak, for instance, of "the attraction of the banks" in reference to the increasing frequency with which public officials take employment with the banks.

"How about the integrity of a state official who in his inmost heart is aspiring to a soft job in the Behrenstrasse?"[2] (the street in Berlin in which the head office of the Deutsche Bank is situated).

In 1909, the publisher of *Die Bank*, Alfred Lansburgh, wrote an article entitled "The Economic Significance of Byzantinism," in which he incidentally referred to Wilhelm II's tour of Palestine, and to "the immediate result of this journey," the construction of the Bagdad railway, that fatal "standard product of German enterprise, which is more responsible for the 'encirclement' than all our political blunders put

---

[1] *Verkehrstrust* (*Transport Trust*) in *Die Bank*, 1914, I, pp. 89-90.
[2] *Der Zug zur Bank* (*The Attraction of the Banks*), in *Die Bank*, 1909, I, p.79.

dominance which the government thus acquired was afterwards (1933) removed by financial manipulation.

In 1933, Citroen, the biggest automobile manufacturing firm in France, was unable to meet its financial obligations. Its condition was temporarily relieved thanks to government assistance in securing it bank subsidies. But the crisis had done its work, and the firm went bankrupt in the beginning of 1935.[1]

---

[1] The Citroen Company was formed in 1923 with a capital stock of 50 million francs. This was increased between August and December, 1924, to 100 million francs, divided into 200,000 shares of 500 francs each. In 1927 Citroen shares were offered on the stock market at 670 francs, but in 1929 they rose to 2,140 francs. After that they began to drop rapidly and in 1934 reached 525 francs. In 1928 the company's capital was increased to 400 million francs. On the day after the shares were admitted on the Stock Exchange, the company issued a 75 million franc loan in 1,000 franc 5.5 per cent bonds at 900 francs per share, redeemable in 1958.

In 1930 the company issued another 125 million franc loan in 1,000 franc 5 per cent bonds, redeemable in 1965, issued at 980 francs. From 1924 onwards, the Citroen Company issued to the public stocks and bonds to a total value of 704 million francs.

The Citroen factories grew rapidly and work was carried on on an American scale. They turned out tens of thousands of automobiles a year, beating the Peugeot works, which was affiliated with Ford. Citroen was connected with, or rather was controlled by, General Motors, a Morgan firm, which is also connected with Deterding. But even these connections did not save the firm.

"The mistake Citroen made," states a certain bourgeois financial organ—"was that, while working for a market with a population of 38 million, it erected plants and set prices as if to supply automobiles to the whole of Europe. Citroen did not foresee that he had created an instrument for his own destruction."

In December 1933, Citroen announced a favourable balance of 31,734,444 francs. Accordingly, on January 15, 1934, the shareholders received their dividends. But the balance sheet had been cooked and the dividends proved to be fictitious. In April 1934, a special audit revealed a deficit of 28 million francs; but Citroen published a report denying the auditors' report, and by means of an extensive press campaign that cost him millions of francs, he succeeded in raising the market price of his shares.

The crash, however, was only postponed for a few months. The crisis and the depression did their work.

From the very first years of its existence the Citroen Co. had been obliged to resort to the banks for assistance. Do what it may, it could not escape from this yoke. The first bank to put its hand on the firm was Lazard Bros. & Co. An administrative council was set up to manage the affairs of the firm. This council consisted of eight members of whom three were representatives of this bank. Soon after two American banking groups put their hands on the victim: Morgan & Co. and the Commercial Investment Trust got hold of one of the firm's most important branches.

In 1929, Mannheimer, a representative of the Morgan-controlled General Motors, became a member of the administrative council. A number of French financial groups rushed to the "aid" of the industrial adventurer: The Daniel-Dreyfus Bank, the Banque de France, the Crédit Lyonnais, etc. Every one of these banks raked in handsome sums in stock exchange speculations, but Citroen went smash.

The holders of Citroen shares lost two billion francs in the crash. This does

together." [1] (By encirclement is meant the policy of Edward VII to isolate Germany by surrounding her with an imperialist anti-German alliance.) In 1912, another contributor to this magazine, Eschwege, to whom we have already referred, wrote an article entitled "Plutocracy and Bureaucracy," in which he exposes the case of a German official named Volker, who was a zealous member of the Cartel Committee and who, some time later, obtained a lucrative post in the biggest cartel, *i.e.*, the Steel Syndicate.[2] Similar cases, by no means casual, forced this bourgeois author to admit that "the economic liberty guaranteed by the German Constitution has become in many departments of economic life, a meaningless phrase" and that under the existing rule of the plutocracy, "even the widest political liberty cannot save us from being converted into a nation of unfree people." [3]

As for Russia, we will content ourselves by quoting one example. Some years ago, all the newspapers announced that Davidov, the director of the Credit Department of the Treasury, had resigned his post to take employment with a certain big bank at a salary which, according to the contract, was to amount to over one million rubles in the course of several years. The function of the Credit Department is to "co-ordinate the activities of all the credit institutions of the country"; it also grants subsidies to banks in St. Petersburg and Moscow amounting to between 800 and 1,000 million rubles. [4]

It is characteristic of capitalism in general that the ownership of capital is separated from the application of capital to production, that money capital is separated from industrial or productive capital, and that the rentier, who lives entirely on income obtained from money capital, is separated from the entrepreneur and from all who are directly concerned in the management of capital. Imperialism, or the domination of finance capital, is that highest stage of capitalism in which this separation reaches vast proportions. The supremacy of finance capital over all other forms of capital means the predominance of the rentier and of the financial oligarchy; it means the crystallisation of a small number of financially "powerful" states from among all the rest. The extent to which this process is going on may be judged from the statistics on emissions, *i.e.*, the issue of all kinds of securities.

---

[1] *Ibid.*, p. 307.
[2] *Die Bank*, 1912, II, p. 825.—*Ed.*
[3] *Ibid.*, 1913, II, p. 962.
[4] E. Agahd, *op. cit.*, p. 202.

The Hydroelectric Combine in Piedmont (Italy), one of the biggest enterprises in the Elettrico-Telefonico group, with a capital of about two billion lire was "reconstructed" at government expense through the medium of a semi-government financial institute, which was especially established for the purpose of "reconstructing" industrial companies.

In connection with the bank crash of 1931 the German government offered a huge subvention to the Dresdner Bank which at the same time absorbed the Darmstädter and National Bank (Danatbank). The government bought shares from the bank for 325 million marks and granted it an "advance" of 200 million marks. Of the 525 million marks, 288 million were utterly lost before 1933. By writing off capital and by other manipulations the shares in the government portfolio were reduced from 325 million to 136 million marks. Government advances to the banks during the crisis are calculated in the report of the commission of enquiry that was set up at 1.5 billion marks, which is an underestimation.

The bankruptcy of the biggest Austrian Bank, the Credit Anstalt, which was closely connected with British and Dutch capital, caused the Austrian government to grant the bank a subsidy of 723 million Austrian schillings, a sum almost equal to its losses. When in 1934 the Credit Anstalt absorbed the other two big Austrian banks, the government again granted it a subsidy of 41 million schillings and wrote off 48 million schillings of a subsidy previously granted to the absorbed banks.

SOURCES: *Die Bank,* 9, XI, 1933 and 28, XI, 1934; *Grünbuch der Aktiengesellschaften,* Bd. IV, 1933, S. 3949, 3950; *Bankers' Almanac,* 1933-34, p. 1141; *Der Oesterreichische Volkswirt,* 28, IV, 1934, S. 668; *Untersuchung des Bankwesens,* 1933, I. Teil, Bd. I, S. 396-97, 418-19.

not include the losses sustained by Citroen's various agents. The extent of these losses can be judged from the fact that the liabilities amounted to 596 billion francs. On the other hand the assets were declared to be 933 million francs, but of this sum 786 million are extremely doubtful. All the numerous branches of the firm, including its industrial enterprises, the Citroen taxi company, the Citroen commercial enterprises in North Africa, Belgium, Holland, Italy, Switzerland and other countries were involved in the crash. (*Pravda,* January 7, 1935).

In the Bulletin of the International Statistical Institute, A. Ney-marck[1] has published very comprehensive and complete comparative figures covering the issue of securities all over the world, which have been repeatedly quoted in economic literature. The following are the totals he gives for four decades:

TOTAL ISSUES IN BILLIONS OF FRANCS
(Decades)

1871-1880	76.1
1881-1890	64.5
1891-1900	100.4
1901-1910	197.8

In the 1870's, the total amount of issues for the whole world was high, owing particularly to the loans floated in connection with the Franco-Prussian War, and the company-promoting boom which set in in Germany after the war. In general, the increase is not very rapid during the three last decades of the nineteenth century, and only in the first ten years of the twentieth century is an enormous increase observed of almost 100 per cent. Thus the beginning of the twentieth century marks the turning point, not only in regard to the growth of monopolies (cartels, syndicates, trusts), of which we have already spoken, but also in regard to the development of finance capital.

Lenin Miscellany, Vol. XXII, p. 144, Russian edition, contains the following table taken from Lenin's notebooks on imperialism:

	Total for Five-Year Periods	Issues (million francs)
	1871/5	45.0
	76/80	31.1
	81/85	24.1
Neymarck, Vol. XIX	86/90	40.4
Part II, p. 206	91/5	40.4
	96/900	60.0
	901/5	83.7
	1906/1910	114.1

---

[1] A. Neymarck, *Bulletin de l'institut international de statistique* (*Bulletin of the International Statistical Institute*), Vol. XIX, Book II, The Hague, 1912. Data concerning small states, second column, are approximately calculated by adding 20 per cent to the 1902 figures.

GROWTH OF CAPITAL ISSUES [1]
TOTAL ISSUES IN BILLION FRANCS

Decades

World total
- 1871-80 .... 76.1
- 1881-90 .... 64.5
- 1891-1900 .... 100.4
- 1901-10 .... 197.8

Four countries whose total share of world issues amounted to 75-80 per cent.....

(in francs of pre-war parity)

U.S.A.	(1921-30)	328.4
England	(1921-30)	80.3
France	(1921-30)	66.2
Germany	(1924-30)	26.4

[1] Figures for all countries include home and foreign issues without conversions; figures for France do not include all foreign issues but only issues for her colonies.

SOURCES: Figures for 1871 to 1910 are quoted from Lenin (world total). Figures for 1921-30 are taken from the *Statistical Abstract of the United States*, 1928, 1932, 1934; *The Economist*, 1925, No. 4245, 1929, No. 4505. 1932, No. 4662; *Annuaire Statistique* (*Stat. Gén. de la France*), 1934; *Statistisches Jahrbuch für das Deutsche Reich*, 1932 (figures expressed in francs of pre-war parity).

TOTAL ISSUES (WHOLE WORLD) IN 5-YEAR PERIODS
(Billion francs of pre-war parity)

- 1896-1900 .... 60.0
- 1901-05 .... 83.7
- 1906-10 .... 114.1
- 1926-30 [1] 358.3

[1] Seventeen most important capitalist countries.

SOURCES: The figures for 1896 to 1910 are quoted from *Lenin Miscellany*, Vol. XXII, Russian ed. Figures for 1926-30 for above four countries are taken from the same sources as above table. Figures for remaining 13 countries are taken from *Statistical Yearbook*, L. of N., 1932-33.

Neymarck estimates the total amount of issued securities current in the world in 1910 at about 815,000,000,000 francs. Deducting from this amounts which might have been duplicated, he reduces the total to 575-600,000,000,000, which is distributed among the various countries as follows: (We will take 600,000,000,000.)

FINANCIAL SECURITIES CURRENT IN 1910
(In billions of francs)

Great, Britain	142
United States	132
France	110
Germany	95
Russia	31
Austria-Hungary	24
Italy	14
Japan	12
Holland	12.5
Belgium	7.5
Spain	7.5
Switzerland	6.25
Denmark	3.75
Sweden, Norway, Rumania, etc.	2.5
Total	600.00

(142, 132, 110, 95 bracketed} 479)

From these figures we at once see standing out in sharp relief four of the richest capitalist countries, each of which controls securities to amounts ranging from 100 to 150 billion francs. Two of these countries, England and France, are the oldest capitalist countries, and, as we shall see, possess the most colonies; the other two, the United States and Germany, are in the front rank as regards rapidity of development and the degree of extension of capitalist monopolies in industry. Together, these four countries own 479,000,000,000 francs, that is, nearly 80 per cent of the world's finance capital. Thus, in one way or another, nearly the whole world is more or less the debtor to and tributary of these four international banker countries, the four "pillars" of world finance capital.

It is particularly important to examine the part which export of capital plays in creating the international network of dependence and ties of finance capital.

As no comparable computations for the post-war period are available, we give below, for the purpose of illustration, the total market values of securities quoted on the New York Stock Exchange for various years, which reveal the enormous increase in securities marketed in the United States since the war.

MARKET VALUE OF SECURITIES ON THE NEW YORK STOCK EXCHANGE

(Billion francs of pre-war parity)

1914		142
1925 (January)		322
1927	,,	393
1929	,,	614
1933	,,	288
1937 [1]	,,	554
1937 [2]	,,	327

The nominal value of securities quoted on the London Stock Exchange in 1937 amounted to £17,846,700,000.

[1] No allowance made for depreciation of dollar.
[2] Allowance made for depreciation of dollar.

Sources: Figures taken from *Survey of Current Business*, Annual Supplements for 1932, 1936 and April, 1937 and from Cartinhour, *Branch, Group and Chain Banking*, New York, Macmillan, 1931; *Economist*, 5, VI, 1937.

CHAPTER IV

THE EXPORT OF CAPITAL

UNDER the old capitalism, when free competition prevailed, the export of *goods* was the most typical feature. Under modern capitalism, when monopolies prevail, the export of *capital* has become the typical feature.

Capitalism is commodity production at the highest stage of development, when labour power itself becomes a commodity. The growth of internal exchange, and particularly of international exchange, is the characteristic distinguishing feature of capitalism. The uneven and spasmodic character of the development of individual enterprises, of individual branches of industry and individual countries, is inevitable under the capitalist system. England became a capitalist country before any other, and in the middle of the nineteenth century, having adopted free trade, claimed to be the "workshop of the world," the great purveyor of manufactured goods to all countries, which in exchange were to keep her supplied with raw materials. But in the last quarter of the nineteenth century, *this* monopoly was already undermined. Other countries, protecting themselves by tariff walls, had developed into independent capitalist states. On the threshold of the twentieth century, we see a new type of monopoly coming into existence. Firstly, there are monopolist capitalist combines in all advanced capitalist countries; secondly, a few rich countries, in which the accumulation of capital reaches gigantic proportions, occupy a monopolist position. An enormous "superabundance of capital" has accumulated in the advanced countries.

It goes without saying that if capitalism could develop agriculture, which today lags far behind industry everywhere, if it could raise the standard of living of the masses, who are everywhere still poverty-stricken and underfed, in spite of the amazing advance in technical knowledge, there could be no talk of a superabundance of capital. This "argument" the petty-bourgeois critics of capitalism advance on every occasion. But if capitalism did these things it would not be capitalism; for uneven development and wretched conditions of the masses are fundamental and inevitable conditions and premises of this mode of production. As long as capitalism remains what it is, surplus capital

ISSUES OF FOREIGN SECURITIES[1]

(Million gold dollars at pre-crisis parity)

Countries	1913	1920-23 (yearly averages)	1924-28	1929	1930	1931	1932	1933	1934	1935	1936
Great Britain	781	446	530	424	473	216	91	118	95	45	75
U.S.A.	442[2]	576	1152	671	905	229	29	10[7]	0	29[7]	14[7]
France[3]	684	86	60	140	303	338	160	182	78	90	—
Holland[4]	—	—	118[6]	45	102	16	9	4	0.04	—	—
Switzerland	—	4[5]	28	20	64	20	30	0.2	1.2	—	—

[1] Issues of foreign securities do not account for the entire export of capital. With the exception of France, the figures for which do not show whether conversions are included or not, the figures in the above table are given exclusive of conversions. Figures for Holland for 1913-24 and those for Switzerland for 1913-22 are not given here since they are not comparable with subsequent figures.

[2] 1914.

[3] Our own computation. It includes long and short-term loans of foreign governments, colonial administrations, foreign and colonial companies and French companies operating abroad. Figures for the period from 1922 to 1928 and since 1932 do not include issues by foreign companies.

[4] Not including Dutch colonies. According to *l'Observation Economique*, for November, 1932, Dutch colonial issues were as follows (in million dollars): 1927, 11.9; 1928, 15.0; 1929, 2.3; 1930, 46.2; 1931, 41.7.

[5] 1923.

[6] 1925-28.

[7] Issues in current dollars were as follows: 1933—$12,000,000; 1935—$48,000,000; 1936—$23,000,000.

SOURCES: For Great Britain, *The Economist*; for U.S.A., *Handbook of American Underwriting of Foreign Securities* and *Federal Reserve Bulletin*; for France, *Bulletin de la Statistique Générale de la France, Revue d'Economie Politique, Note du Ministère des Finances (Temps, 2, III, 1932)*; for Holland, *Statistical Yearbook*, L. of N.; for Switzerland, *Statistisches Jahrbuch der Schweiz*.

FOREIGN INVESTMENTS

(Million dollars)

Countries	1913	1929-30
China	1,610	3,243
India	1,844[1]	3,445
Canada	2,114[1]	6,126
South America	4,006	6,780
Caribbean America	2,217	4,698

[1] 1910.

SOURCES: Figures for China—Remer, *Foreign Investments in China*, 1933, p. 76; India—1910 figures of British investments from the estimates of Sir George Paish; for 1930, from Financial Times, 9, I, 1930; figures of non-British investments for 1930 are based on the estimates of *The Statist* for 1931; Canada—1910 figures based on estimates of Sir George Paish; 1930 figures from *Canada Yearbook* 1933; figures for South and Caribbean America include only U.S. and British investments—M. Winkler, *Investments of U.S. Capital in Latin America*, 1929, pp. 284-85.

will never be utilised for the purpose of raising the standard of living of the masses in a given country, for this would mean a decline in profits for the capitalists; it will be used for the purpose of increasing those profits by exporting capital abroad to the backward countries. In these backward countries profits are usually high, for capital is scarce, the price of land is relatively low, wages are low, raw materials are cheap. The possibility of exporting capital is created by the fact that numerous backward countries have been drawn into international capitalist intercourse; main railways have either been built or are being built there; the elementary conditions for industrial development have been created, etc. The necessity for exporting capital arises from the fact that in a few countries capitalism has become "over-ripe" and (owing to the backward state of agriculture and the impoverished state of the masses) capital cannot find "profitable" investment.

Here are approximate figures showing the amount of capital invested abroad by the three principal countries: [1]

CAPITAL INVESTED ABROAD
(In billions of francs)

Year	Great Britain	France	Germany
1862	3.6	—	—
1872	15.0	10 (1869)	—
1882	22.0	15 (1880)	?
1893	42.0	20 (1890)	?
1902	62.0	27-37	12.5
1914	75-100	60	44.0

This table shows that the export of capital reached formidable dimensions only in the beginning of the twentieth century. Before the war the capital invested abroad by the three principal countries amounted to between 175,000,000,000 and 200,000,000,000 francs. At the mod-

---

[1] Hobson, *Imperialism*, London, 1902, p. 58; Riesser, *op. cit.*, pp. 395 and 404; P. Arndt in *Weltwirtschaftliches Archiv* (*World Economic Archive*), Vol. VII, 1916, p. 35; Neymarck in *Bulletin de l'institut international de statistique*; Hilferding, *Finanzkapital*, p. 437; Lloyd George, Speech in the House of Commons, May 4, 1915, reported in *Daily Telegraph*, May 5, 1915; B. Harms *Probleme der Weltwirtschaft* (*Problems of World Economy*), Jena, 1912, p. 235, et seq.; Dr. Sigmund Schilder, *Entwicklungstendenzen der Weltwirtschaft* (*Trends of Development of World Economy*), Berlin, 1912, Vol. I, p. 150; George Paish, Great Britain's Capital Investments, etc., in *Journal of the Royal Statistical Society*. Vol. LXXIV, 1910-11, p. 167; Georges Diouritch, *L'expansion des banques allemandes à l'étranger, ses rapports avec le développement économique de l'Allemagne* (*Expansion of German Banks Abroad, in connection with the Economic Development of Germany*), Paris, 1909, p. 84.

EXPORT OF BRITISH AND U.S. CAPITAL IN COLONIAL AND DEPENDENT COUNTRIES DURING THE PERIOD 1924 to 1931

(Million dollars)

	U.S.A.	Great Britain
South and Caribbean America..........	1,758.4	655.0
British Colonies & Dominions..........	1,885.3	3,474.4
Australasia	252.4	1,011.3
India	—	373.2
Canada & Newfoundland	1,632.9	349.2
Africa	—	603.2

SOURCES: For Great Britain—*Balances of Payments, 1931-32*, L. of N.; for U.S.A.—*ibid.*, also, *Handbook of American Underwriting of Foreign Securities*, 1931.

CAPITAL INVESTED ABROAD
(In billion francs of pre-war parity)

Year	By Great Britain	By France	By Germany	By U.S.A.
1862	3.6	—	—	—
1872	15	10 (1869)	—	—
1882	22	15 (1880)	?	—
1893	42	20 (1890)	?	—
1902	62	27-37	12.5	2.6 (1900)
1914	75-100	60	44.0	9.9 (1912)
1930	94	31-40	4.9-6.1	81.0
1935[1].........	94[4]	40-49	—	70.5[3]
1935[2].........	58[4]	—	—	41.9

[1] No allowance made for depreciation of pound and dollar.
[2] Allowance made for depreciation of pound and dollar.
[3] During the period of crisis United States foreign debtors (Germany and others) took advantage of the depreciation of the dollar to pay off part of their debts.
[4] 1934.

Considerable changes took place in capital exports from imperialist countries after the war. In order to finance the war Great Britain sold about 25 per cent of her foreign investments (25,000,000,000 francs of pre-war parity), but after the war British capital exports again increased considerably, so that British foreign investments are now approximately equal to pre-war.

As a result of the World War France lost (according to Moulton, who estimated France's pre-war foreign investments at 45,000,000,000 francs) 23,000,000,000 francs and sold foreign securities amounting to about

est rate of 5 per cent, this sum should have brought in from 8 to 10 billions a year. This provided a solid basis for imperialist oppression and the exploitation of most of the countries and nations of the world; a solid basis for the capitalist parasitism of a handful of wealthy states!

3,500,000,000 francs. Basing himself on these figures, Moulton calculates French foreign investments in 1924 at 27,000,000,000 francs of pre-war parity. From 1924 to 1930 foreign issues in France amounted to about 4,000,000,000 pre-war francs. Thus, taking Moulton's figures as a basis, French foreign investments in 1930 may be roughly estimated at 31,000,000,000 pre-war francs. During the period 1931-35, foreign issues in France amounted to about 5,000,000,000 pre-war francs. If we calculate that of the total French capital which fled abroad 20,000,000,000 francs, *i.e.*, about 4,000,000,000 francs of pre-war parity represented long-term investments, the amount of French foreign investments in 1935 may be approximately estimated at 40,000,000,000 pre-war francs. In so far as Moulton's estimate of French foreign investments before the war (45,000,000,000 francs) is very much lower than the figure quoted by Lenin (60,000,000,000 francs), the loss during the war estimated by Moulton at 23,000,000,000 francs should amount to 30,000,000,000 pre-war francs on the basis of the figures quoted by Lenin. Thus, in 1924 French foreign investments must have amounted, not to 27,000,000,000, but to 35,000,000,000 pre-war francs. The corresponding figures for 1930 would be 40,000,000,000 pre-war francs and for 1935—49,000,000,000 pre-war francs.

Germany was transformed after the World War from a capital-exporting country into a capital-importing country. Her entire capital investments abroad amounted approximately to 5 billion marks in 1930. This is obviously an underestimation.

The foreign investments of the U.S.A. in post-war years assumed colossal proportions.

It must be noted that the figures for the post-war period have been taken from sources other than those from which Lenin took his. The reason for this is that the authors whom Lenin quoted did not continue their computations. However, although there is no direct continuity between Lenin's figures and the post-war figures, the latter, nevertheless, indicate the changes in the roles played by the different countries in the world capital market.

SOURCES: Pre-war figures quoted from Lenin; we have reduced those for 1930 and 1935 in francs of pre-war parity; for England, on the basis of the data in *Statistical Summary, Bank of England,* July 1933, p. 79, Dec. 1936, p. 155; for France—*The French Debt Problem,* by H. Moulton and C. Lewis, pp. 27, 45; for Germany—*Wirtschaft und Statistik,* No. 22, 1930, S. 893; for the U.S.A.—*A New Estimate of American Investments Abroad,* p. 24; *Balances of Payments,* L. of N., 1935, p. 17.

How is this capital invested abroad distributed among the various countries? *Where* does it go? Only an approximate answer can be given to this question, but sufficient to throw light on certain general relations and ties of modern imperialism.

APPROXIMATE DISTRIBUTION OF FOREIGN CAPITAL
(About 1910)

(In billions of marks)

Continent	Gt. Britain	France	Germany	Total
Europe	4	23	18	45
America	37	4	10	51
Asia, Africa and Australia	29	8	7	44
Total	70	35	35	140

The principal spheres of investment of British capital are the British colonies, which are very large also in America (for example, Canada) not to mention Asia, etc. In this case, enormous exports of capital are bound up with the possession of enormous colonies, of the importance of which for imperialism we shall speak later. In regard to France, the situation is quite different. French capital exports are invested mainly in Europe, particularly in Russia (at least ten billion francs). This is mainly *loan* capital, in the form of government loans and not investments in industrial undertakings. Unlike British colonial imperialism, French imperialism might be termed usury imperialism. In regard to Germany, we have a third type; the German colonies are inconsiderable, and German capital invested abroad is divided fairly evenly between Europe and America.

The export of capital greatly affects and accelerates the development of capitalism in those countries to which it is exported. While,

RENTIER STATES

Countries	National wealth (bill. marks)	Foreign investments (net) (bill. marks)	(%) of national wealth)
Gt. Britain	450-455	80-85	18
U.S.A.	1,760-1,765	60-65	4
France	295-300	40-50	15
Holland ...... approx.	75	approx. 15	approx. 20
Switzerland	50-55	6-7	12
Belgium	45-50	5-6	12

The ratio of capital invested abroad to the national wealth of the respective countries as given in the table is undoubtedly underestimated, because the figures of the national wealth are exaggerated (they include value of land, etc.), while the figures of foreign investments understate the actual position.

SOURCE: *Die wirtschaftlichen Kräfte der Welt,* published by Dresdner Bank, Berlin, 1930.

APPROXIMATE DISTRIBUTION OF FOREIGN CAPITAL

(In billions of marks)

Continent	Gt. Britain 1910	Germany 1910	U.S.A. 1912	Gt. Britain 1930	Germany 1930	U.S.A. 1930
Europe	4	18	0.8	6	2.3-2.7	21
America	37	10	6.9	30	1.5-2.1	38
Asia, Africa and Australia	29	7	0.3	40	0.2	7
Total	70	35	8.0	76	4.0-5.0	66

The figures of the distribution of foreign investments by continents are quoted: for England, from the calculations of Sir Robert Kindersley; for the U.S.A., from the computations of the Department of Commerce. From the table it will be seen that U.S. investments abroad, which grew very rapidly after the war, flowed mainly to South America and Canada where Great Britain already had large investments before the war. This is characteristic of the growing acuteness of the imperialist struggle between the U.S.A. and Great Britain since the war.

SOURCES: The figures for 1910 are quoted from Lenin; for 1930 the figures are compiled as follows: for Great Britain, from *Statistical Summary, Bank of England,* July 1933, p. 79; for the U.S.A., from *A New Estimate of American Investments Abroad,* p. 24; for Germany, from *Wirtschaft und Statistik,* No. 22, 1930, S. 893.

therefore, the export of capital may tend to a certain extent to arrest development in the countries exporting capital, it can only do so by expanding and deepening the further development of capitalism throughout the world.

The countries which export capital are nearly always able to obtain "advantages," the character of which throws light on the peculiarities of the epoch of finance capital and monopoly. The following passage, for instance, occurred in the Berlin review, *Die Bank*, for October 1913:

"A comedy worthy of the pen of Aristophanes is being played just now on the international capital market. Numerous foreign countries, from Spain to the Balkan states, from Russia to the Argentine, Brazil and China, are openly or secretly approaching the big money markets demanding loans, some of which are very urgent. The money market is not at the moment very bright and the political outlook is not yet promising. But not a single money market dares to refuse a foreign loan for fear that its neighbour might first anticipate it and so secure some small reciprocal service. In these international transactions the creditor nearly always manages to get some special advantages: an advantage of a commercial-political nature, a coaling station, a contract to construct a harbour, a fat concession, or an order for guns." [1]

Finance capital has created the epoch of monopolies, and monopolies introduce everywhere monopolist methods: the utilisation of "connections" for profitable transactions takes the place of competition on the open market. The most usual thing is to stipulate that part of the loan that is granted shall be spent on purchases in the country of issue, particularly on orders for war materials, or for ships, etc. In the course of the last two decades (1890-1910), France often resorted to this method. The export of capital abroad thus becomes a means for encouraging the export of commodities. In these circumstances transactions between particularly big firms assume a form "bordering on corruption," as Schilder[2] "delicately" puts it. Krupp in Germany, Schneider in France, Armstrong in England are instances of firms which have close connections with powerful banks and governments and cannot be "ignored" when arranging a loan.

France granted loans to Russia in 1905 and by the commercial treaty of September 16, 1905, she "squeezed" concessions out of her to run till 1917. She did the same thing when the Franco-Japanese commercial treaty was concluded on August 19, 1911. The tariff war between Austria and Serbia, which lasted with a seven months' interval, from 1906 to 1911, was partly caused by competition between Austria and France for

---

[1] *Die Bank*, 1913, pp. 1024-25.
[2] Schilder, *op. cit.*, Vol. I., pp 346, 350 and 371.

EXPORT OF CAPITAL AS A MEANS OF INCREASING THE EXPORT OF COMMODITIES

The terms of seventeen of the railway loans granted to China between 1902 and 1928 contained special clauses providing for the purchase of railway materials from the country which furnished the loan. The lenders were British, French, Belgian, German and American capitalists. In twenty-one cases the terms of railway loans granted to China stipulated that the lenders were to act as agents in the purchasing of all materials required for the construction of the railways.

U.S. investments in ten South American countries increased from 173 million dollars in 1913 to *2,294 million dollars* in 1929. Of the total sum invested in these countries by Great Britain and the U.S.A., the latter's share was *4.3 per cent in 1913, and 33.8 per cent in 1929.* Simultaneously the United States' share of the imports to South America increased from 16.1 per cent in 1913 to 31.5 per cent in 1929, *i.e.,* nearly doubled.

According to the German investigator, G. Tacke, in 1925-29 the U.S.A. invested in electrical companies in Argentina, Brazil and Chile a sum equal to 1,027,000,000 German marks. During the same period, the U.S.A. exported to the same countries electrical equipment and materials to the amount of 242,900,000 marks, or 24 per cent of the sum invested.

In the period 1928-31 France granted 4 loans to Rumania, 2 loans to Jugoslavia, 3 loans to Poland, 1 loan to Czechoslovakia, and 1 loan to Finland—a total of over 4,500,000,000 francs. During the same period France exported war materials and aeroplanes alone to the amount of 1,276,000,000 francs, primarily to the countries just enumerated.

In July 1923, the question of a loan to India was discussed in the British House of Commons. In the course of the debate the Under-Secretary of State for India stated that 95 per cent of the loans that had been granted to the Indian Administration up to that time had been expended in Great Britain on the purchase of British goods.

In the spring of 1931 the French consortium of the Banque des Pays du Nord, and Schneider-Creusot undertook the financing as well as the construction of the Upper Silesia-Gdynia railroad in Poland.

In 1931 Poland received from the General Limited Trust in England a loan of 11,000,000 German marks for 12 years, for the construction of

10*

supplying Serbia with war materials. In January 1912, Paul Deschanel stated in the Chamber of Deputies that from 1908 to 1911 French firms had supplied war materials to Serbia to the value of 45,000,000 francs.

A report from the Austro-Hungarian Consul at Sao-Paulo (Brazil) states:

"The construction of the Brazilian railways is being carried out chiefly by French, Belgian, British and German capital. In the financial operations connected with the construction of these railways the countries involved also stipulate for orders for the necessary railway materials."

Thus, finance capital, almost literally, one might say, spreads its net over all countries of the world. Banks founded in the colonies, or their branches, play an important part in these operations. German imperialists look with envy on the "old" colonising nations which are "well established" in this respect. In 1904, Great Britain had 50 colonial banks with 2,279 branches (in 1910 there were 72 banks with 5,449 branches); France had 20 with 136 branches; Holland 16 with 68 branches; and Germany had a "mere" 13 with 70 branches.[1] The American capitalists, in their turn, are jealous of the English and German: "In South America," they complained in 1915, "five German banks have forty branches and five English banks have seventy branches. . . . England and Germany have invested in Argentina, Brazil, and Uruguay in the last twenty-five years approximately four thousand million dollars, and as a result enjoy together 46 per cent of the total trade of these three countries."[2]

The capital exporting countries have divided the world among themselves in the figurative sense of the term. But finance capital has also led to the *actual* division of the world.

---

[1] Riesser, *op. cit.*, fourth edition, pp. 374-75; Diouritch, p. 283.

[2] *The Annals of the American Academy of Political and Social Science*, Vol. LIX, May 1915, p. 301. In the same volume on p. 331, we read that the well-known statistician Paish, in the last annual issue of the financial magazine *Statist*, estimated the amount of capital exported by England, Germany, France, Belgium and Holland at 40,000,000,000 dollars, *i.e.*, 200,000,000,000 francs.

a telephone system. Poland on her part undertook during the first six years to purchase British materials to an amount equal to 6,000,000 German marks at contract prices.

SOURCES: G. Tacke, *Kapitalausfuhr und Warenausfuhr*, 1933, S. 76-77, 116-17, 170; M. Winkler, *Investments of U.S. Capital in Latin America*, 1929, p. 284; *The Magazine of Wall Street*, 9, VII, 1932; *Foreign Commerce Handbook*, 1933; Fies, *Europe—the World's Banker*, 1930, p. 94.

INCOME OF IMPERIALIST COUNTRIES FROM LONG-TERM INVESTMENTS ABROAD [1]

(Million gold dollars)

	1929
Great Britain (minimum)	1,219
U.S.A.	876
France	179
Japan	45

[1] Exclusive of war debts.

INTEREST AND DIVIDENDS ON FOREIGN INVESTMENTS PAID BY COLONIAL AND DEPENDENT COUNTRIES

(Million gold dollars)

	1928-29
Union of South Africa	77.4
Argentina	190.6
Canada	299.1
British India	125.6
Dutch East Indies	147.5
Australia	173.4
New Zealand	43.4

SOURCE: *Balances of Payments*, 1930, League of Nations, Geneva, 1932.

BANKS OF IMPERIALIST COUNTRIES IN THE COLONIES

In 1933 Great Britain had 46 colonial banks with 7,209 branches;[1] France had 31 with 542 branches, Holland 9 with 126 branches, and Germany only 4 with 38 branches.

[1] Following Lenin, we have included not only colonial banks proper, but all banks operating in dependent countries.

SOURCES: *The Economist*, Banking Supplement, 14, X, 1933, p. 24; *Banker's Almanac*, 1933-34.

CHAPTER V

THE DIVISION OF THE WORLD AMONG CAPITALIST COMBINES

MONOPOLIST capitalist combines—cartels, syndicates, trusts—divide among themselves, first of all, the whole internal market of a country, and impose their control, more or less completely, upon the industry of that country. But under capitalism the home market is inevitably bound up with the foreign market. Capitalism long ago created a world market. As the export of capital increased, and as the foreign and colonial relations and the "spheres of influence" of the big monopolist combines expanded, things "naturally" gravitated towards an international agreement among these combines, and towards the formation of international cartels.

This is a new stage of world concentration of capital and production, incomparably higher than the preceding stages. Let us see how this super-monopoly develops.

The electrical industry is the most typical of the modern technical achievements of capitalism of the *end* of the nineteenth and beginning of the twentieth centuries. This industry has developed most in the two most advanced of the new capitalist countries, the United States and Germany. In Germany, the crisis of 1900 gave a particularly strong impetus to its concentration. During the crisis, the banks, which by this time had become fairly well merged with industry, greatly accelerated and deepened the collapse of relatively small firms and their absorption by the large ones.

"The banks," writes Jeidels, "in refusing a helping hand to the very companies which are in greatest need of capital bring on first a frenzied boom and then the hopeless failure of the companies which have not been attached to them closely long enough." [1]

As a result, after 1900, concentration in Germany proceeded by leaps and bounds. Up to 1900 there had been seven or eight "groups" in the electrical industry. Each was formed of several companies (altogether there were twenty-eight) and each was supported by from two to

---

[1] Jeidels, *op. cit.*, p. 232.

150

eleven banks. Between 1908 and 1912 all the groups were merged into two, or possibly one. The diagram below shows the process:

GROUPS IN THE GERMAN ELECTRICAL INDUSTRY

Prior to 1900 :	Felten & Lah-Guillaume meyer	Union A.E.G.	Siemens Schuckert & Halske & Co.	Berg-mann	Kum-mer
	Felten & Lahmeyer	A.E.G.	Siemens & Halske-Schuckert	Berg-mann	Failed in 1900
By 1912:	A.E.G. (General Electric Co.)		Siemens & Halske Schuckert		

(In close "co-operation" since 1908)

The famous A.E.G. (General Electric Company), which grew up in this way, controls 175 to 200 companies (through shareholdings), and a total capital of approximately 1,500,000,000 marks. Abroad, it has thirty-four direct agencies, of which twelve are joint stock companies, in more than ten countries. As early as 1904 the amount of capital invested abroad by the German electrical industry was estimated at 233,000,000 marks. Of this sum, 62,000,000 were invested in Russia. Needless to say, the A.E.G. is a huge combine. Its manufacturing companies alone number no less than sixteen, and their factories make the most varied articles, from cables and insulators to motor cars and aeroplanes.

But concentration in Europe was a part of the process of concentration in America, which developed in the following way:

MONOPOLIES IN THE ELECTRICAL INDUSTRY IN GERMANY

The relation of forces between AEG and Siemens has changed in the post-war period. At the present time Siemens plays the predominant role in the electrical industry, as can be seen from the following main indices: In 1929 AEG owned a share capital of 199 million marks; it had a gross turnover of 580 million marks and employed 60,000 workers. The corresponding figures for Siemens are: 227 million marks share capital, 800 million marks gross turnover and 137,000 workers employed. In addition, by means of its holdings Siemens controls a larger capital than AEG.

AEG controlled:

in 1912, 175 to 200 companies;
in 1930, 280 to 290 companies,
including 50 companies controlled jointly with Siemens.

The capital of the controlled companies amounted to:

in 1912, approximately 1.50 billion marks;
in 1930, approximately 1.62 billion marks,
including 165 million marks controlled jointly with Siemens.

AEG investments abroad:

in 1904, 233 million marks;
in 1930, 280 million marks.

The present influence of United States electrical monopolies can be seen from the following chart: (p. 155.)

GENERAL ELECTRIC COMPANY

| United States: | Thomson-Houston Co. establishes a firm in Europe | Edison Co. establishes in Europe the French Edison Co. which transfers its patents to the German firm |
| Germany: | Union Electric Co. | Gen'l Electric Co. (A.E.G.) |

GENERAL ELECTRIC CO. (A.E.G.)

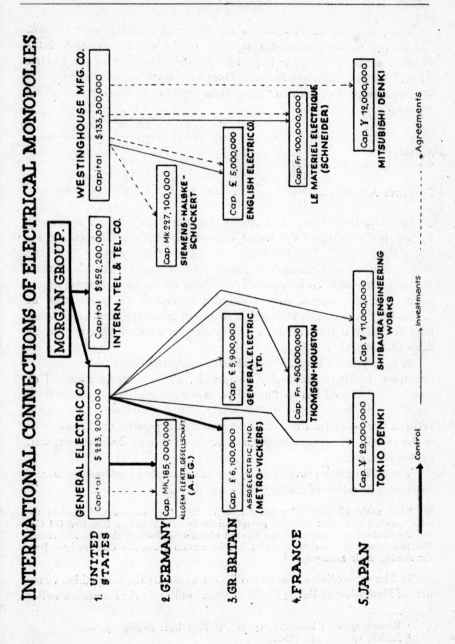

INTERNATIONAL CONNECTIONS OF ELECTRICAL MONOPOLIES

MORGAN GROUP.

1. UNITED STATES

GENERAL ELECTRIC CO. Capital $223,200,000

WESTINGHOUSE MFG. CO. Capital $133,300,000

INTERN. TEL. & TEL. CO. Capital $252,200,000

2. GERMANY

Cap. Mk.185,000,000 ALLGEM. ELEKTR. GESELLSCHAFT (A.E.G.)

Cap. Mk 227,100,000 SIEMENS-HALSKE-SCHUCKERT

3. GR. BRITAIN

Cap. £ 6,100,000 ASSO. ELECTRIC. IND. (METRO-VICKERS)

Cap. £ 5,900,000 GENERAL ELECTRIC LTD.

Cap. £ 5,000,000 ENGLISH ELECTRIC CO.

4. FRANCE

Cap. Fn 450,000,000 THOMSON-HOUSTON

Cap. Fn 100,000,000 LE MATERIEL ELECTRIQUE (SCHNEIDER)

5. JAPAN

Cap. ¥ 29,000,000 TOKIO DENKI

Cap. ¥ 11,000,000 SHIBAURA ENGINEERING WORKS

Cap. ¥ 12,000,000 MITSUBISHI DENKI

Control
Investments
Agreements

Thus, *two* "Great Powers" in the electrical industry were formed. "There are no other electric companies in the world *completely* independent of them," wrote Heinig in his article "The Path of the Electric Trust." An idea, although far from complete, of the turnover and the size of the enterprises of the two "trusts" can be obtained from the following figures:

		Turnover (mill. marks)	No. of employees	Net profits (mill. marks)
AMERICA:				
General Electric Co. ...	1907...........	252	28,000	35.4
	1910..........	298	32,000	45.6
GERMANY: A.E.G.	1907...........	216	30,700	14.5
	1911..........	362	60,800	21.7

In 1907, the German and American trusts concluded an agreement by which they divided the world between themselves. Competition between them ceased. The American General Electric Company "got" the United States and Canada. The A.E.G. "got" Germany, Austria, Russia, Holland, Denmark, Switzerland, Turkey and the Balkans. Special agreements, naturally secret, were concluded regarding the penetration of "subsidiary" companies into new branches of industry, into "new" countries formally not yet allotted. The two trusts were to exchange inventions and experiments.[1]

It is easy to understand how difficult competition has become against this trust, which is practically world-wide, which controls a capital of several billion, and has its "branches," agencies, representatives, connections, etc., in every corner of the world. But the division of the world between two powerful trusts does not remove the possibility of re-division, if the relation of forces changes as a result of uneven development, war, bankruptcy, etc.

The oil industry provides an instructive example of attempts at such a redivision, or rather of a struggle for redivision.

"The world oil market," wrote Jeidels in 1905, "is even today divided in the main between two great financial groups—Rockefeller's American Standard Oil Co., and the controlling interests of the Russian oilfields in Baku, Rothschild and Nobel. The two groups are in close alliance. But for several years, five enemies have been threatening their monopoly:"[2]

1) The exhaustion of the American oil wells; 2) the competition of the firm of Mantashev of Baku; 3) the Austrian wells; 4) the Rumanian wells;

---

[1] Riesser, *op. cit.*; Diouritch, *op. cit.*, p. 239; Kurt Heinig, *op. cit.*
[2] Jeidels, *op. cit.*, pp. 192-93.

THE STRUGGLE OF MONOPOLIES IN ELECTRICAL ENGINEERING

	Year	Turnover (mill. marks)	No. of employees	Net profits (mill. marks)
AMERICA: General Electric Co.....	1907	252	28,000	35.4
	1910	298	32,000	45.6
	1929	1,744	78,000 [1]	282.6
GERMANY: A.E.G.	1907	216	30,700	14.5
	1911	362	60,800	21.7
	1929	580	60,000	19.2

The change in the relation of forces between the various monopolist groups brought about by the war and post-war development resulted in a *redivision* of the world market for electrical equipment. The role and importance of the American monopoly, the General Electric Co., has increased enormously. In 1922 the GE and the AEG concluded a 20-year agreement which to a certain degree restored the pre-war relationship between the two firms. The agreement provided for the exchange of patents and the division of the world market whereby GE "obtained" the markets of the U.S.A., Central America, and partly, Canada, while the Central and East European markets were allocated to the German trust. Unlike the position in pre-war times, however, the AEG ceased to be an equal participant in this agreement. As far back as 1920 the General Electric Co. acquired 25 per cent of the newly issued stock of the AEG. This connection was greatly strengthened in 1929, when the American trust took over 30 per cent of all the shares of the German monopoly.

Of the other international monopolist agreements concluded in the sphere of electrical engineering, the ten-year agreement concluded between the second largest American electrical engineering firm, Westinghouse, and the German group of Siemens-Schuckert should be noted. This agreement provides for the division of the world market for electrical equipment.

The international electric bulb cartel (Glühlampenkartell Phönix) embraces the whole of the electric bulb industry of Germany, France, Great Britain, Holland, the United States, the Scandinavian countries, Italy, Austria, Hungary and Czechoslovakia. This cartel, which combines

---

[1] 1927.

5) the overseas oilfields, particularly in the Dutch colonies (the extremely rich firms, Samuel and Shell, also connected with British capital). The three last groups are connected with the great German banks, principally, the Deutsche Bank. These banks independently and systematically developed the oil industry in Rumania, in order to have a foothold of their "own." In 1907, 185,000,000 francs of foreign capital were invested in the Rumanian oil industry, of which 74,000,000 came from Germany.[1]

A struggle began, which in economic literature is fittingly called "the struggle for the division of the world." On one side, the Rockefeller trust, wishing to conquer *everything*, formed a subsidiary company *right in* Holland, and bought up oil wells in the Dutch Indies, in order to strike at its principal enemy, the Anglo-Dutch Shell trust. On the other side, the Deutsche Bank and the other German banks aimed at "retaining" Rumania "for themselves" and at uniting it with Russia against Rockefeller. The latter controlled far more capital and an excellent system of oil transport and distribution. The struggle had to end, and did end in 1907, with the utter defeat of the Deutsche Bank, which was confronted with the alternative: either to liquidate its oil business and lose millions, or to submit. It chose to submit, and concluded a very disadvantageous agreement with the American trust. The Deutsche Bank agreed "not to attempt anything which might injure American interests." Provision was made, however, for the annulment of the agreement in the event of Germany establishing a state oil monopoly.

Then the "comedy of oil" began. One of the German finance kings, von Gwinner, a director of the Deutsche Bank, began through his private secretary, Strauss, a campaign *for* a state oil monopoly. The gigantic machine of the big German bank and all its wide "connections" were set in motion. The press bubbled over with "patriotic" indignation against the "yoke" of the American trust, and, on March 15, 1911, the Reichstag by an almost unanimous vote, adopted a motion asking the government to introduce a bill for the establishment of an oil monopoly. The government seized upon this "popular" idea, and the game of the Deutsche Bank, which hoped to cheat its American partner and improve its business by a state monopoly, appeared to have been won. The German oil magnates saw visions of wonderful profits, which would not be less than those of the Russian sugar refiners. . . . But, firstly, the big

---

[1] Diouritch, *op. cit.*, p. 245.

over 90 per cent of the world output of electric bulbs, is one of the largest
post-war international monopolies.

SOURCES: *Grünbuch der Aktiengesellschaften*, 1931; *Spezialarchiv der deutschen
Wirtschaft; Der AEG Konzern, Der Siemens Konzern; Moody's Industrials*, 1935.

THE STRUGGLE FOR OIL MARKETS

At the present time, the world oil market is, in the main, divided
among three groups: Standard Oil, Royal Dutch-Shell, and Anglo-Per-
sian-Burma Oil.

The last two groups are very closely connected. For a long time, the
raw material base of the Standard Oil was concentrated in the United
States. After the war, however, the Standard Oil gradually bought up
Mexican and Central and South American oil fields. The Standard Oil
group is also striving to penetrate into countries "belonging" to Shell and
Anglo-Persian by buying up shares in the Dutch-British group. A particularly fierce struggle is going on in the Far-Eastern markets, where the
Standard Oil, after the merger of the Standard Oil Co. of New York with
the Vacuum Oil Co., has gained a very solid position, but the Royal
Dutch-Shell is fighting hard to strengthen its position in the regions in
which the Standard Oil Co. is operating.

The Standard Oil group dominates the oil industry in the United
States, where it controls about 60 per cent of all prospected oil-bearing
territories, 25-30 per cent of the output of crude oil, 45-50 per cent of the
refining, 60 per cent of the transportation and of the entire tanker fleet
and 70 per cent of the entire foreign trade. Standard Oil has penetrated into
Venezuela and has there reduced the share of Shell output to 50 per cent.
It also controls 50 per cent of the Mexican oil output, almost the entire
output of Colombia, Canada, Peru, a considerable share of the Argentine
and Bolivian output, and 12 per cent of the Rumanian output. According
to the figures for 1926 (precise data of more recent date are not available), this American oil trust controls 26 per cent of the world's output.
Its chief competitor is the Anglo-Dutch concern, the Royal Dutch-Shell,
of which Sir Henry Deterding is the head, which controls 12 per cent of
the world oil output (together with the Anglo-Persian Co. and the Burma Oil Co. which is connected with the Royal Dutch-Shell, it controls 16
per cent). It occupies a predominant place in the oil output of the Dutch
East Indies, India, Egypt, Rumania, and also controls a considerable share

German banks quarrelled among themselves over the division of the spoils. The Disconto-Gesellschaft exposed the covetous aims of the Deutsche Bank; secondly, the government took fright at the prospect of a struggle with Rockefeller; it was doubtful whether Germany could be sure of obtaining oil from other sources. (The Rumanian output was small.) Thirdly, just at that time the 1913 credits of a billion marks were voted for Germany's war preparations. The project of the oil monopoly was postponed. The Rockefeller trust came out of the struggle, for the time being, victorious.

The Berlin review, *Die Bank,* said in this connection that Germany could only fight the oil trust by establishing an electricity monopoly and by converting water power into cheap electricity.

"But," the author added, "the electricity monopoly will come when the producers need it, that is to say, on the eve of the next great crash in the electrical industry, and when the powerful, expensive electric stations which are now being put up at great cost everywhere by private electrical concerns, which obtain partial monopolies from the state, from towns, etc., can no longer work at a profit. Water power will then have to be used. But it will be impossible to convert it into cheap electricity at state expense; it will have to be handed over to a 'private monopoly controlled by the state,' because of the immense compensation and damages that would have to be paid to private industry. . . . So it was with the nitrate monopoly, so it is with the oil monopoly; so it will be with the electric power monopoly. It is time for our state socialists, who allow themselves to be blinded by beautiful principles, to understand once and for all that in Germany monopolies have never pursued the aim, nor have they had the result, of benefiting the consumer, or of handing over to the state part of the *entrepreneurs'* profits; they have served only to facilitate, at the expense of the state, the recovery of private industries which were on the verge of bankruptcy."[1]

Such are the valuable admissions which the German bourgeois economists are forced to make. We see plainly here how private monopolies and state monopolies are bound up together in the age of finance capital; how both are but separate links in the imperialist struggle between the big monopolists for the division of the world.

In mercantile shipping, the tremendous development of concentration has ended also in the division of the world. In Germany two powerful companies have raised themselves to first rank, the Hamburg-Amerika and the Norddeutscher Lloyd, each having a capital of 200,000,000 marks (in stocks and bonds) and possessing 185 to 189 million marks worth of shipping tonnage. On the other side, in America, on January 1, 1903, the Morgan trust, the International Mercantile Marine Co., was

---

[1] *Die Bank*, 1912, p. 1036; *cf.* also *ibid.*, p. 629 *et. seq.*; 1913, I, p. 388.

of the output of Mexico, Venezuela, Argentina, Iraq and a small part (5 to 6 per cent) of the American output.

A sharp struggle is also going on for the Persian oil fields. The Anglo-Persian oil concession (in which the British government is interested) was annulled by the Persian government, undoubtedly under the influence of agents in the pay of Standard Oil, and was subsequently renewed only after protracted negotiations.

Another struggle is going on for the Mossul oil wells in Iraq. After a prolonged struggle control over the Iraq Petroleum Co., which up to the end of 1936 was in the hands of Italian, German, French and other capitalists with a small holding by the Shell group, passed into the hands of the latter as a result of the purchase of the control block of shares from the Italian semi-state concern AGIP.

SOURCES: Ludwell Denny, *The Struggle for Oil*, 1934; *Petroleum*, 1930-34; *Petrol Times*, 15, VIII, 1936; *World Petroleum*, 1936.

MONOPOLIES IN THE SHIPPING TRADE

After the war, the German steamship companies, mentioned by Lenin, lost the greater part of their tonnage as a result of the Versailles Treaty. Subsequently, their tonnage began to grow again as a result of the purchase of ships from other companies and the building of new tonnage. By the end of 1931 their tonnage almost reached that of 1913. This is shown in the following table.

	1913	1920	1931	1935
		(1,000 register tons)		
Hamburg-Amerika Line	1,360	397	1,087	744
Norddeutscher Lloyd	983	57	955	607

The changes in the capital of these companies revealed in the following table were caused in 1924 by the revaluation of assets that followed inflation, and in 1931 and 1935 by depreciation resulting from the crisis.

formed which united nine British and American steamship companies, and which controlled a capital of 120,000,000 dollars (480,000,000 marks). As early as 1903, the German giants and the Anglo-American trust concluded an agreement and divided the world in accordance with the division of profits. The German companies undertook not to compete in the Anglo-American traffic. The ports were carefully "allotted" to each; a joint committee of control was set up, etc. This contract was concluded for twenty years, with the prudent provision for its annulment in the event of war.[1]

---

[1] Riesser, *op. cit.*, p. 125.

	1913	1924	1926	1930	1931	1935
			(million marks)			
Hamburg-Amerika						
Stocks	180.0	55.1	131.4	161.4	54.5	46.4
Bonds	69.5	—	29.6	43.5	20.2	16.6
Norddeutscher Lloyd						
Stocks	125.0	33.0	125.0	165.0	54.4	46.7
Bonds	65.6	4.0	23.2	81.6	78.1	38.2

The Hamburg-Amerika Line controls 10 subsidiary steamship companies and has an interest in 12 others. The Norddeutscher Lloyd controls 10 subsidiary steamship companies. In 1930, the Hamburg-Amerika Line and the Norddeutscher Lloyd entered into a close union by concluding a fifty-year agreement, and are now operating as parts of a single group, under the name of Hapag-Lloyd.[1]

The International Mercantile Marine Co., the Morgan trust, mentioned by Lenin, has lost its pre-war monopoly position. In 1931 this trust combined six companies owning 57 ships with an aggregate tonnage of 493,000 gross tons. It is now merged with the more powerful steamship company, the American International Corporation, which controls a tonnage of 1,200,000 gross tons, of which 500,000 tons sail under the British flag.

The division of the world between German and Anglo-American groups, noted by Lenin, was brought about in the post-war period by the North Atlantic Conference, an international combine of sixteen of the biggest international companies, in which the Hapag-Lloyd, the British Cunard-White Star Line and Royal Mail and the United States Lines participated. These were joined by the French Compagnie Générale Transatlantique and by other steamship companies.

The number of international agreements in the shipping trade now exceeds fifty. In 1929 these agreements covered over 50 per cent of the passenger traffic and 80 per cent of the freight traffic.

The biggest international shipping monopoly today is the Baltic and International Maritime Conference. In June 1930, it represented a combination of 650 steamship companies, with 3,532 steamships and an aggregate tonnage of 9.88 million gross tons, *i.e.*, approximately 15 per cent of the world's tonnage.

---

[1] In the beginning of 1935 the Hapag-Lloyd union was officially dissolved although the cartel agreement between the two companies, which continued under the joint control of the Deutsche Bank—Disconto-Gesellschaft, remained in force.

Sources: *Grünbuch der Aktiengesellschaften*, 1933; *Stock Exchange Yearbook*, 1934; *Der Aktienführer*, 1936-37.

11*

Extremely instructive also is the story of the creation of the International Rail Cartel. The first attempt of the British, Belgian and German rail manufacturers to create such a cartel was made as early as 1884, at the time of a severe industrial depression. The manufacturers agreed not to compete with one another for the home markets of the countries involved, and they divided the foreign markets in the following quotas: Great Britain 66 per cent; Germany 27 per cent; Belgium 7 per cent. India was reserved entirely for Great Britain. Joint war was declared against a British firm which remained outside the cartel. The cost of this economic war was met by a percentage levy on all sales. But in 1886 the cartel collapsed when two British firms retired from it. It is characteristic that agreement could not be achieved in the period of industrial prosperity which followed.

At the beginning of 1904, the German steel syndicate was formed. In November 1904, the International Rail Cartel was revived, with the following quotas for foreign trade: England 53.5 per cent; Germany 28.83 per cent; Belgium 17.67 per cent. France came in later with 4.8 per cent, 5.8 per cent and 6.4 per cent in the first, second and third years respectively, in excess of the 100 per cent limit, *i.e.*, when the total was 104.8 per cent, etc. In 1905, the United States Steel Corporation entered the cartel; then Austria; then Spain.

"At the present time," wrote Vogelstein in 1910, "the division of the world is completed, and the big consumers, primarily the state railways—since the world has been parcelled out without consideration for their interests—can now dwell like the poet in the heaven of Jupiter." [1]

We will mention also the International Zinc Syndicate, established in 1909, which carefully apportioned output among three groups of factories: German, Belgian, French, Spanish and British.

---

[1] Th. Vogelstein, *Organisationsformen* (*Forms of Organisation*), p. 100.

THE INTERNATIONAL RAIL CARTEL

This refers to the International Railmakers' Association, known as IRMA. This cartel broke up in 1914, but was reorganised in 1926. The export quotas follow (per cent):

	1904	1929
Great Britain	53.5	24.75
United States	—	18.50
Germany	28.83	19.55
France	4.8 to 6.4	17.60
Belgium	17.67	14.35
Luxemburg	—	4.95
Central European group	—	4.30

This table illustrates the changed relation of forces of the industry in the various countries, resulting from the increasing unevenness of their development.

The main object of the cartel is to divide the foreign markets among its members and to fix export prices; it does not undertake to regulate production. Unlike the European steel cartel, which collapsed during the crisis and was restored only in April 1933, IRMA has managed to hold on continuously to this day.

Sources: 1904 figures are quoted from Lenin; figures for 1926 are taken from *Kartellrundschau*.

THE INTERNATIONAL ZINC SYNDICATE

This syndicate was formed in 1909. It collapsed during the war, but was reorganised in 1928. It comprised German, Polish, Belgian, French, British, Spanish, Italian and Norwegian zinc firms, controlling in the aggregate approximately 95 per cent of the European and 50 per cent of the world zinc output. The agreement, which was concluded for a period of six months, provided for a reduction of output in the event of prices dropping below a specified level. In December 1928 Canada and Australia joined the syndicate, and the biggest United States monopolists declared that they would co-operate. The object of this syndicate was to restrict production and raise prices. Immediately on the outbreak of the crisis sharp disagreements arose among the members of the syndicate and on January 1, 1930, the agreement was dissolved. The syndicate was reorganised in 1931, but on a narrower basis, *i.e.*, without the participation of the transatlantic producers. The agreement, renewed in 1933, provided

Then there is the International Dynamite Trust, of which Liefmann says that it is

"quite a modern, close alliance of all the manufacturers of explosives who, with the French and American dynamite manufacturers who have organised in a similar manner, have divided the whole world among themselves, so to speak." [1]

Liefmann calculated that in 1897 there were altogether about forty international cartels in which Germany had a share, while in 1910 there were about a hundred.

Certain bourgeois writers (with whom K. Kautsky, who has completely abandoned the Marxist position he held, for example, in 1909, has now associated himself) express the opinion that international cartels are the most striking expressions of the internationalisation of capital, and, therefore, give the hope of peace among nations under capitalism. Theoretically, this opinion is absurd, while in practice it is sophistry and a dishonest defence of the worst opportunism. International cartels show to what point capitalist monopolies have developed, and they *reveal the object* of the struggle between the various capitalist groups. This last circumstance is the most important; it alone shows us the historico-economic significance of events; for the *forms* of the struggle may and do constantly change in accordance with varying, relatively particular, and temporary causes, but the *essence* of the struggle, its class *content, cannot* change while classes exist. It is easy to understand, for example, that it is in the interests of the German bourgeoisie, whose theoretical arguments have now been adopted by Kautsky (we will deal with this later), to obscure the *content* of the present economic struggle

---

[1] R. Liefmann, *Kartelle und Trusts*, Second ed., p. 161.

for the restriction of production by 45 per cent of the pre-crisis level. The syndicate has not functioned since the end of 1934.

SOURCES: C. Lammers, *Internationale Industriekartelle*, 1932; E. Ertel, *Internationale Kartelle und Konzerne der Industrie*, 1930; *Frankfurter Zeitung*; *Bergwerkszeitung*; *Kartellrundschau*

THE INTERNATIONAL DYNAMITE TRUST

The International Dynamite Trust, mentioned by Lenin, existed up to the World War. It was revived in 1925 in the form of an agreement between the big explosives manufacturers—the Nobel group of Great Britain, duPont de Nemours of the United States, and the Dynamit Fabrik A. G. of Germany (formerly Nobel in Hamburg, and Köln Rottweil in Berlin). The last two concerns merged with the German I. G. Farbenindustrie. The agreement provides for *technical collaboration*, particularly for the exchange of patents and improvements. The contracting groups also exchanged shares in their respective companies.

SOURCE: Fox, *Imperial Chemical Industries*, London, 1934.

TOTAL NUMBER OF INTERNATIONAL CARTELS

1897	1910	1931
40	100	320

NUMBER OF INTERNATIONAL CARTELS IN DIFFERENT INDUSTRIES (1931)

Mining	12	Textiles	27
Ferrous metals	50	Food	11
Non-ferrous metals	10	Other industries	30
Building materials	25	Transport and communications	80
Wood and paper	15	Insurance	10
Chemicals	51		

During the crisis many international monopolies (the European Steel Cartel, the International Copper Syndicate, the Zinc Syndicate, etc.) collapsed. Nevertheless, strenuous efforts have been made, particularly of late, to revive the old cartels and to form a number of new ones. The European Steel Export Cartel, which collapsed during the crisis, was reorganised in 1933-34. An international agreement has been concluded among the rubber producers, an agreement has been concluded between the synthetic nitrogen producers and the Chile nitrate producers, etc. In 1935 Great Britain joined the European Steel Cartel.

SOURCES: The figures for 1897 and 1910 are quoted from Lenin. The 1897 figure includes only those cartels in which Germany participated. The figures for 1931 are based on the estimate of Wagenführ, "Statistik der Kartelle," *Allg. Statistisches Archiv*, 1932, Bd. 22, H. II, S. 252.

(the division of the world) and to emphasise this or that *form* of the struggle. Kautsky makes the same mistake. Of course, we have in mind not only the German bourgeoisie, but the bourgeoisie all over the world. The capitalists divide the world, not out of any particular malice, but because the degree of concentration which has been reached forces them to adopt this method in order to get profits. And they divide it in proportion to "capital," in proportion to "strength," because there cannot be any other system of division under commodity production and capitalism. But strength varies with the degree of economic and political development. In order to understand what takes place, it is necessary to know what questions are settled by this change of forces. The question as to whether these changes are "purely" economic or *non*-economic (*e.g.,* military) is a secondary one, which does not in the least affect the fundamental view on the latest epoch of capitalism. To substitute for the question of the *content* of the struggle and agreements between capitalist combines the question of the *form* of these struggles and agreements (today peaceful, tomorrow war-like, the next day war-like again) is to sink to the role of a sophist.

The epoch of modern capitalism shows us that certain relations are established between capitalist alliances, *based* on the economic division of the world; while parallel with this fact and in connection with it, certain relations are established between political alliances, between states, on the basis of the territorial division of the world, of the struggle for colonies, of the "struggle for economic territory."

CHAPTER VI

THE DIVISION OF THE WORLD AMONG THE GREAT POWERS

In his book, *The Territorial Development of the European Colonies*, A. Supan,[1] the geographer, gives the following brief summary of this development at the end of the nineteenth century:

PERCENTAGE OF TERRITORIES BELONGING TO THE EUROPEAN COLONIAL POWERS (INCLUDING UNITED STATES)

	1876	1900	Increase or Decrease
Africa	10.8	90.4	+79.6
Polynesia	56.8	98.9	+42.1
Asia	51.5	56.6	+ 5.1
Australia	100.0	100.0	—
America	27.5	27.2	— 0.3

"The characteristic feature of this period," he concludes, "is, therefore, the division of Africa and Polynesia."

As there are no unoccupied territories—that is, territories that do not belong to any state—in Asia and America, Mr. Supan's conclusion must be carried further, and we must say that the characteristic feature of this period is the final partition of the globe—not in the sense that a *new partition* is impossible—on the contrary, new partitions are possible and inevitable—but in the sense that the colonial policy of the capitalist countries has *completed* the seizure of the unoccupied territories on our planet. For the first time the world is completely divided up, so that in the future *only* redivision is possible; territories can only pass from one "owner" to another, instead of passing as unowned territory to an "owner."

Hence, we are passing through a peculiar period of world colonial policy, which is closely associated with the "latest stage in the development of capitalism," with finance capital. For this reason, it is essential first of all to deal in detail with the facts, in order to ascertain exactly what

---

[1] A. Supan, *Die territoriale Entwicklung der europäischen Kolonien*, Gotha, 1906, p. 254.

PERCENTAGE OF TERRITORIES BELONGING TO EUROPEAN COLONIAL POWERS, UNITED STATES AND JAPAN

1932	Changes compared with 1900	
96.6[1]	+ 6.2	Africa
100.0	+ 1.1	Polynesia
20.6[2]	— 36.0	Asia (exclusive of Asiatic part of U.S.S.R.)
100.0	—	Australia
30.4[3]	+ 3.2	America

[1] In 1936, after the seizure of Abyssinia by Italy, the African territory belonging to colonial powers amounted to nearly 100 per cent (the only exception being Liberia which, formally, is independent, but actually is a dependency of the United States).

[2] After the seizure of a number of provinces in China by Japan after 1930, this percentage increased.

[3] The discrepancy between these and Lenin's figures is due mainly to the correction of the figures relating to American countries and the American continent as a whole. Minor corrections have also been made in the above table and in the two following tables concerning a number of other countries.

SOURCES: Figures for 1932 are calculated on the basis of data from *Statistical Yearbook of the League of Nations*, 1932-33.

distinguishes this period from those preceding it, and what the present situation is. In the first place, two questions of fact arise here. Is an intensification of colonial policy, an intensification of the struggle for colonies, observed precisely in this period of finance capital? And how, in this respect, is the world divided at the present time?

The American writer, Morris, in his book on the history of colonisation,[1] has made an attempt to compile data on the colonial possessions of Great Britain, France and Germany during different periods of the nineteenth century. The following is a brief summary of the results he has obtained:

COLONIAL POSSESSIONS
(Million square miles and million inhabitants)

	Great Britain		France		Germany	
	Area	Pop.	Area	Pop.	Area	Pop.
1815-30	?	126.4	0.02	0.5	—	—
1860	2.5	145.1	0.2	3.4	---	—
1880	7.7	267.9	0.7	7.5	—	—
1899	9.3	309.0	3.7	56.4	1.0	14.7

For Great Britain, the period of the enormous expansion of colonial conquests is that between 1860 and 1880, and it was also very considerable in the last twenty years of the nineteenth century. For France and Germany this period falls precisely in these last twenty years. We saw above that the apex of pre-monopoly capitalist development, of capitalism in which free competition was predominant, was reached in the sixties and seventies of the last century. We now see that it is *precisely after that period* that the "boom" in colonial annexations begins, and that the struggle for the territorial division of the world becomes extraordinarily keen. It is beyond doubt, therefore, that capitalism's transition to the stage of monopoly capitalism, to finance capital, is *bound up* with the intensification of the struggle for the partition of the world.

---

[1] Henry C. Morris, *The History of Colonisation*, New York, 1900, II, p. 88; I, pp. 304, 419.

COLONIAL POSSESSIONS

(Million square miles and million inhabitants)

	Great Britain		France		Germany		U.S.A.		Japan	
	Area	Pop.	Area	Pop.	Area	Pop.	Area	Pop.	Area	Pop.
1815-30	?	126.4	0.02	0.5	—	—				
1860........	2.5	145.1	0.2	3.4	—	—				
1880........	7.7	267.9	0.7	7.5	—	—				
1899........	9.3	309.0	3.7	56.4	1.0	14.7	0.06	10.6		
1932........	13.5	466.5	4.6	65.1	—	—	0.7	14.6	0.1	28.0

exclusive of recently occupied Chinese territory

SOURCES: For 1815-30, 1860, 1880, 1899 the figures for Britain, Germany and France are quoted from Lenin. U.S.A. figures for 1899 are taken from *Statesman's Yearbook*, 1901: 1932 figures are taken from *International Statistical Yearbook*, L. of N., 1932-33.

LATEST EXAMPLES OF PROPAGANDA IN FAVOUR OF COLONIAL PLUNDER

The cynical arguments of the outspoken advocates of colonial plunder at the end of the nineteenth century, such as Cecil Rhodes, Joseph Chamberlain, and their ilk, are repeated almost verbatim by the politicians and ideologists of present-day imperialism. Particularly shameless propaganda in favour of colonial plunder is conducted by German and Italian fascists and Japanese militarists. Spurious, inhuman and barbarous racial "theories" constitute the official ideology of the fascist aggressors. While pursuing a policy of enslavement of other peoples in the interests of a handful of monopolists the aggressors try to screen this policy by phrases about the interests of the nation, the need to feed the so-called "surplus" population and similar lies. Actually, the fascist policy of aggression condemns the German, Japanese and Italian peoples to distressing privations, to say

Hobson, in his work on imperialism, marks the years 1884-1900 as the period of the intensification of the colonial "expansion" of the chief European states. According to his estimate, Great Britain during these years acquired 3,700,000 square miles of territory with a population of 57,000,000; France acquired 3,600,000 square miles with a population of 36,500,000; Germany 1,000,000 square miles with a population of 16,700,000; Belgium 900,000 square miles with 30,000,000 inhabitants; Portugal 800,000 square miles with 9,000,000 inhabitants. The quest for colonies by all the capitalist states at the end of the nineteenth century and particularly since the 1880's is a commonly known fact in the history of diplomacy and of foreign affairs.

When free competition in Great Britain was at its zenith, *i.e.*, between 1840 and 1860, the leading British bourgeois politicians were opposed to colonial policy and were of the opinion that the liberation of the colonies and their complete separation from Britain was inevitable and desirable. M. Beer, in an article, "Modern British Imperialism,"[1] published in 1898, shows that in 1852, Disraeli, a statesman generally inclined towards imperialism, declared: "The colonies are millstones round our necks." But at the end of the nineteenth century the heroes of the hour in England were Cecil Rhodes and Joseph Chamberlain, open advocates of imperialism, who applied the imperialist policy in the most cynical manner.

It is not without interest to observe that even at that time these leading British bourgeois politicians fully appreciated the connection between what might be called the purely economic and the politico-social roots of modern imperialism. Chamberlain advocated imperialism by calling it a "true, wise and economical policy," and he pointed particularly to the German, American and Belgian competition which Great Britain was encountering in the world market. Salvation lies in monopolies, said the capitalists as they formed cartels, syndicates and trusts. Salvation lies in monopolies, echoed the political leaders of the bourgeoisie, hastening to appropriate the parts of the world not yet shared out. The journalist, Stead, relates the following remarks uttered by his close friend Cecil Rhodes, in 1895, regarding his imperialist ideas:

"I was in the East End of London yesterday and attended a meeting of the unemployed. I listened to the wild speeches, which were just a cry for 'bread,' 'bread,' 'bread,' and on my way home I pondered over the scene and I became more than ever convinced of the importance of imperialism. . . . My cherished idea is a solution for the social problem, *i.e.*, in order to save the 40,000,000 inhabitants of the

---

[1] *Die Neue Zeit*, XVI, I, 1898, p. 302.

nothing of the indescribable suffering of the peoples who have become victims of aggression. Below we quote a few examples of this cynical propaganda:

An appeal issued by the German Imperial Colonial League *(Reichskolonialbund)* and published in the *Deutsche Tageszeitung* on March 17, 1934, declared that:

"The Leader" (Hitler) "has advanced the following demands in point 3 of the party programme: 'We demand lands and territories (colonies) for the sustenance of our people and for the settlement of our surplus population.' In the speech he delivered in the Reichstag on March 23, 1933, he declared: 'We know that the geographical position of Germany, which is poor in raw materials, does not guarantee autarchy for our state.' On February 11, 1933, he declared to a representative of the *Sunday Express* that Germany had not by any means renounced her colonial aspirations. 'Germany needs a great number of things which she must obtain from colonies, and we need colonies just as much as any other power.' "

In a special supplement devoted to colonial propaganda, the *Kölnische Zeitung* of April 24, 1934, says:

"The value of owning colonies cannot be overestimated. They ensure for the nation raw materials in accordance with national interests. It is an advantage which a state with exporting requirements cannot dispense with for any length of time. Has not Japan on these grounds recently secured for herself the riches of Manchuria; does she not lease whole regions in Abyssinia and Turkey, where she intends to develop her own cotton plantations? Of still greater importance, perhaps, is the fact that possession of colonies is the nation's most important foundation for overseas national activity. . . ."

"The spaceless German people in an overpopulated Europe is directly confronted with the African territories—*space without a people*. Africa lies at the gates of Europe and she still has for Europe the significance she had at the time of the Roman Empire, and which she again acquired in the age of discoveries: She was and remains a *colonial region. . . .* "

"It is precisely at the present time that we realise so clearly how important it is for us to have our own cotton, our own hemp, our own rubber and our own vegetable oils, for which we can pay with German currency. It is precisely these raw materials that we used to obtain from our tropical colonies. . . ."

In an article published in *Deutsche Bergwerkszeitung* in 1933 Professor Henning even thought fit to advance as an argument for the return of the colonies to Germany her superior ability to keep the native population in a state of subjection. He wrote:

United Kingdom from a bloody civil war, we colonial statesmen must acquire new lands to settle the surplus population, to provide new markets for the goods produced by them in the factories and mines. The Empire, as I have always said, is a bread and butter question. If you want to avoid civil war, you must become imperialists."[1]

This is what Cecil Rhodes, millionaire, king of finance, the man who was mainly responsible for the Boer War, said in 1895. His defence of imperialism is just crude and cynical, but in substance it does not differ from the "theory" advocated by Messrs. Maslov, Südekum, Potresov, David and the founder of Russian Marxism and others. Cecil Rhodes was a somewhat more honest social-chauvinist.

To tabulate as exactly as possible the territorial division of the world, and the changes which have occurred during the last decades, we will take the data furnished by Supan in the work already quoted on the colonial possessions of all the powers of the world. Supan examines the years 1876 and 1900; we will take the year 1876—a year aptly selected, for it is precisely at that time that the pre-monopolist stage of development of West European capitalism can be said to have been completed, in the main, and we will take the year 1914, and in place of Supan's figures we will quote the more recent statistics of Hübner's *Geographical and Statistical Tables*. Supan gives figures only for colonies: we think it useful in order to present a complete picture of the division of the world to add brief figures on non-colonial and semi-colonial countries like Persia, China and Turkey. Persia is already almost completely a colony; China and Turkey are on the way to becoming colonies. We thus get the following summary:

---

[1] *Ibid.*, p. 304.

"The British Mandate administration in the present territory of Tanganyika (formerly German East Africa) ... spoils the blacks ... it panders to them too much.... The planters feel instinctively that these senseless methods irresponsibly undermine white rule in Africa. That is why they so persistently demand that Germany should return to German East Africa, because she pursued a more sensible policy, and one that was more beneficial for the natives themselves, than the administration of the 'Mandated Territory of Tanganyika' which, notwithstanding its indulgent methods, has not won the hearts of the blacks, and has only made them stubborn and worthless."

From Japanese documents, which advance arguments in favour of colonial plunder, we shall quote a few passages from the notorious Tanaka Memorandum, which was submitted to the Emperor in 1927.

"In order to conquer China, we must first conquer Manchuria and Mongolia; in order to conquer the world, we must first conquer China. If we succeed in conquering China, the rest of the Asiatic countries and the South Seas countries will fear us and surrender to us.

"According to the last will of Meiji, our first step was to conquer Formosa and the second step to annex Korea. Having completed both of these, the third step is yet to be taken and that is the conquest of Manchuria, Mongolia and China. When this is done, the rest of Asia including the South Sea Islands will be at our feet. . . .

"The iron deposits in Manchuria and Mongolia are estimated at 1,200,000,000 tons, and coal deposits, 2,500,000,000. . . . We shall save the expense of 120,000,000 yen which we pay for the importation of steel every year. When we can have sufficient iron and steel for our own industries, we shall have acquired the secret for becoming the leading nation in the world. Thus strengthened, we can conquer both the East and the West. In order to attain this goal, the iron works must be separated from the South Manchuria Railway.

"Another important commodity which we lack is petroleum. It is also essential to the existence of a nation. Fortunately there lie in the Fushun Coal Mine 5,200,000 tons of shale oil from every hundred catties of which six catties of crude oil may be extracted. . . .

"This will be a great industrial revolution for us. From the standpoint of national defence and national wealth, petroleum is a great factor. Having the iron and petroleum of Manchuria, our army and navy will become impregnable walls of defence. That Manchuria and Mongolia are the heart and liver of our empire, is a truthful saying."

SOURCES: "The Tanaka Memorial," *The China Critic*, 24, IX, 1931, pp. 923, 927-28, 932.

COLONIAL POSSESSIONS OF THE GREAT POWERS

(Million square kilometres and million inhabitants)

	Colonies				Home countries		Total	
	1876		1914		1914		1914	
	Area	Pop.	Area	Pop.	Area	Pop.	Area	Pop.
Great Britain.....	22.5	251.9	33.5	393.5	0.3	46.5	33.8	440.0
Russia	17.0	15.9	17.4	33.2	5.4	136.2	22.8	169.4
France	0.9	6.0	10.6	55.5	0.5	39.6	11.1	95.1
Germany	—	—	2.9	12.3	0.5	64.9	3.4	77.2
U.S.A.	—	—	0.3	9.7	9.4	97.0	9.7	106.7
Japan	—	—	0.3	19.2	0.4	53.0	0.7	72.2
Total	40.4	273.8	65.0	523.4	16.5	437.2	81.5	960.6
Colonies of other powers (Belgium, Holland, etc.)							9.9	45.3
Semi-colonial countries (Persia, China, Turkey)							14.5	361.2
Other countries							28.0	289.2
Total area and population of the world							133.9	1,657.0

We see from these figures how "complete" was the partition of the world at the end of the nineteenth and beginning of the twentieth centuries. After 1876 colonial possessions increased to an enormous degree, more than one and a half times, from 40,000,000 to 65,000,000 square kilometres in area for the six biggest powers, an increase of 25,000,000 square kilometres, that is, one and a half times greater than the area of the "home" countries, which have a total of 16,500,000 square kilometres. In 1876 three powers had no colonies, and a fourth, France, had scarcely any. In 1914 these four powers had 14,100,000 square kilometres of colonies, or an area one and a half times greater than that of Europe, with a population of nearly 100,000,000. The unevenness in the rate of expansion of colonial possessions is very marked. If, for instance, we compare France, Germany and Japan, which do not differ very much in area and population, we will see that the first has annexed almost three times as much colonial territory as the other two combined. In regard to finance capital, also, France, at the beginning of the period we are considering, was perhaps several times richer than Germany and Japan put together. In addition to, and on the basis of, purely economic causes, geographical conditions and other factors also affect the dimensions of colonial possessions. However strong the process of levelling the world, of levelling the economic and living conditions in different countries, may have been in the past decades as a result of the pressure of large-scale industry, exchange and finance capital, great differences still

(Million square kilometres and million inhabitants)

Colonies		Home countries		Total		
		1932				
Area	Pop.	Area	Pop.	Area	Pop.	
34.9	466.5	0.25[1]	46.2	35.1	512.7	Great Britain
11.9	65.1	0.55[2]	42.0	12.45	107.1	France
—	—	0.47[3]	64.8	0.47	64.8	Germany
0.3	14.6	9.4[4]	124.6	9.7	139.2	United States
0.3[5]	28.0	0.4	65.5	0.7	93.5	Japan (excl. of recently occupied Chinese provinces)
47.4	574.2	11.02	343.1	58.42	917.3	Total for 5 Great Powers
9.6	87.6	—	—	9.6	87.6	Colonies of other powers (Belgium, Holland, Denmark, Italy, Spain, Norway and Portugal)
—	—	—	—	34.9	600.0	Semi-colonial and dependent countries—China,[6] Arabia, Siam, countries of Central and South America, Abyssinia[7] and Liberia
—	—	—	—	3.0	30.7	Countries which have entirely or almost entirely freed themselves from imperialist dependence (Turkey, Iran and Afghanistan)
—	—	—	—	3.98	224.1	Other countries (capitalist)
—	—	—	—	1.4	1.6	Mongolian and Tanna Tuva People's Republics
—	—	—	—	111.3	1861.3	World total (excl. U.S.S.R.)
—	—	—	—	21.2	163.2	U.S.S.R.
—	—	—	—	132.5	2,024.5	World total

[1] The discrepancy between these and Lenin's figures (0.3 million square kilometres in 1914) is due to the exclusion of the Irish Free State. If the area of Great Britain in 1932 (244,000 sq. km.) is added to the area of the Irish Free State (69,000 sq. km.) we shall get the figure of 0.3 million sq. km., as given by Lenin.

[2] The pre-war area of France was 536,000 sq. km.; post-war area, 551,000 sq. km.

[3] The pre-war area of Germany was 541,000 sq. km.; post-war area 469,000 sq. km.

[4] Including Alaska, as given by Lenin in 1914.

[5] According to *Statistical Yearbook*, L. of N., 1927, 1932-33, the area of the Japanese colonies was 296,000 sq. km. in 1914 and 299,000 sq. km. in 1932.

[6] At present China is waging a heroic struggle against Japanese aggression and is on the way to becoming an independent country.

[7] In 1936 Italy seized Abyssinia.

remain; and among the six powers, we see, firstly, young capitalist powers (America, Germany, Japan) which progressed very rapidly; secondly, countries with an old capitalist development (France and Great Britain), which, of late, have made much slower progress than the previously mentioned countries, and thirdly, a country (Russia) which is economically most backward, in which modern capitalist imperialism is enmeshed, so to speak, in a particularly close network of pre-capitalist relations.

Alongside the colonial possessions of these great powers, we have placed the small colonies of the small states, which are, so to speak, the next possible and probable objects of a new colonial "share-out." Most of these little states are able to retain their colonies only because of the conflicting interests, frictions, etc., among the big powers, which prevent them from coming to an agreement in regard to the division of the spoils. The "semi-colonial states" provide an example of the transitional forms which are to be found in all spheres of nature and society. Finance capital is such a great, it may be said, such a decisive force in all economic and international relations, that it is capable of subordinating to itself, and actually does subordinate to itself even states enjoying complete political independence. We shall shortly see examples of this.

The following are the most important changes that have taken place in the division of the world since 1914:

1) As a result of national liberation revolutions a number of former colonial and semi-colonial countries secured independence. The October Revolution put an end to the subjugation of the numerous national minorities in former tsarist Russia and, in particular, it freed from colonial exploitation the Asiatic part of the U.S.S.R. which in Lenin's table is included in the category of colonies. The Mongolian and Tanna Tuva People's Republics also gained their independence. The victorious Chinese revolution brought about the formation of Soviet districts (now special regions) in China. At present the great Chinese people is waging a heroic struggle against the Japanese aggressors for its national independence. Turkey, Iran and Afghanistan have entirely, or almost entirely, freed themselves from imperialist dependence.

2) On the other hand, a number of formerly independent countries have been transformed into colonies or semi-colonies (*cf.* list of latest colonial conquests on page 183).

3) As a result of the redivision of the world under the Versailles Treaty, Great Britain, France and Italy, as well as other powers, greatly enlarged their colonial possessions by seizing the colonies of the defeated countries.

4) Japan has practically grabbed Manchuria and a number of other provinces of China, and is now fighting to keep these as her colonies and to seize additional Chinese territory. These conquests of Japanese imperialism are merely a prelude to the war that is maturing among the imperialist powers for a new redivision of the world and for a counter-revolutionary war on the Soviet Union.

5) Italy invaded and forcibly annexed Abyssinia.

6) Germany in 1938 seized Austria by force, turning it into her colony.

7) The Italian and German interventionists do what they like in the part of Spain occupied by them and treat it as their colony.

COLONIES OF THE SMALL POWERS

Of the small powers who possess colonies in the post-war period, Portugal and Holland are under the powerful influence of Great Britain, while Belgium (Belgian Congo) is under the influence of France. The colonial possessions of Spain are a matter of rivalry between all European imperialist great powers.

Naturally, however, finance capital finds it most "convenient," and is able to extract the greatest profit from a subordination which involves the loss of the political independence of the subjected countries and peoples. In this connection, the semi-colonial countries provide a typical example of the "middle stage." It is natural that the struggle for these semi-dependent countries should have become particularly bitter during the period of finance capital, when the rest of the world had already been divided up.

Colonial policy and imperialism existed before this latest stage of capitalism, and even before capitalism. Rome, founded on slavery, pursued a colonial policy and achieved imperialism. But "general" arguments about imperialism, which ignore, or put into the background the fundamental difference of social-economic systems, inevitably degenerate into absolutely empty banalities, or into grandiloquent comparisons like: "Greater Rome and Greater Britain." [1] Even the colonial policy of capitalism in its *previous* stages is essentially different from the colonial policy of finance capital.

The principal feature of modern çapitalism is the domination of monopolist combines of the big capitalists. These monopolies are most firmly established when *all* the sources of raw materials are controlled by the one group. And we have seen with what zeal the international capitalist combines exert every effort to make it impossible for their rivals to compete with them; for example, by buying up mineral lands. oil fields, etc. Colonial possession alone gives complete guarantee of success to the monopolies against all the risks of the struggle with competitors, including the risk that the latter will defend themselves by means of a law establishing a state monopoly. The more capitalism is developed, the more the need for raw materials is felt, the more bitter competition becomes, and the more feverishly the hunt for raw materials proceeds throughout the whole world, the more desperate becomes the struggle for the acquisition of colonies.

Schilder writes:

"It may even be asserted, although it may sound paradoxical to some, that in the more or less discernible future the growth of the urban industrial population is more likely to be hindered by a shortage of raw materials for industry than by a shortage of food."

For example, there is a growing shortage of timber—the price of which is steadily rising—of leather, and raw materials for the textile industry.

---

[1] A reference to the book by C. P. Lucas, *Greater Rome and Greater Britain*, Oxford, 1912, or the Earl of Cromer's *Ancient and Modern Imperialism*, London, 1910.

IMPORTANT COLONIAL CONQUESTS IN THE 20TH CENTURY

1899–1900..Division of Samoan Islands among Germany, U.S.A. and Great Britain.

1900–02....Anglo-Boer War and British annexation of the Boer Republics in South Africa.

1903.......Seizure by U.S. of part of Colombia and establishment of "independent" Republic of Panama which turned over the Panama Canal Zone to the U.S.

1903–04....Complete subjugation of Somaliland by Great Britain.

1904.......Anglo-French agreement concerning the division of spheres of influence in Africa.

1904.......Great Britain establishes *de facto* protectorate over Tibet.

1905.......United States establishes *de facto* protectorate over Santo Domingo.

1905.......Japan annexes southern half of Sakhalin.

1908.......The Congo Free State is transformed from the private domain of Leopold, King of the Belgians, into a Belgian colony.

1907.......Anglo-Russian agreement concerning the division of spheres of influence in Persia.

1907.......France annexes three provinces in Siam.

1907–10....Japan annexes Korea.

1911.......Franco-German agreement concerning Morocco and the Congo.

1911-12....Italy annexes Tripoli and Cirenaica.

1912.......French protectorate established over Morocco and latter finally divided up between France and Spain.

1912–13....Italy seizes the Dodecanese Islands (formal annexation in 1923).

1914.......Great Britain proclaims formal protectorate over Egypt, actually seized in the 'eighties (Egypt's independence was formally restored in 1922).

REDIVISION OF GERMAN COLONIES BY VERSAILLES TREATY

1919.......Tanganyika allocated to Great Britain.
Ruanda and Urundi allocated to Belgium.
Kionga allocated to Portugal.
The Cameroons and Togoland divided between Great Britain and France.
German Southwest Africa allocated to the Union of South Africa (British Empire).

"As instances of the efforts of associations of manufacturers to create an equilibrium between industry and agriculture in world economy as a whole, we might mention the International Federation of Cotton Spinners' Associations in the most important industrial countries, founded in 1904, and the European Federation of Flax Spinners' Associations, founded on the same model in 1910." [1]

The bourgeois reformists, and among them particularly the present-day adherents of Kautsky, of course, try to belittle the importance of facts of this kind by arguing that it "would be possible" to obtain raw materials in the open market without a "costly and dangerous" colonial policy; and that it would be "possible" to increase the supply of raw materials to an enormous extent "simply" by improving agriculture. But these arguments are merely an apology for imperialism, an attempt to embellish it, because they ignore the principal feature of modern capitalism: monopoly. Free markets are becoming more and more a thing of the past; monopolist syndicates and trusts are restricting them more and more every day, and "simply" improving agriculture reduces itself to improving the conditions of the masses, to raising wages and reducing profits. Where, except in the imagination of the sentimental reformists, are there any trusts capable of interesting themselves in the condition of the masses instead of the conquest of colonies?

Finance capital is not only interested in the already known sources of raw materials; it is also interested in potential sources of raw materials, because present-day technical development is extremely rapid, and because land which is useless today may be made fertile tomorrow if new methods are applied (to devise these new methods a big bank can equip a whole expedition of engineers, agricultural experts, etc.), and large amounts of capital are invested. This also applies to prospecting for minerals, to new methods of working up and utilising raw materials, etc., etc. Hence, the inevitable striving of finance capital to extend its economic territory and even its territory in general. In the same way that the trusts capitalise their property by estimating it at two or three times its value, taking into account its "potential" (and not present) returns, and the further results of monopoly, so finance capital strives to seize the largest possible amount of land of all kinds and in any place it can, and by any means, counting on the possibilities of finding raw materials there, and fearing to be left behind in the insensate struggle for the last available scraps of undivided territory, or for the repartition of that which has been already divided.

---

[1] Schilder, *op. cit.*, pp. 38 and 42.

Caroline, Marshall and Marianne Islands allocated to Japan.
German New Guinea allocated to Australia (British Empire).
German Samoan Islands allocated to New Zealand (British
Empire).

REDIVISION OF POSSESSIONS OF THE FORMER OTTOMAN EMPIRE

1919.......Seizure of Syria by France.
Seizure of Palestine and Transjordania by Great Britain.
Seizure of Iraq by Great Britain (since 1931, Iraq has been
formally independent).

1923......Formal annexation of the Dodecanese Islands by Italy.

1926.......Final seizure of the Riff zones in Morocco by France and
Spain.

1931-36....Occupation of Manchuria and parts of the Northern Provinces of China by Japan.

1936.......Occupation of Abyssinia by Italy.

SOURCES: *Annual Register,* 1900-32; *Schultheiss Jahrbücher,* 1900-32; A.
Toynbee, *Survey of International Affairs,* 1925-32.

IMPERIALIST EXPANSION OF THE PRODUCTION OF RAW MATERIALS IN THE COLONIES

The efforts of the imperialists to develop the production of raw materials in their own colonies have been greatly increased in the post-war
period, as is shown by the data given below.

Striving to free herself from dependence on American cotton, Great
Britain is extensively developing the cultivation of cotton in Egypt, the
Anglo-Egyptian Sudan and in Uganda. This can be seen from the follow-
ing table:

AREA UNDER COTTON IN BRITISH COLONIES
(thousand hectares)

	1904	1909-13	1930-31	1932-33	1936-37
Egypt	600	705	875	459	721
Anglo-Egyptian Sudan	—	18	157	133	192
Uganda	—	23	299	434	602

Owing to the crisis the area under cotton in Egypt and the Sudan was
reduced in 1931-32 and 1932-33. Since 1933, however, the area has been
increasing. In Uganda the area kept on increasing even during the crisis.

France is also making efforts to create her own cotton base in her colonies, primarily in French Equatorial Africa. This is illustrated in the
following table:

The British capitalists are exerting every effort to develop cotton growing in *their* colony, Egypt (in 1904, out of 2,300,000 hectares of land under cultivation, 600,000, or more than one-fourth, were devoted to cotton growing); the Russians are doing the same in *their* colony, Turkestan; and they are doing so because in this way they will be in a better position to defeat their foreign competitors, to monopolise the sources of raw materials and form a more economical and profitable textile trust in which *all* the processes of cotton production and manufacturing will be "combined" and concentrated in the hands of a single owner.

The necessity of exporting capital also gives an impetus to the conquest of colonies, for in the colonial market it is easier to eliminate competition, to make sure of orders, to strengthen the necessary "connections," etc., by monopolist methods (and sometimes it is the only possible way).

The non-economic superstructure which grows up on the basis of finance capital, its politics and its ideology, stimulates the striving for colonial conquest. "Finance capital does not want liberty, it wants domination," as Hilferding very truly says. And a French bourgeois writer, developing and supplementing, as it were, the ideas of Cecil Rhodes, which we quoted above, writes that social causes should be added to the economic causes of modern colonial policy.

"Owing to the growing difficulties of life which weigh not only on the masses of the workers, but also on the middle classes, impatience, irritation and hatred are accumulating in all the countries of the old civilisation and are becoming a menace to public order; employment must be found for the energy which is being hurled out of the definite class channel; it must be given an outlet abroad in order to avert an explosion at home." [1]

Since we are speaking of colonial policy in the period of capitalist imperialism, it must be observed that finance capital and its corresponding foreign policy, which reduces itself to the struggle of the Great Powers for the economic and political division of the world, give rise to a number of *transitional* forms of national dependence. The division of the world into two main groups—of colony-owning countries on the one hand and colonies on the other—is not the only typical feature of this period; there is also a variety of forms of dependent countries; countries which, officially, are politically independent, but which are, in fact, enmeshed in the net of financial and diplomatic dependence. We

---

[1] Wahl, *La France aux colonies* (*France in the Colonies*), quoted by Henri Bussier, *Le partage de l'Océanie* (*The Partition of Oceania*), Paris, 1905, pp. 165-66.

AREA UNDER COTTON IN FRENCH COLONIES
(hectares)

	1909-13	1922-23	1929	1934-35
All French colonies	1,854	54,374	263,367	354,766
Equatorial Africa only	—	2.810	15,000	117,200

During the crisis the area under cotton in the French colonies was reduced. This, however, does not apply to French Equatorial Africa, where the increase of the area under cotton continued.

In 1932 a special Cotton Committee, consisting of representatives of French companies operating in the French colonies in Africa, drew up in conjunction with the government a programme for the maintenance and further development of cotton growing, which provided, among other things, for fixed purchase prices, subsidies, etc.

Japan is developing the cultivation of cotton in Korea where the area under cotton increased from 59,000 hectares in the period 1909-13 to 192,000 hectares in 1934-35. At the same time she is trying to develop the cultivation of cotton in Manchuria and North China. In the latter territory the area under cotton from 1933 to 1936 increased by almost 53 per cent.

The United States, the principal consumer of rubber, is waging a fierce struggle against the British rubber monopoly. In 1929 over 70 per cent of the world's rubber exports—622,000 l. tons out of a total of 861,000 l. tons—was exported from plantations under British control. The United States acquired land for rubber plantations in Brazil (1927), Liberia (1929), Sumatra and the Malay Peninsula. She has also developed the rubber reclaiming industry. The biggest American companies formed a buying syndicate in order to resist the British price policy, particularly during the operation of the Stevenson scheme of 1922-28, which restricted the export of rubber from British possessions for the purpose of keeping up the price. The opposition of this syndicate greatly contributed to the collapse of that scheme. Simultaneously, there was a large increase in the consumption of reclaimed rubber in the United States.

France is also creating her own rubber base in her colonies, primarily in Indo-China, where the production of rubber increased from 7,400, l. tons in 1925 to 40,830 l. tons in 1936. The capital invested in rubber plantations in Indo-China in 1928-29 was no less than 400 million francs. In order to maintain the new plantations during the crisis the French Government in 1930 began to grant subsidies, which by 1935 were to have amounted to a total of 100,000,000 francs. It also introduced the payment

have already referred to one form of dependence—the semi-colony. Another example is provided by Argentina.

"South America, and especially Argentina," writes Schulze-Gaevernitz in his work on British imperialism, "is so dependent financially on London that it ought to be described as almost a British commercial colony."[1]

Basing himself on the report of the Austro-Hungarian consul at Buenos Aires for 1909, Schilder estimates the amount of British capital invested in Argentina at 8,750,000,000 francs. It is not difficult to imagine the solid bonds that are thus created between British finance capital (and its faithful "friend," diplomacy) and the Argentine bourgeoisie, with the leading businessmen and politicians of that country.

A somewhat different form of financial and diplomatic dependence, accompanied by political independence, is presented by Portugal. Portugal is an independent sovereign state. In actual fact, however, for more than two hundred years, since the war of the Spanish Succession (1700-14), it has been a British protectorate. Great Britain has protected Portugal and her colonies in order to fortify her own positions in the fight against her rivals, Spain and France. In return she has received commercial advantages, preferential import of goods, and, above all, of capital into Portugal and the Portuguese colonies, the right to use the ports and islands of Portugal, her telegraph cables, etc.[2] Relations of this kind have always existed between big and little states. But during the period of capitalist imperialism they become a general system, they form part of the process of "dividing the world"; they become a link in the chain of operations of world finance capital.

In order to complete our examination of the question of the division of the world, we must make the following observation. This question was raised quite openly and definitely not only in American literature after the Spanish-American War, and in English literature after the Boer War, at the very end of the nineteenth century and the beginning of the twentieth; not only has German literature, which always "jealously" watches "British imperialism," systematically given its appraisal of this fact, but it has also been raised in French bourgeois literature in terms as

---

[1] Schulze-Gaevernitz, *Britischer Imperialismus und englischer Freihandel zu Beginn des 20. Jahrhunderts* (*British Imperialism and English Free Trade at the Beginning of the Twentieth Century*), Leipzig, 1906, p. 318. Sartorius von Waltershausen says the same in *Das volkswirtschaftliche System der Kapitalanlage im Auslande* (*The National Economic System of Capital Investments Abroad*), Berlin, 1907, p. 46.

[2] Schilder, *op. cit.*, Vol. I, pp. 159-61.

of rubber export bonuses. Similar measures are being employed in connection with the rubber plantations in the French colonies in Africa.

The colonial sources of oils and fats are largely monopolised by Anglo-Dutch capital (Unilever). In order to create her own supply base France is intensively developing vegetable oil cultivation, particularly ground nuts in French Equatorial and West Africa. The area under cultivation of ground nuts increased from 40,000 hectares in 1909-13, to 1,202,000 hectares in 1931. Owing to the crisis the area began to diminish, but in 1933 a number of measures were introduced for the purpose of stimulating the cultivation of oil producing crops in the French colonies, such as restricting imports of foreign raw materials into France, construction of roads in Africa, etc.

In addition, France is creating a food supplies base in her African colonies. The area under wheat and other grains is being continually enlarged in Algiers, Tunis and Morocco, thanks to the large subsidies the government paid to the French colonists, particularly during the crisis. In Morocco, for example, the area under wheat increased from 628,000 hectares in 1915-18, to 1,218,000 hectares in 1929; in 1935-36 the area was 1,463,000 hectares.

Japan is pursuing a similar policy of creating a fats and food supplies base in her colonies. Korea and Formosa are used primarily for the cultivation of food supplies (rice and other grain). By the seizure of Manchuria Japan secured the monopoly in the production of soya beans. In 1929 the soya bean harvest in Manchuria amounted to 4,849,400 tons out of a total world harvest of 6,121,000 tons, *i.e.*, 79.2 per cent. During the last few years Japan has been developing cotton raising and sheep breeding in Korea and Manchuria.

SOURCES: *Annuaire International de la Statistique Agricole*, 1925, 1932-33; *Revue Internationale d'Agriculture*, Février 1937; *Ostasiatische Rundschau*, 1, II, 1937; J. W. F. Rowe "Studies in the Artificial Control of Raw Material Supplies," No. 2, *Rubber*, April 1931, p. 86; Statistical Bulletin of the International Rubber Regulation Committee, February 1937; *Bulletin de la Statistique Générale de la France, Janvier-Mars*, 1934; *Semaine Coloniale*, 20 Avril, 1934; *The Economist*, May 5, 1934; Denny, *America Conquers Britain*, 1930.

THE STRUGGLE BETWEEN THE UNITED STATES AND GREAT BRITAIN FOR THE CARIBBEANS AND SOUTH AMERICA

After the war American capitalism strengthened its positions in South America and especially in the Caribbeans and outstripped Great Britain in regard to the speed and dimensions of its investments. This is seen from the following tables:

wide and clear as they can be made from the bourgeois point of view. We will quote Driault, the historian, who, in his book, *Political and Social Problems at the End of the Nineteenth Century,* in the chapter "The Great Powers and the Division of the World," wrote the following:

"During recent years, all the free territory of the globe, with the exception of China, has been occupied by the powers of Europe and North America. Several conflicts and displacements of influence have already occurred over this matter, which foreshadow more terrible outbreaks in the near future. For it is necessary to make haste.   The nations which have not yet made provision for themselves run the risk of never receiving their share and never participating in the tremendous exploitation of the globe which will be one of the essential features of the next century " (*i.e.,* the twentieth). "That is why all Europe and America has lately been afflicted with the fever of colonial expansion, of 'imperialism,' that most characteristic feature of the end of the nineteenth century."

And the author added:

"In this partition of the world, in this furious pursuit of the treasures and of the big markets of the globe, the relative power of the empires founded in this nineteenth century is totally out of proportion to the place occupied in Europe by the nations which founded them.   The dominant powers in Europe, those which decide the destinies of the Continent, are *not* equally preponderant in the whole world. And, as colonial power, the hope of controlling hitherto unknown wealth, will obviously react to influence the relative strength of the European powers, the colonial question—'imperialism,' if you will—which has already modified the political conditions of Europe, will modify them more and more."[1]

---

[1] Ed. Driault, *Problèmes politiques et sociaux,* Paris, 1907, p. 289.

BRITISH AND UNITED STATES INVESTMENTS IN SOUTH AMERICA AND THE CARIBBEANS

(Million dollars)

Countries	British 1913	British 1929	U.S.A. 1913	U.S.A. 1929
SOUTH AMERICA				
Argentina	1,861	2,140	40	611
Bolivia	2	13	10	133
Brazil	1,162	1,414	50	476
Chile	332	390	15	396
Colombia	34	38	2	261
Ecuador	15	23	10	25
Paraguay	16	18	3	15
Peru	133	141	35	151
Uruguay	240	217	5	64
Venezuela	41	92	3	162
Total	3,836	4,486	173	2,294
THE CARIBBEANS (including Cuba, Mexico and West Indies)				
Costa Rica	33	27	7	36
Guatemala	52	58	20	38
Honduras	16	25	3	13
Nicaragua	6	4	3	24
Salvador	11	10	3	15
Panama	—	8	5	36
Cuba	222	238	220	1,526
Haiti	—	—	4	31
Mexico	808	1,035	800	1,550
Dominican Republic	—	—	4	24
Total	1,148	1,405	1,069	3,293
Grand Total	4,984	5,891	1,242	5,587

SOURCES: M. Winkler, *Investments of U.S. Capital in Latin America*, 1929, pp. 284-85, in round figures.

BRITISH AND UNITED STATES SHARE OF ABC COUNTRIES' IMPORTS (%)

Countries	Argentina 1913	Argentina 1931	Brazil 1913	Brazil 1931	Chile 1913	Chile 1931
Great Britain	31.0	20.1	24.5	17.5	30.0	16.0
United States	14.7	16.0	15.7	25.0	16.7	34.3

SOURCES: *Wochenbericht des Instituts für Konjunkturforschung*, No. 28, 1934; Max Winkler, *Investments of U.S. Capital in Latin America*, 1929, pp. 274, 279.

CHAPTER VII

IMPERIALISM AS A SPECIAL STAGE OF CAPITALISM

WE must now try to sum up and put together what has been said above on the subject of imperialism. Imperialism emerged as the development and direct continuation of the fundamental attributes of capitalism in general. But capitalism only became capitalist imperialism at a definite and very high stage of its development, when certain of its fundamental attributes began to be transformed into their opposites, when the features of a period of transition from capitalism to a higher social and economic system began to take shape and reveal themselves all along the line. Economically, the main thing in this process is the substitution of capitalist monopolies for capitalist free competition. Free competition is the fundamental attribute of capitalism, and of commodity production generally. Monopoly is exactly the opposite of free competition; but we have seen the latter being transformed into monopoly before our very eyes, creating large-scale industry and eliminating small industry, replacing large-scale industry by still larger-scale industry, finally leading to such a concentration of production and capital that monopoly has been and is the result: cartels, syndicates and trusts, and merging with them, the capital of a dozen or so banks manipulating thousands of millions. At the same time monopoly, which has grown out of free competition, does not abolish the latter, but exists over it and alongside of it, and thereby gives rise to a number of very acute, intense antagonisms, friction and conflicts. Monopoly is the transition from capitalism to a higher system.

If it were necessary to give the briefest possible definition of imperialism we should have to say that imperialism is the monopoly stage of capitalism. Such a definition would include what is most important, for, on the one hand, finance capital is the bank capital of a few big monopolist banks, merged with the capital of the monopolist combines of manufacturers; and, on the other hand, the division of the world is the transition from a colonial policy which has extended without hindrance to territories unoccupied by any capitalist power, to a colonial

192

THE UNEVENNESS OF CAPITALIST DEVELOP-
MENT UNDER IMPERIALISM

COMPARATIVE LEVELS OF BASIC INDUSTRIES
OF PRINCIPAL COUNTRIES

Countries	1880	1900	1913	1929	1932	1936
COAL OUTPUT (million tons)						
Great Britain (coal).................	149.0	228.8	292.0	262.0	212.1	232.2
Germany „	47.0	109.3	190.1	163.4	104.7	158.4[1]
United States (coal and lignite)	64.9	244.6	517.0	552.3	326.2	441.5
France „ „ „	19.4	33.4	40.8	53.8	46.3	45.2
Japan (coal)	0.8	7.5	21.3	34.3	28.1	38.4
PIG IRON OUTPUT (million tons)						
Great Britain	7.7	9.0	10.3 ·	7.7	3.6	7.8
Germany............................	2.5	7.5	19.3	13.4	3.9	15.3[2]
United States	3.8	13.8	31.0	43.3	8.9	31.5
France.............................	1.7	2.7	5.2	10.4	5.5	6.2
Japan..............................	—	0.02	0.2	1.5	1.5	2.9
STEEL OUTPUT (million tons)						
Great Britain	1.3	4.9	7.7	9.8	5.3	11.9
Germany............................	0.7	6.4	18.9	16.2	5.8	19.2[2]
United States	1.2	10.2	31.3	57.3	13.9	47.7
France.............................	0.4	1.6	4.7	9.7	5.6	6.7
Japan (open hearth)	—	—	0.2	2.3	2.4	5.0
COTTON CONSUMPTION (million quintals)						
Great Britain	6.4	7.0	8.7	6.3	5.0	6.0
Germany............................	1.4	3.1	4.9	3.0	3.3	1.1[2]
United States	4.2	8.2	13.5	16.0	11.6	16.5
France.............................	0.9	1.6	2.7	3.6	2.4	2.7
Japan..............................	—	1.4	3.3	5.9	5.9	7.5

[1] Including the Saar.
[2] For second half-year only.

SOURCES: For 1880-1913, from *Annuaire Statistique, Stat. Générale de la France,* 1934; *National Federation of Iron and Steel Manufacturers,* 1932; figures from 1929 on, from *International Cotton Statistics,* and *Statistical Yearbook of the League of Nations,* 1935-36; *Cotton,* 20, III, 1937; *Monthly Bulletin of Statistics,* League of Nations, No. 3, 1937.

policy of monopolistic possession of the territory of the world which has been completely divided up.

But very brief definitions, although convenient, for they sum up the main points, are nevertheless inadequate, because very important features of the phenomenon that has to be defined have to be especially deduced. And so, without forgetting the conditional and relative value of all definitions, which can never include all the concatenations of a phenomenon in its complete development, we must give a definition of imperialism that will embrace the following five essential features:

1) The concentration of production and capital developed to such a high stage that it created monopolies which play a decisive role in economic life.

2) The merging of bank capital with industrial capital, and the creation, on the basis of this "finance capital," of a financial oligarchy.

3) The export of capital, which has become extremely important, as distinguished from the export of commodities.

4) The formation of international capitalist monopolies which share the world among themselves.

5) The territorial division of the whole world among the greatest capitalist powers is completed.

Imperialism is capitalism in that stage of development in which the dominance of monopolies and finance capital has established itself; in which the export of capital has acquired pronounced importance; in which the division of the world among the international trusts has begun; in which the division of all territories of the globe among the great capitalist powers has been completed.

We shall see later that imperialism can and must be defined differently if consideration is to be given, not only to the basic, purely economic factors—to which the above definition is limited—but also to the historical place of this stage of capitalism in relation to capitalism in general, or to the relations between imperialism and the two main trends in the working class movement. The point to be noted just now is that imperialism, as interpreted above, undoubtedly represents a special stage in the development of capitalism. In order to enable the reader to obtain as well grounded an idea of imperialism as possible, we deliberately quoted largely from *bourgeois* economists who are obliged to admit the particularly incontrovertible facts regarding modern capitalist economy. With the same object in view, we have produced detailed statistics which reveal the extent to which bank capital, etc., has developed.

UNEVENNESS OF DEVELOPMENT OF "OLD" AND "NEW" INDUSTRIES

AVERAGE ANNUAL OUTPUT OF CAPITALIST WORLD

Period	"Old" Industries					"New" Industries				
	Coal and lignite	Pig iron	Steel	Ships launched	Cotton consumption	Oil output	Aluminium	Nitrogen[9]	Artificial silk	Automobiles
	Million tons			mill. reg. tons	million quintals	mill. tons	thousand tons			thous. units
1875-84 ..	—	17	4	—	—	3.3	—	—	—	—
1885-94 ..	533[1]	24	11	—	24.5[3]	9.2	—	—	—	—
1895-1904	735	39	28	2.0[2]	32.1[3]	20.3	6.4	—	2.3[4]	8[6]
1905-13 ..	1133	63	57	2.5	43.6[3]	40.2	35.3	178.2	16.2[5]	263[7]
1914-18 ..	1252	66	73	2.9	41.7	63.6	95.7	459.5	—	1241[8]
1919-23 ..	1228	56	64	4.4	40.6	103.9	114.0	565.9	31.8	2534
1924-29 ..	1398	80	95	2.3	50.9	161.7	209.9	1090.3	122.9	4957
1930-32 ..	1186	57	66	1.7	45.3	169.2	211.0	1555.5[10]	218.4	3037
1933-36 ..	1149	57	80	1.2	46.2	201.3	213.3	—	380.8	4302

Indices (1913=100)

Period	Coal and lignite	Pig iron	Steel	Ships launched	Cotton consumption	Oil output	Aluminium	Nitrogen[9]	Artificial silk	Automobiles
1875-84 ..	—	21	5	—	—	6	—	—	—	—
1885-94 ..	34[1]	30	14	—	50[3]	18	—	—	—	—
1895-1904	55	49	37	59[2]	66[3]	39	10	—	14[4]	14[6]
1905-13 ..	85	80	75	75	89[3]	78	56	51.5	100[5]	46[7]
1914-18 ..	96	83	96	87	85	123	151	132.8	—	214[8]
1919-23 ..	92	71	84	132	83	202	180	163.5	196	438
1924-29 ..	104	101	124	69	104	314	332	315.0	759	858
1930-32 ..	89	72	86	51	92	328	334	449.4[10]	1348	525
1933-36 ..	86	72	104	36	94	390	338	—	2351	743

[1] Up to 1894—total for U.S.A., Great Britain, France and Germany. [2] Total for 15 countries. [3] From 1885 to 1904—total for 11 countries; from 1905—total for 12 countries. [4] 1902. [5] 1913. [6] Annual average for U.S.A. for period 1897-1904. [7] Annual average total for Great Britain, France, Germany, U.S.A., for 1907-13. [8] Output of U.S.A. and Canada. [9] Nitrogen compounds, exclusive of Chilian nitrates, reduced to units of pure nitrogen. [10] Agricultural years, from August 1 to July 31.

SOURCES: *Annuaire Statistique, Stat. Générale de la France*, 1931, 1932; *Statistical Yearbook*, L. of N., 1933-34; *Report of the National Federation of Iron and Steel Manufacturers*, 1932, pp. 137-39; *British and Foreign Trade and Industry*, Board of Trade, 1908; *Lloyd's Register of Shipping*, 1924-25, 1930-31, 1936-37; *Statistisches Jahrbuch für das Deutsche Reich*, 1915, 1928, 1931, 1932; *Wirtshaft des Auslandes*, 1900-27, Berlin, 1928; *Monthly Return of Foreign Trade of Japan*, 1929-32; *Die Kunstseide*, April 1933; *Motor Industry of Great Britain*, p. 79; *Facts and Figures of the Automobile Industry*, U.S. Chamber of Commerce, 1931; *Gesamtbericht Weltkonferenz*, Berlin 1930. Bd. II, S. 147; *Reports of the British Sulphate of Ammonia Federation*, 1928-29, 1931-32; *Monthly Bulletin of Statistics*, League of Nations, No. 3, 1937; *Cotton*, 20, III, 1937; *Pester Lloyd*, 25, II, 1937.

showing how the transformation of quantity into quality, of developed capitalism into imperialism, has expressed itself. Needless to say, all boundaries in nature and in society are conditional and changeable, and, consequently, it would be absurd to discuss the exact year or the decade in which imperialism "definitely" became established.

In this matter of defining imperialism, however, we have to enter into controversy, primarily, with K. Kautsky, the principal Marxian theoretician of the epoch of the so-called Second International—that is, of the twenty-five years between 1889 and 1914.

Kautsky, in 1915 and even in November 1914, very emphatically attacked the fundamental ideas expressed in our definition of imperialism. Kautsky said that imperialism must not be regarded as a "phase" or stage of economy, but as a policy; a definite policy "preferred" by finance capital; that imperialism cannot be "identified" with "contemporary capitalism"; that if imperialism is to be understood to mean "all the phenomena of contemporary capitalism"—cartels, protection, the domination of the financiers and colonial policy—then the question as to whether imperialism is necessary to capitalism becomes reduced to the "flattest tautology"; because, in that case, "imperialism is naturally a vital necessity for capitalism," and so on. The best way to present Kautsky's ideas is to quote his own definition of imperialism, which is diametrically opposed to the substance of the ideas which we have set forth (for the objections coming from the camp of the German Marxists, who have been advocating such ideas for many years already, have been long known to Kautsky as the objections of a definite trend in Marxism).

Kautsky's definition is as follows:

"Imperialism is a product of highly developed industrial capitalism. It consists in the striving of every industrial capitalist nation to bring under its control and to annex increasingly big *agrarian*" (Kautsky's italics) "regions irrespective of what nations inhabit those regions."[1]

This definition is utterly worthless because it one-sidedly, *i.e.*, arbitrarily, brings out the national question alone (although this is extremely important in itself as well as in its relation to imperialism), it arbitrarily and *inaccurately* relates this question *only* to industrial capital in the countries which annex other nations, and in an equally arbitrary and inaccurate manner brings out the annexation of agrarian regions.

Imperialism is a striving for annexations—this is what the *political* part of Kautsky's definition amounts to. It is correct, but very incom-

---

[1]*Die Neue Zeit*, 32nd year (1913-14), II, p. 909; *cf.* also 34th year (1915-16), II, p. 107 *et seq.*

UNEVEN DEVELOPMENT OF INDUSTRY IN PRINCIPAL COUNTRIES
PER CENT OF INCREASE OR DECREASE IN INDUSTRIAL PRODUCTION
(Annual Average)

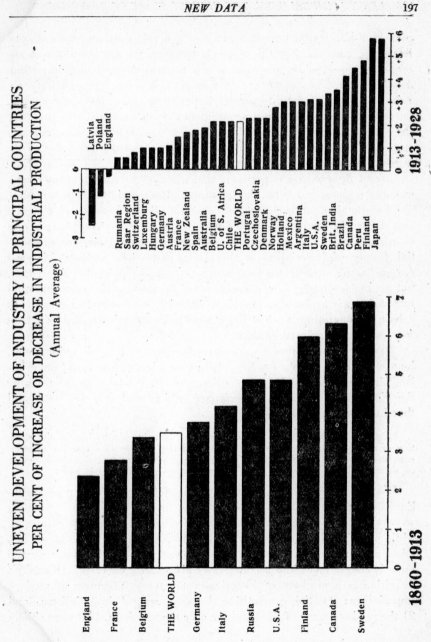

1913 - 1928

Latvia
Poland
England
Rumania
Saar Region
Switzerland
Luxemburg
Hungary
Germany
Austria
France
New Zealand
Spain
Australia
Belgium
U. of S. Africa
Chile
THE WORLD
Portugal
Czechoslovakia
Denmark
Norway
Holland
Mexico
Argentina
Italy
U.S.A.
Sweden
Brit. India
Brazil
Canada
Peru
Finland
Japan

1860 - 1913

England
France
Belgium
THE WORLD
Germany
Italy
Russia
U.S.A.
Finland
Canada
Sweden

plete, for politically, imperialism is, in general, a striving towards violence and reaction. For the moment, however, we are interested in the *economic* aspect of the question, which Kautsky *himself* introduced into *his* definition. The inaccuracy of Kautsky's definition is strikingly obvious. The characteristic feature of imperialism is *not* industrial capital, *but* finance capital. It is not an accident that in France it was precisely the extraordinarily rapid development of *finance* capital, and the weakening of industrial capital, that, from 1880 onwards, gave rise to the extreme extension of annexationist (colonial) policy. The characteristic feature of imperialism is precisely that it strives to annex *not only* agricultural regions, but even highly industrialised regions (German appetite for Belgium; French appetite for Lorraine), because 1) the fact that the world is already divided up obliges those contemplating a *new* division to reach out for *any kind* of territory, and 2) because an essential feature of imperialism is the rivalry between a number of great powers in the striving for hegemony, *i.e.,* for the conquest of territory, not so much directly for themselves as to weaken the adversary and undermine *his* hegemony. (Belgium is chiefly necessary to Germany as a base for operations against England; England needs Bagdad as a base for operations against Germany, etc.)

Kautsky refers especially—and repeatedly—to English writers who, he alleges, have given a purely political meaning to the word "imperialism" in the sense that Kautsky understands it. We take up the work by the Englishman Hobson, *Imperialism,* which appeared in 1902, and therein we read:

"The new imperialism differs from the older, first, in substituting for the ambition of a single growing empire the theory and the practice of competing empires, each motivated by similar lusts of political aggrandisement and commercial gain; secondly, in the dominance of financial or investing over mercantile interests." [1]

We see, therefore, that Kautsky is absolutely wrong in referring to English writers generally (unless he meant the vulgar English imperialist writers, or the avowed apologists for imperialism). We see that Kautsky, while claiming that he continues to defend Marxism, as a matter of fact takes a step backward compared with the *social-liberal* Hobson, who *more correctly* takes into account two "historically concrete" (Kautsky's definition is a mockery of historical concreteness) features of modern imperialism: 1) the competition between *several* imperialisms, and 2) the predominance of the financier over the merchant. If it were chiefly

---

[1] J. A. Hobson, *Imperialism—a Study,* London, 1902, p. 324.

DISTRIBUTION OF WORLD COAL AND LIGNITE OUTPUT (%)

Countries	1881-90	1891-1900	1901-10	1911-13	1914-18	1919-23	1924-29	1930-32	1933-35
United States	26.2	30.0	36.8	38.4	42.9	42.2	38.9	33.9	31.6
Great Britain	39.2	32.5	25.5	22.0	20.0	19.0	16.8	19.2	19.0
Germany[1] ..	17.6	18.4	19.0	20.3	19.7	18.7	21.0	21.6	22.7
France......	5.1	4.8	3.6	3.2	1.9	3.2	4.6	5.3	4.7
Other countries.......	11.9	14.3	15.1	16.1	15.5	16.9	18.7	20.0	22 0
Whole capitalist world ...	100.0	100.0	100.0	100.0	100.0	100.0	100.0	100.0	100.0

[1] Including the Saar.

SOURCES: *Annuaire Statistique, Stat. Générale de la France*, 1932, 1936. *Monthly Bulletin of Statistics*, League of Nations, No. 3, 1937. Figures not otherwise available were estimated by the "Konjunktur" Dept. of the Institute of World Economics and World Politics, Moscow.

DISTRIBUTION OF WORLD PIG IRON OUTPUT (%)

Countries	1881-90	1891-1900	1901-10	1911-13	1914-18	1919-23	1924-29	1930-32	1933-36
United States	26.0	32.0	40.9	39.6	52.2	55.3	47.2	37.9	37.3
Great Britain	36.2	26.3	18.0	13.4	13.8	11.1	7.9	8.7	11.1
Germany[1] ..	15.2	17.6	18.8	21.3	17.0	12.7	13.6	12.5	18.9
France......	8.1	7.3	6.0	6.7	2.4	7.1	11.4	15.1	11.1
Other countries.......	14.5	16.8	16.3	19.0	14.6	13.8	19.9	25.8	21.6
Whole capitalist world ..	100.0	100.0	100.0	100.0	100.0	100.0	100.0	100.0	100.0

[1] Including the Saar.

SOURCES: Reports of the National Federation of Iron and Steel Manufacturers, 1932; *Annuaire Statistique, Stat. Générale de la France*, 1936; *Monthly Bulletin of Statistics*, L. of N., No. 3, 1937.

a question of the annexation of agrarian countries by industrial countries, the role of the merchant would be predominant.

Kautsky's definition is not only wrong and un-Marxian. It serves as a basis for a whole system of views which run counter to Marxian theory and Marxian practice all along the line. We shall refer to this again later. The argument about words which Kautsky raises as to whether the modern stage of capitalism should be called "imperialism" or "the stage of finance capital" is of no importance. Call it what you will, it matters little. The fact of the matter is that Kausky detaches the politics of imperialism from its economics, speaks of annexations as being a policy "preferred" by finance capital, and opposes to it another bourgeois policy which, he alleges, is possible on this very basis of finance capital. According to his argument, monopolies in economics are compatible with non-monopolistic, non-violent, non-annexationist methods in politics. According to his argument, the territorial division of the world, which was completed precisely during the period of finance capital, and which constitutes the basis of the present peculiar forms of rivalry between the biggest capitalist states, is compatible with a non-imperialist policy. The result is a slurring-over and a blunting of the most profound contradictions of the latest stage of capitalism, instead of an exposure of their depth; the result is bourgeois reformism instead of Marxism.

Kautsky enters into controversy with the German apologist of imperialism and annexations, Cunow, who clumsily and cynically argues that: imperialism is modern capitalism, the development of capitalism is inevitable and progressive; therefore imperialism is progressive; therefore, we should cringe before and eulogise it. This is something like the caricature of Russian Marxism which the Narodniki drew in 1894-95. They used to argue as follows: if the Marxists believe that capitalism is inevitable in Russia, that it is progressive, then they ought to open a public-house and begin to implant capitalism! Kautsky's reply to Cunow is as follows: imperialism is not modern capitalism. It is only one of the forms of the policy of modern capitalism. This policy we can and should fight; we can and should fight against imperialism, annexations, etc.

The reply seems quite plausible, but in effect it is a more subtle and more disguised (and therefore more dangerous) propaganda of conciliation with imperialism; for unless it strikes at the economic basis of the trusts and banks, the "struggle" against the policy of the trusts and banks

DISTRIBUTION OF WORLD STEEL OUTPUT (%)

Countries	1881-90	1891-1900	1901-10	1911-13	1914-18	1919-23	1924-29	1930-32	1933-36
United States	30.9	35.0	43.1	41.8	52.4	56.1	50.2	41.1	41.5
Great Britain	31.7	20.5	12.9	9.8	12.4	11.1	8.2	9.1	12.1
Germany [1] ..	17.6	22.5	22.1	23.0	19.4	13.6	14.1	12.9	17.4
France......	6.5	5.8	5.3	6.2	2.7	5.6	8.7	11.6	8.2
Italy........	2.5	1.2	1.3	1.4	1.5	1.3	1.8	2.3	2.7
Japan	—	—	—	—	0.9	1.4	1.7	3.4	5.3
Other countries.......	10.8	15.0	15.3	17.8	10.7	10.9	15.3	19.6	12.8
Whole capitalist world ..	100.0	100.0	100.0	100.0	100.0	100.0	100.0	100.0	100.0

[1] Including the Saar.

SOURCES: Reports of the National Federation of Iron and Steel Manufacturers, 1932; *Monthly Bulletin of Statistics*, L. of N., No. 3, 1937.

DISTRIBUTION OF WORLD COTTON CONSUMPTION (%)

Countries	1882-1891	1892-1901	1902-10	1911-13	1914-18	1919-23	1924-29	1930-32	1933-36
United States	24.3	24.8	26.6	27.0	38.0	36.2	33.8	28.1	28.7
Great Britain	33.4	24.1	20.2	19.8	19.3	16.1	14.1	11.9	11.3
Germany	9.0	9.9	10.1	9.9	—	5.2	6.7	6.7	6.8 [2]
France......	5.6	5.7	5.2	5.5	4.8	5.2	6.4	6.1	5.1
Italy........	2.9	3.8	4.3	4.1	4.9	4.2	4.0	4.1	4.0 [2]
Japan.......	0.5	3.7	5.1	7.0	10.3	12.4	12.6	14.8	14.6
India	6.2	8.3	8.5	7.4	9.1	9.2	7.5	10.6	10.2
China......	—	—	—	—	—	—	5.1	8.9	7.5
Other countries	18.1	19.7	20.0	19.3	13.6	11.5	9.8	8.8	11.8
Whole capitalist world [1]..	100.0	100.0	100.0	100.0	100.0	100.0	100.0	100.0	100.0

[1] Total for 24 countries. Figures otherwise not available estimated by the "Konjunktur" Dept. of the Institute of World Economics and World Politics, Moscow.

[2] As figures for 1935-36 are not available, the percentage has been computed on the basis of figures for 1933-34.

SOURCES: Tugan-Baranovsky, *The Russian Factory* (3rd Russ. ed.), 1908; *Annuaire Statistique, Stat. Générale de la France*, 1932; *Statistical Abstract of the U.K.*; *Statistisches Jahrbuch für das Deutsche Reich*; *Wirtschaft des Auslandes*, 1900-27; *Monthly Return of Foreign Trade of Japan; Industrie du Coton*, Société des Nations, 1927; *International Cotton Statistics; Indian Yearbook*, 1933; *Cotton*, 20, III, 1937.

reduces itself to bourgeois reformism and pacifism, to an innocent and benevolent expression of pious hopes. Kautsky's theory means refraining from mentioning existing contradictions, forgetting the most important of them, instead of revealing them in their full depth; it is a theory that has nothing in common with Marxism. Naturally, such a "theory" can only serve the purpose of advocating unity with the Cunows.

Kautsky writes

"from the purely economic point of view it is not impossible that capitalism will yet go through a new phase, that of the extension of the policy of the cartels to foreign policy, the phase of ultra-imperialism," [1]

i.e., of a super-imperialism, a union of world imperialisms and not struggles among imperialisms; a phase when wars shall cease under capitalism, a phase of

"the joint exploitation of the world by internationally combined finance capital." [2]

We shall have to deal with this "theory of ultra-imperialism" later on in order to show in detail how definitely and utterly it departs from Marxism. In keeping with the plan of the present work, we shall examine the exact economic data on this question. Is "ultra-imperialism" possible "from the purely economic point of view" or is it ultra-nonsense?

If, by purely economic point of view a "pure" abstraction is meant, then all that can be said reduces itself to the following proposition: evolution is proceeding towards monopoly; therefore the trend is towards a single world monopoly, to a universal trust. This is indisputable, but it is also as completely meaningless as is the statement that "evolution is proceeding" towards the manufacture of foodstuffs in laboratories. In this sense the "theory" of ultra-imperialism is no less absurd than a "theory of ultra-agriculture" would be.

If, on the other hand, we are discussing the "purely economic" conditions of the epoch of finance capital as an historically concrete epoch which opened at the beginning of the twentieth century, then the best reply that one can make to the lifeless abstractions of "ultra-imperialism" (which serve an exclusively reactionary aim: that of diverting attention from the depth of *existing* antagonisms) is to contrast them with the concrete economic realities of present-day world economy. Kautsky's utterly meaningless talk about ultra-imperialism encourages, among other things, that profoundly mistaken idea which only brings grist to the mill of the apologists of imperialism, *viz.*, that the rule of finance capital *lessens* the unevenness

---

[1] *Die Neue Zeit*, 32nd year (1913-14), II, Sept. 11, 1914, p. 909; *cf.* also 34th year (1915-16), II, p. 107 *et seq.*

[2] *Die Neue Zeit*, 33rd year, II (April 30, 1915), p. 144.

EXPORTS OF MANUFACTURES

(Million dollars)

Countries	Average for 1895-99	Average for 1909-13	Average for 1925-29	1932	1936
Great Britain	980.5	1750.3	2788.6	966.3	1003.6
Germany	566.6	1277.8	1913.6	1064.0	1136.7
France..................	383.5	704.3	1238.6	480.7	309.4
U.S.A..................	185.0	597.0	2114.8	624.2	681.4
Japan..................	—	73.5	374.5	196.8	268.9

Indices (average 1909-13 = 100)

Great Britain	56.0	100.0	159.3	55.2	57.3
Germany	44.3	100.0	149.8	83.3	89.0
France..................	54.4	100.0	175.9	68.2	43.9
U.S.A..................	31.0	100.0	354.2	104.6	114.1
Japan..................	—	100.0	509.5	267.7	365.9

SOURCES: Customs statistics of the respective countries.

DISTRIBUTION OF WORLD TRADE (%)

SPECIAL TRADE

Countries	Averages for five-year periods				1932	1936
	1886-90	1900-04	1909-13	1925-29		
World trade	100.0	100.0	100.0	100.0	100.0	100.0
Great Britain	20.2	18.6	16.2	13.6	13.4	15.4
Germany	11.6	12.8	13.6	8.7	9.3	9.1
U.S.A.	10.8	11.8	11.7	14.0	10.9	12.1
Japan.............	0.7	1.4	1.6	3.0	2.9	3.9
France...........	10.9	8.5	8.5	6.4	7.3	6.1
Colonies of 8 imperialist powers	—	17.3	19.3	24.3	—	—

SOURCES: For 1886-1913—Soltau, *Vierteljahrshefte zur Konjunkturforschung*, 1926, Erg. Heft; for 1925-29, 1932-36—*Statistical Yearbook,* L. of N., 1929, 1930-31, 1932-33; *Monthly Bulletin of Statistics of the League of Nations*, No. 4, 1934; Nos. 8-12, 1936; Nos. 1-3, 1937.

and contradictions inherent in world economy, whereas in reality it *increases* them.

R. Calwer, in his little book, *An Introduction to World Economics*,[1] attempted to compile the main, purely economic, data required to understand in a concrete way the internal relations of world economy at the end of the nineteenth and beginning of the twentieth centuries. He divides the world into five "main economic areas," as follows: 1) Central Europe (the whole of Europe with the exception of Russia and Great Britain); 2) Great Britain; 3) Russia; 4) Eastern Asia; 5) America; he includes the colonies in the "areas" of the state to which they belong and "leaves out" a few countries not distributed according to areas, such as Persia, Afghanistan and Arabia in Asia; Morocco and Abyssinia in Africa, etc.

Here is a brief summary of the economic data he quotes on these regions:

Principal economic areas	Area Million sq. km.	Pop. Millions	Transport		Trade	Industry		
			Railways (thous. km.)	Mercantile fleet (million tons)	Imports and exports (billion marks)	Output of coal (million tons)	Output of pig iron (million tons)	No. of cotton spindles (million)
1) Central European ..	27.6 (23.6)[2]	388 (146)	204	8	41	251	15	26
2) British	28.9 (28.6)[2]	398 (355)	140	11	25	249	9	51
3) Russian ...	22	131	63	1	3	16	3	7
4) East Asian .	12	389	8	1	2	8	0.02	2
5) American ..	30	148	379	6	14	245	14	19

We notice three areas of highly developed capitalism with a high development of means of transport, of trade and of industry, the Central European, the British and the American areas. Among these are three states which dominate the world: Germany, Great Britain, the United States. Imperialist rivalry and the struggle between these countries have become very keen because Germany has only a restricted area and few colonies (the creation of "Central Europe" is still a matter for the future; it is being born in the midst of desperate struggles). For the moment the distinctive feature of Europe is political disintegration. In

---

[1] R. Calwer, *Einführung in die Weltwirtschaft*, Berlin, 1906.

[2] The figures in parentheses show the area and population of the colonies.

UNEVEN DEVELOPMENT OF JAPAN, U.S.A. AND GREAT BRITAIN

The rapid development of Japan referred to by Lenin continued in the post-war period, as can be seen from the following figures:

	Index of industrial production (1913=100)			Capacity of electric motors in industry (million h.p.)			Value of exports (million dollars)		
	Japan	U.S.A.	Great Britain	Japan	U.S.A.	Great Britain[2]	Japan[3]	U.S.A.	Great Britain
1913.....	100	100	100	0.2[1]	8.8[1]	2.2	311	2448	2556
1925.....	222	151	87	1.8	26.1	7.6	910	4819	3734
1929.....	297	170	99	4.9	35.2	10.2	969	5157	3549
1936.....	450	150	115	—	—	—	463	2416	1297
% 1929 to 1913....	—	—	—	2450	400	464	312	211	139

[1] 1914.

[2] 1912, 1924, 1930.

[3] Japan managed to keep her exports at a comparatively high level during the crisis by resorting to colossal dumping based on the depreciated yen: calculated in paper yen her export dropped from 1929 to 1933 only 13.2 per cent compared with a much sharper drop in the principal capitalist countries. Calculated in gold currency, however, her exports dropped 56 per cent.

SOURCES: *Vierteljahrshefte zur Konjunkturforschung, Die Industriewirtschaft,* Sonderheft 31, S. 64-66; *Monthly Bulletin of Statistics of the League of Nations,* No. 7-8, 1934; No. 3, 1937; *Statistical Yearbook,* L. of N., 1927, p. 128; 1928, p. 128; 1932-33, p. 168; *Financial and Economic Annual of Japan,* 1916, p. 57; 1923, p. 89; *Fourteenth Census of the U.S.,* 1920, Vol. VIII, "Manufactures," General Report, p. 122; *Statistical Abstract of the U.S.,* 1931, p. 815; 1933, p. 694; H. Butler, *The United Kingdom,* Washington, 1930, p. 127; *The Economist,* 11, III, 1933.

the British and American areas, on the other hand, political concentration is very highly developed, but there is a tremendous disparity between the immense colonies of the one and the insignificant colonies of the other. In the colonies, capitalism is only beginning to develop. The struggle for South America is becoming more and more acute.

There are two areas where capitalism is not strongly developed: Russia and Eastern Asia. In the former, the density of population is very low, in the latter it is very high; in the former political concentration is very high, in the latter it does not exist. The partition of China is only beginning, and the struggle between Japan, U.S.A., etc., in connection therewith is continually gaining in intensity.

Compare this reality, the vast diversity of economic and political conditions, the extreme disparity in the rate of development of the various countries, etc., and the violent struggles of the imperialist states, with Kautsky's silly little fable about "peaceful" ultra-imperialism. Is this not the reactionary attempt of a frightened philistine to hide from stern reality? Are not the international cartels which Kautsky imagines are the embryos of "ultra-imperialism" (with as much reason as one would have for describing the manufacture of tabloids in a laboratory as ultra-agriculture in embryo) an example of the division and the *redivision* of the world, the transition from peaceful division to non-peaceful division and *vice versa*? Is not American and other finance capital, which divided the whole world peacefully, with Germany's participation, for example, in the international rail syndicate, or in the international mercantile shipping trust, now engaged in *redividing* the world on the basis of a new relation of forces, which has been changed by methods *by no means* peaceful?

Finance capital and the trusts are increasing instead of diminishing the differences in the rate of development of the various parts of world economy. When the relation of forces is changed, how else, *under capitalism*, can the solution of contradictions be found, except by resorting to *violence*? Railway statistics [1] provide remarkably exact data on the different rates of development of capitalism and finance capital in world economy. In the last decades of imperialist development, the total length of railways has changed as follows:

---

[1] *Statistisches Jahrbuch für das Deutsche Reich* (*Statistical Yearbook for the German Empire*), 1915, Appendix pp. 46, 47, *Archiv für Eisenbahnwesen*, 1892 (*Railroad Archive*). Minor detailed figures for the distribution of railways among the colonies of the various countries in 1890 had to be estimated approximately.

UNEVEN DEVELOPMENT OF DIFFERENT INDUSTRIAL REGIONS

One of the characteristic illustrations of the uneven development of industry in different regions in capitalist countries is the post-war spasmodic shifting of the United States cotton textile industry from the North to the South, with its cheap labour and the proximity of raw material. Before the war, two thirds of the total spindles in the United States were located in the North. Today, the positions of North and South have been reversed, as can be seen from the following table:

UNEVEN DEVELOPMENT IN COTTON INDUSTRY IN SOUTH AND NORTH U.S.A.

	Total number of spindles (in place)						Number of spindles (active)					
	New England States		Southern States		Total U.S.A.		New England States		Southern States		Total U.S.A.	
	millions	% of total	millions	% of total	millions	% of total	millions	% of total in place	millions	% of total in place	millions	% of total in place
1911	17.0	55.2	11.7	38.0	30.8	100.0	16.5	97.1	11.1	94.9	29.5	95.8
1922	18.9	51.2	16.1	43.6	36.9	100.0	17.9	94.7	15.9	98.8	35.7	96.7
1932	11.4	36.0	19.1	60.3	31.7	100.0	8.6	75.4	17.6	92.1	27.3	86.1
1935	10.5	34.0	19.4	62.8	30.9	100.0	7.8	74.3	18.1	93.3	26.7	86.4

SOURCES: *Statistical Abstract of the United States*, 1926, pp. 797-98; 1933, pp. 741-42; Kennedy, *Profits and Losses in Textiles*, N. Y., 1936, p. 235.

RAILWAYS
(thousand kilometres)

	1890	1913	Increase
Europe	224	346	122
U.S.A.	268	411	143
Colonies (total)	82 ⎫	210 ⎫	128 ⎫
Independent and semi-dependent states of Asia and America	43 ⎭ 125	137 ⎭ 347	94 ⎭ 222
Total	617	1,104	

Thus, the development of railways has been more rapid in the colonies and in the independent (and semi-dependent) states of Asia and America. Here, as we know, the finance capital of the four or five biggest capitalist states reigns undisputed. Two hundred thousand kilometres of new railways in the colonies and in the other countries of Asia and America represent more than 40,000,000,000 marks in capital, newly invested on particularly advantageous terms, with special guarantees of a good return and with profitable orders for steel works, etc., etc.

Capitalism is growing with the greatest rapidity in the colonies and in overseas countries. Among the latter, *new* imperialist powers are emerging (*e.g.*, Japan). The struggle of world imperialism is becoming more acute. The tribute levied by finance capital on the most profitable colonial and overseas enterprises is increasing. In sharing out this "booty," an exceptionally large part goes to countries which, as far as the development of productive forces is concerned, do not always stand at the top of the list. In the case of the biggest countries, considered with their colonies, the total length of railways was as follows (in thousands of kilometres):

	1890	1913	Increase
U.S.A.	268	413	145
British Empire	107	208	101
Russia	32	78	46
Germany	43	68	25
France	41	63	22
Total	491	830	339

Thus, about 80 per cent of the total existing railways are concentrated in the hands of the five Great Powers. But the concentration of the *ownership* of these railways, of finance capital, is much greater still:

RAILWAYS
(thousand kilometres)

1913 (exclusive of railways within present boundaries of U.S.S.R.)	1930	changes compared with 1913	
303	344	+ 41	Europe
411	402	— 9	U.S.A.
194 ⎫	288 ⎫	+ 94 ⎫	Colonies (total)
⎬ 331	⎬ 458	⎬ + 127	Independent and semi-de-
137 ⎭	170 ⎭	+ 33 ⎭	pendent states of Asia and
1,045	1,204		America
			Total

In supplementing Lenin's tables with the figures for 1930, we first established clearly the composition of each group of countries in these tables by examining Lenin's original sources, *Statistisches Jahrbuch für das Deutsche Reich*, 1915, and *Archiv für Eisenbahnwesen*, 1892 and 1915. This grouping was used as the basis for the 1930 figures.

The computation of the distribution of railways for 1930 was made on the basis of figures taken from *Archiv für Eisenbahnwesen*, H. I, 1933, *i.e.*, on the basis of the same sources used by Lenin. The computation:

1. Excludes the railways of the European part of the U.S.S.R. from the figures of European railways;

2. Excludes the railways of the Asiatic part of the U.S.S.R. from figures of colonial railways;

3. The railways of Iraq, Palestine, Syria, the Lebanon (parts of the former Ottoman Empire), Cuba and Korea were transferred from the group of "independent and semi-dependent states of Asia and America" to the "colonies" group. This group includes also the railways in other Japanese colonies such as Formosa and South Sakhalin and the South Manchurian Railway, which were not included in Lenin's tables.

	1890	1913 (thous. km.)	Increase in period 1890-1913 (thous. km.)	1930 [1]	Changes in period 1913-30
U.S.A.	268	413	+ 145	410	— 3
British Empire...........	107	208	+ 101	279	+71
Russia..................	32	78	+ 46	—	—
Germany	43	68	+ 25	—	—
France...................	41	63	+ 22	84	+21
Total 5 Powers.......	491	830	+ 339	—	—
Japan...................	—	12	—	28	+ 16
Total 4 Powers[2]	—	696	—	801	+ 105

[1] Within present boundaries, including mandate territories acquired by the British Empire and France from Germany and Turkey as a result of the war of 1914-18.

[2] United States, the British Empire, France and Japan.

French and English millionaires, for example, own an enormous amount of stocks and bonds in American, Russian and other railways.

Thanks to her colonies, Great Britain has increased the length of "her" railways by 100,000 kilometres, four times as much as Germany. And yet, it is well known that the development of productive forces in Germany, and especially the development of the coal and iron industries, has been much more rapid during this period than in England—not to mention France and Russia. In 1892, Germany produced 4,900,000 tons of pig iron and Great Britain produced 6,800,000 tons; in 1912, Germany produced 17,600,000 tons and Great Britain, 9,000,000 tons. Germany, therefore, had an overwhelming superiority over England in this respect.[1] We ask, is there *under capitalism* any means of removing the disparity between the development of productive forces and the accumulation of capital on the one side, and the division of colonies and "spheres of influence" for finance capital on the other side—other than by resorting to war?

---

[1] *Cf.* also Edgar Crummond, "The Economic Relation of the British and German Empires," in *Journal of the Royal Statistical Society*, July 1914, p. 777, *et seq.*

Whereas the length of railways of the *entire capitalist world* increased by 15 per cent from 1913 to 1930, that of *all the colonies* increased by 48 per cent and that of *independent and semi-dependent states in Asia and America* increased by 24 per cent in the same period.

Of the five imperialist powers indicated by Lenin, Russia has dropped out as a result of the October Revolution. Imperialist Germany lost her colonies as a result of the Versailles Treaty. In this period, however, another imperialist power has risen in importance, *viz.*, Japan. Today the U.S.A., the British Empire, France and Japan—the four biggest imperialist powers together with their colonies—possess 66.5 per cent of the total railway mileage in the capitalist world. In pursuit of her policy of colonial conquest on the continent of Asia, the young and aggressive imperialist power, Japan, has developed considerable railway construction both at home and in her old colonies, Korea, Formosa and South Sakhalin. During the past few years she has seized the railways of Manchuria and partly of North China. In Manchuria she is now feverishly engaged in the construction of strategic railways in preparation for war against the Soviet Union.

At the same time considerable railway construction was carried on in Kuomintang China in the period of 1934-36, financed mainly by British and also by German and French capital.

During the period of 1913 to 1930 the unevenness in the development of railways became still more acute. Railway development in capitalist Europe has almost ceased since the war (only small sections are being built, and these are mainly of a strategic nature). In the United States the length of railways is continually decreasing. World imperialism in postwar years is building railways mainly in the colonies, semi-colonies and in dependent countries for the purpose of further facilitating the exploitation of these countries; but even in the colonies, railway construction is not proceeding on the same scale as before the war: *the rate of growth of railways has diminished considerably all over the capitalist world.*

In the U.S.S.R. hundreds and thousands of kilometres of new railways are annually being put into operation. (The length of railways in the Soviet Union increased from 58.5 thousand kilometres in 1913 to 85.0 thousand kilometres in 1937.)

SOURCES: For both railway tables: the figures for 1913 are taken from *Statistisches Jahrbuch für das Deutsche Reich*, 1915, S. 47; for 1930 from *Archiv für Eisenbahnwesen*, 1933, H. 1, S. 4-11, with certain corrections from *Statesmen's Yearbook*. Figures on Japan and the Japanese colonies for 1913 are taken partly from *Financial and Economic Annual of Japan*, 1914; for 1930 they have been taken in full from *The Annual Report* for 1931, Department of Railways, Government of Japan.

CHAPTER VIII

THE PARASITISM AND DECAY OF CAPITALISM

WE have to examine yet another very important aspect of imperialism to which, usually, too little importance is attached in most of the arguments on this subject. One of the shortcomings of the Marxist Hilferding is that he takes a step backward compared with the non-Marxist Hobson. We refer to parasitism, which is a feature of imperialism.

As we have seen, the most deep-rooted economic foundation of imperialism is monopoly. This is capitalist monopoly, *i.e.*, monopoly which has grown out of capitalism and exists in the general environment of capitalism, commodity production and competition, and remains in permanent and insoluble contradiction to this general environment. Nevertheless, like all monopoly, this capitalist monopoly inevitably gives rise to a tendency to stagnation and decay. As monopoly prices become fixed, even temporarily, so the stimulus to technical and, consequently, to all progress, disappears to a certain extent, and to that extent, also, the *economic* possibility arises of deliberately retarding technical progress. For instance, in America, a certain Mr. Owens invented a machine which revolutionised the manufacture of bottles. The German bottle manufacturing cartel purchased Owens' patent, but pigeon-holed it, refrained from utilising it. Certainly, monopoly under capitalism can never completely, and for a long period of time, eliminate competition in the world market (and this, by the by, is one of the reasons why the theory of ultra-imperialism is so absurd). Certainly the possibility of reducing cost of production and increasing profits by introducing technical improvements operates in the direction of change. Nevertheless, the *tendency* to stagnation and decay, which is the feature of monopoly, continues, and in certain branches of industry, in certain countries, for certain periods of time, it becomes predominant.

The monopoly of ownership of very extensive, rich or well-situated colonies, operates in the same direction.

Even to this day, *Owens' bottle-making machine*, to which Lenin refers, although greatly improved during the last 15 to 20 years, is employed only to a comparatively limited extent, and its wider employment is still hindered by monopolies. By a special convention the European Bottle Syndicate regulates in a number of countries the transition from hand work to machine methods.

In Germany, the Compulsory Cartelisation Act of February 1934 prohibited the installation of new automatic glass-blowing machines and presses until the end of 1935.

SOURCES: *Kartellrundschau*, H. 3, 1934, S. 187; E. F. Solovyov, *Reconstruction of Fixed Capital in Glass and Porcelain Industry* (Russ.), Moscow-Leningrad, 1926, pp. 26-30; Dr. Ing. L. Springer, *Die Fortschritte der Glastechnik in den letzten Jahrzehnten* (Russ. ed.), Moscow, 1928, p. 193.

Further, imperialism is an immense accumulation of money capital in a few countries, which, as we have seen, amounts to 100-150 billion francs in various securities. Hence the extraordinary growth of a class, or rather of a category, of *bondholders* (*rentiers*), *i.e.*, people who live by "clipping coupons," who take no part whatever in production, whose profession is idleness. The export of capital, one of the most essential economic bases of imperialism, still more completely isolates the *rentiers* from production and sets the seal of parasitism on the whole country that lives by the exploitation of the labour of several overseas countries and colonies.

"In 1893," writes Hobson, "the British capital invested abroad represented about 15 per cent of the total wealth of the United Kingdom." [1]

Let us remember that by 1915 this capital had increased about two and a half times.

"Aggressive imperialism," says Hobson further on, "which costs the taxpayer so dear, which is of so little value to the manufacturer and trader . . . is a source of great gain to the investor.... The annual income Great Britain derives from commissions in her whole foreign and colonial trade, import and export, is estimated by Sir R. Giffen at £18,000,000 for 1899, taken at 2½ per cent, upon a turnover of £800,000,000." [2]

Great as this sum is, it does not explain the aggressive imperialism of Great Britain. This is explained by the 90 to 100 million pounds sterling income from "invested" capital, the income of the rentiers.

The income of the bondholders is *five times greater* than the income obtained from the foreign trade of the greatest "trading" country in the world. This is the essence of imperialism and imperialist parasitism.

For that reason the term, "rentier state" (*Rentnerstaat*), or usurer state, is passing into current use in the economic literature that deals with imperialism. The world has become divided into a handful of usurer states on the one side, and a vast majority of debtor states on the other.

"The premier place among foreign investments," says Schulze-Gaevernitz, "is held by those placed in politically dependent or closely allied countries. Great Britain grants loans to Egypt, Japan, China and South America. Her navy plays here the part of bailiff in case of necessity. Great Britain's political power protects her from the indignation of her debtors." [3]

Sartorius von Walterhausen in his book, *The National Economic System of Foreign Investments*, cites Holland as the model "rentier state" and

---

[1] *Op. cit.*, p. 59.—*Ed.*
[2] *Op. cit.* pp. 62-3.—*Ed.*
[3] Schulze-Gaevernitz, *Britischer Imperialismus*, p. 320 *et seq.*

INCREASE IN THE AMOUNT OF SECURITIES IN GREAT BRITAIN

There are no precise figures of the amount of securities in circulation in Great Britain in the post-war period, but there is no doubt that it has increased enormously. This is evidenced by the fact that the amount of internal government loan bonds alone (mainly war loan) has increased by nearly £7,000,000,000. This alone would account for an increase of 1½ to 2 times at least. In addition, however, during 1910 to 1932, the issues of new home (private and municipal) securities alone amounted to 2 to 2½ billion pounds sterling. Hence, even if allowance is made for depreciation and the writing off of capital, the total amount of securities now in circulation should be two and a half times the amount given by Lenin in 1910.

SOURCES: *Statistical Abstract for the United Kingdom*, 1934, p. 146; *The Economist*, 1934.

GREAT BRITAIN'S INCOME FROM FOREIGN TRADE AND INVESTMENTS

(£000,000)

	1899	1912	1929	1932
Income from foreign trade	18	33	51	28
Income from foreign investments	90-100	176	250	145
Income from foreign investments plus income from short-term investments abroad, bankers' and brokers' commissions, etc.	—	—	378	—

The income from foreign trade for 1912, 1929 and 1932 is computed at the same rate (2.5 per cent for the entire foreign trade turnover) which served as the basis for estimating income in the figures given by Lenin for 1899.

The figures show that while income from foreign investments in 1899 exceeded the income from foreign trade by £70,000,000 to £80,000,000, this difference increased to £200,000,000 in 1929, exclusive of income from short-term investments abroad, bankers' and brokers' commissions, etc. If the latter is included, the difference will amount to £327,000,000.

SOURCES: 1899 figures are quoted from Lenin. Income from foreign investments for 1912 are computed on the basis of figures given by Chas. K. Hobson in his *Export of Capital*, 1927. Figures for 1929 to 1932 are taken from the *Board of Trade Journal*, 18, II, 1932, p. 218 and 23, II, 1933, p. 295. The more complete figures on income from foreign investments for 1929 are taken from Clark's "The National Income in 1932," *The Economic Journal*, June 1933, p. 205.

points out that Great Britain and France have taken the same road.[1] Schilder believes that five industrial nations have become "pronounced creditor nations": Great Britain, France, Germany, Belgium and Switzerland. Holland does not appear on this list simply because she is "industrially less developed." [2] The United States is creditor only of the other American countries.

"Great Britain," says Schulze-Gaevernitz, "is gradually becoming transformed from an industrial state into a creditor state. Notwithstanding the absolute increase in industrial output and the export of manufactured goods, the relative importance of income from interest and dividends, issues of securities, commissions and speculation is on the increase in the whole of the national economy. In my opinion it is precisely this that forms the economic basis of imperialist ascendancy. The creditor is more permanently attached to the debtor than the seller is to the buyer." [3]

In regard to Germany, A. Lansburgh, the editor of *Die Bank*, in 1911, in an article entitled "Germany—a Rentier State," wrote the following:

"People in Germany are ready to sneer at the yearning to become rentiers that is observed among the people in France. But they forget that as far as the middle class is concerned the situation in Germany is becoming more and more like that in France." [4]

The rentier state is a state of parasitic, decaying capitalism, and this circumstance cannot fail to influence all the social-political conditions of the countries affected generally, and the two fundamental trends in the working class movement, in particular. To demonstrate this in the clearest possible manner we will quote Hobson, who will be regarded as a more "reliable" witness, since he cannot be suspected of leanings towards "orthodox Marxism"; moreover, he is an Englishman who is very well acquainted with the situation in the country which is richest in colonies, in finance capital, and in imperialist experience.

With the Boer War fresh in his mind, Hobson describes the connection between imperialism and the interests of the "financiers," the growing profits from contracts, etc., and writes:

"While the directors of this definitely parasitic policy are capitalists, the same motives appeal to special classes of the workers. In many towns, most important trades are dependent upon government employment or contracts; the imperialism of the metal and shipbuilding centres is attributable in no small degree to this fact." [5]

---

[1] Sartorius von Waltershausen, *Das volkswirtschaftliche System, etc.* (*The National Economic System, etc.*), Book IV, B. 1907.

[2] Schilder, *op. cit.*, pp. 392-93.

[3] Schulze-Gaevernitz, *op. cit.*, p. 122.—*Ed.*

[4] *Die Bank*, 1911, I, pp. 10-11.

[5] *Op. cit.*, p. 103.—*Ed.*

UNITED STATES INCOME FROM FOREIGN TRADE AND INVESTMENTS

Prior to the World War the United States was a debtor country. Foreign capital invested in the United States in 1913 amounted to $7,000,000,000, while American capital invested abroad amounted to $2,600,000,000. As a result, the adverse balance of the United States on the payment of interest and dividends in the period from 1896 to 1914 amounted on the average to $160,000,000 per annum.

After the war the United States rose to second place among the capital exporting countries and came close to Great Britain in the amount of foreign investments (see table on page 141). Income from American investments abroad has greatly increased; it considerably exceeds United States payments to other countries and exceeds several fold the income from foreign trade, as can be seen from the following table.

	1922	1929	1932
	($000,000)		
Income from foreign trade (2.5% of the turnover)	174	241	73
Income from foreign investments			
a) exclusive of war debt payments	530	979	461
b) including war debt payments	756	1,186	560
Interest and dividends paid by U.S. to other countries[1]	120	414	68

[1] The bulk of the interest and dividend payments by U.S. to other countries constitute profits from speculative short-term investments by foreign capitalist investors in American securities. The large sum of payments under this heading in 1929 reflects the peak of the stock market speculation fever that was reached before the crash of October 1929.

SOURCES: *The Annalist,* 27, VII, 1934, p. 123; National Industrial Conference Board, "The International Financial Position of the United States," 1929, p. 55.

GROWTH OF RENTIERS' INCOMES
INTEREST AND DIVIDENDS PAID IN THE U.S.A.
(Including banks, trust companies, also U.S. federal gov't and New York City gov't interest payments)

Years	Billion dollars	Index (1913=100)	Index of national income (1913=100)
1913	1.8	100	100
1917	3.4	189	158
1922	3.4	189	183
1929	6.9	383	246
1931	8.1	450	162
1932	7.0	389	117
1933	6.3	350	124
1934	6.1	339	141

In this writer's opinion there are two causes which weakened the older empires: 1) "economic parasitism," and 2) the formation of armies composed of subject races.

"There is first the habit of economic parasitism, by which the ruling state has, used its provinces, colonies, and dependencies in order to enrich its ruling class and to bribe its lower classes into acquiescence." [1]

And we would add that the economic possibility of such corruption, whatever its form may be, requires high monopolist profits.

As for the second cause, Hobson writes:

"One of the strangest symptoms of the blindness of imperialism is the reckless indifference with which Great Britain, France and other imperial nations are embarking on this perilous dependence. Great Britain has gone farthest. Most of the fighting by which we have won our Indian Empire has been done by natives; in India, as more recently in Egypt, great standing armies are placed under British commanders; almost all the fighting associated with our African dominions, except in the southern part, has been done for us by natives." [2]

Hobson gives the following economic appraisal of the prospect of the partition of China:

"The greater part of Western Europe might then assume the appearance and character already exhibited by tracts of country in the South of England, in the Riviera, and in the tourist-ridden or residential parts of Italy and Switzerland, little clusters of wealthy aristocrats drawing dividends and pensions from the Far East, with a somewhat larger group of professional retainers and tradesmen and a large body of personal servants and workers in the transport trade and in the final stages of production of the more perishable goods; all the main arterial industries would have disappeared, the staple foods and manufactures flowing in as tribute from Asia and Africa." [3]

"We have foreshadowed the possibility of even a larger alliance of Western States, a European federation of great powers which, so far from forwarding the cause of world civilisation, might introduce the gigantic peril of a Western parasitism, a group of advanced industrial nations, whose upper classes drew vast tribute from Asia and Africa, with which they supported great, tame masses of retainers, no longer engaged in the staple industries of agriculture and manufacture, but kept in the performance of personal or minor industrial services under the control of a new financial aristocracy. Let those who would scout such a theory as undeserving of consideration examine the economic and social condition of districts in Southern England today which are already reduced to this condition, and reflect upon the vast extension of such a system which might be rendered feasible by the subjection of China to the economic control of similar groups of financiers, investors, and political and business officials, draining the greatest potential reservoir of profit the world has ever known, in order to consume it in Europe. The situation is far too complex, the play of world forces far too incalculable, to render this or any other single interpretation of the future very probable: but the influences which govern the imperialism of Western Europe today are moving in this direction, and, unless counteracted or diverted, make towards some such consummation." [4]

[1] *Op. cit.*, p. 205.
[2] *Op. cit.*, p. 144.
[3] *Op. cit.*, p. 335.
[4] *Op. cit.*, pp. 385-86.

PAYMENTS ON INTERNAL PRIVATE AND GOVERNMENT DEBTS IN THE U.S.A.

(including redemption)

1913-14	1921	1929	1932-33
($000,000)			
2,143	4,953	7,642	7,910
(% of national income)			
6	7	9	20

INCOME FROM SECURITIES IN GREAT BRITAIN

1913-14	1924-25	1930-31	1931-32
(£000)			
128,416	297,628	363,221	343,743
(% of national income)			
5.7	8.3	9.2	10.0

SOURCES: For U.S.A.—*Conference Board Bulletin*, April 1935; *The World Almanac and Book of Facts*, 1936, p. 287; E. Clark, *The Internal Debts of the United States*, 1933, p. 13. Figures of the national income of Great Britain are based on the estimates of Stamp and Bowley (*cf.* Woytinsky, "Die Welt in Zahlen," Bd. I, S. 161, Berlin, 1925); figures for 1924 are taken from Colin Clark, *The National Income, 1924-31*, p. 72, and *Statistical Abstract for the United Kingdom*, 1934, pp. 174-77.

INCOME FROM FOREIGN INVESTMENTS AND TOTAL NATIONAL INCOME OF U.S.A.

Years	National Income		Income from foreign investments [1]			
			Not including payments on war debts		Including payments on war debts (post-war years)	
	Billion dollars	Index (1915=100)	Million dollars	Index (1915=100)	Million dollars	Index (1915=100)
1915	34.5	100	160	100	160	100
1922	61.7	179	530	331	756	478
1929	83.0	241	978	612	1,128	705
1932	39.4	114	456	283	523	333
1934	47.6	132	493	308	494	309

[1] Including income from short-term investments.

SOURCES: National income: *Conference Board Bulletin*, April 1935; figures of income from foreign investments for 1915 and 1922—from "The International Financial Position of the United States," National Industrial Conference Board, pp. 36, 55. For other years, *Annalist*, July 27, 1934, p. 123; *Balances of Payments*, L. of N., 1935, p. 157.

Hobson in quite right. *Unless* the forces of imperialism are counteracted they will lead precisely to what he has described. He correctly appraises the significance of a "United States of Europe" in the present conditions of imperialism. He should have added, however, that, *even within* the working class movement, the opportunists, who are for the moment predominant in most countries, are "working" systematically and undeviatingly in this very direction. Imperialism, which means the partition of the world, and the exploitation of other countries besides China, which means high monopoly profits for a handful of very rich countries, creates the economic possibility of corrupting the upper strata of the proletariat, and thereby fosters, gives form to, and strengthens opportunism. However, we must not lose sight of the forces which counteract imperialism in general, and opportunism in particular, which, naturally, the social-liberal Hobson is unable to perceive.

The German opportunist, Gerhard Hildebrand, who was expelled from the Party for defending imperialism, and who would today make a leader of the so-called "Social-Democratic" Party of Germany, serves as a good supplement to Hobson by his advocacy of a "United States of Western Europe" (without Russia) for the purpose of "joint" action . . . against the African Negroes, against the "great Islamic movement," for the upkeep of a "powerful army and navy," against a "Sino-Japanese coalition," etc.[1]

The description of "British imperialism" in Schulze-Gaevernitz's book reveals the same parasitical traits. The national income of Great Britain approximately doubled from 1865 to 1898, while the income "from abroad" increased *ninefold* in the same period. While the "merit" of imperialism is that it "trains the Negro to habits of industry" (not without coercion of course . . .), the "danger" of imperialism is that:

"Europe . . . will shift the burden of physical toil—first agricultural and mining, then the more arduous toil in industry—on to the coloured races, and itself be content with the role of rentier, and in this way, perhaps, pave the way for the economic, and later, the political emancipation of the coloured races."

An increasing proportion of land in Great Britain is being taken out of cultivation and used for sport, for the diversion of the rich.

"Scotland," says Schulze-Gaevernitz, "is the most aristocratic playground in the world—it lives . . . on its past and on Mr. Carnegie."

On horse-racing and fox-hunting alone Britain annually spends £14,000,000. The number of rentiers in England is about one million.

---

[1] Gerhard Hildebrand, *Die Erschütterung der Industrieherrschaft und des Industriesozialismus,* Jena, 1910, p. 229 et seq.

INCOME FROM FOREIGN INVESTMENTS AND TOTAL NATIONAL INCOME OF GREAT BRITAIN

The more rapid increase of the incomes "from abroad" of the rentier class compared with the total national income is observed also in the post-war years. Basing our computation on Colin Clark's calculations (absolute figures), the respective changes in the national income and the "net income from abroad" may be presented as follows:

Years	Index of national income	Index of "net income from abroad"
1924.....	100.0	100.0
1926.....	102.7	125.9
1927.....	108.4	148.7
1928.....	107.3	149.2
1929.....	111.4	155.1
1930.....	109.8	139.5

But Clark manifestly underestimates the "net income from abroad," as is proved by the Board of Trade figures of balance of payments, according to which the net income from foreign investments, short-term loans and commissions amounted to £315,000,000 in 1929 and to £275,000,000 in 1930, whereas Clark gives the figures of £287,000,000 and £258,000,000 for the respective years. It is interesting to note that in his endeavour to arrive at a more complete estimate of the net income from abroad Clark gives for 1929 the huge figure of £378,000,000, compared with a national income of £3,996,000,000 for the same year.

SOURCES: Colin Clark, *The National Income* 1924-31, London, 1932, p. 72 and his article "The National Income in 1932," in *The Economic Journal*, June 1933, p. 205; *Board of Trade Journal*, 18, II, 1932, pp. 218-19.

The percentage of the productively employed population to the total population is becoming smaller.

Year	Population (millions)	No. of workers in basic industries (millions)	Per cent of total population
1851	17.9	4.1	23
1901	32.5	4.9	15

And in speaking of the British working class the bourgeois student of "British imperialism at the beginning of the twentieth century" is obliged to distinguish systematically between the *"upper stratum"* of the workers and the *"lower stratum of the proletariat proper."* The upper stratum furnishes the main body of members of co-operatives, of trade unions, of sporting clubs and of numerous religious sects. The electoral system, which in Great Britain is still *"sufficiently restricted to exclude the lower stratum of the proletariat proper,"* is adapted to their level!! In order to present the condition of the British working class in the best possible light, only this upper stratum—which constitutes only a *minority* of the proletariat—is generally spoken of. For instance, "the problem of unemployment is mainly a London problem and that of the lower proletarian stratum, *which is of little political moment* for politicians." [1] It would be better to say: which is of little political moment for the bourgeois politicians and the "socialist" opportunists.

Another special feature of imperialism, which is connected with the facts we are describing, is the decline in emigration from imperialist countries, and the increase in immigration into these countries from the backward countries where lower wages are paid. As Hobson observes, emigration from Great Britain has been declining since 1884. In that year the number of emigrants was 242,000, while in 1900, the number was only 169,000. German emigration reached the highest point between 1880 and 1890, with a total of 1,453,000 emigrants. In the course of the following two decades, it fell to 544,000 and even to 341,000. On the other hand, there was an increase in the number of workers entering Germany from Austria, Italy, Russia and other countries. According to the 1907 census, there were 1,342,294 foreigners in Germany, of whom 440,800 were industrial workers and 257,329 were agricultural workers.[2]

---

[1] Schulze-Gaevernitz *Britischer Imperialismus*, pp. 246, 301, 317, 323, 324, 361.
[2] *Statistik des Deutschen Reichs* (*Statistics of the German Empire*), Vol. 211.

DECLINE IN PERCENTAGE OF PRODUCTIVELY EMPLOYED POPULATION TO TOTAL POPULATION IN ENGLAND

Year	Population	No. of workers in basic industries (millions)	Per cent of total population	No. of workers and office employees in basic industries, including chemical industry (millions)	Per cent of total population
1851.....	17.9	4.1	23	—	—
1901......	32.5	4.9	15	—	—
1929.....	39.6	5.4	13.6	5.6	14.1
1932.....	40.2	4.6	11.4	4.8	11.9

The difficulty in supplementing Lenin's tables lay in determining the industries he included under the heading "basic industries." In our computations we took into account the economic importance of the various industries and the number of workers employed in them. We were able to single out seven industries: mining, metal industries, woodworking, building, textile, clothing and food industries. The metal industries include electrical engineering and the automobile industry.

Hence the figures for 1929 and 1932 do not include one of the new industries, *viz.,* the chemical industry, which played a small part in the economy of the country in the second half of the nineteenth century. In view of the increased importance of this industry in the twentieth century, and particularly during the post-war period, we included in the table parallel figures for 1929 and 1932 which include the chemical industry. Owing to the relatively low level of unemployment in 1851 and 1901 and the sharp increase in unemployment in the post-war years, we have given, for 1929 and 1932, only the number of *employed* workers and office employees in the respective industries, and not the total number of workers and office employees in these occupations as is the case with the figures for 1851 and 1901.

Furthermore, it was necessary to exclude Scotland from the data furnished by the Ministry of Labour, since Lenin's figures only cover England and Wales without Scotland and Ireland. (The inclusion of Northern Ireland does not materially affect the results.)

SOURCES: Figures for 1851 and 1901 are quoted from Lenin; figures for 1929 and 1932 are computed by the "Konjunktur" Dept. of the Institute of World Economics and World Politics, Moscow. Owing to the absence of census figures for these years we utilised the unemployment insurance figures published in *The Ministry of Labour Gazette*. Population figures are taken from the *Statistical Abstract for the United Kingdom*, 1936, pp. XII-XIII, 4-5.

In France, the workers employed in the mining industry are, "in great part," foreigners: Polish, Italian and Spanish.[1] In the United States, immigrants from Eastern and Southern Europe are engaged in the most poorly paid occupations, while American workers provide the highest percentage of overseers or of the better paid workers.[2] Imperialism has the tendency to create privileged sections even among the workers, and to detach them from the main proletarian masses.

It must be observed that in Great Britain the tendency of imperialism to divide the workers, to encourage opportunism among them and to cause temporary decay in the working class movement, revealed itself much earlier than the end of the nineteenth and the beginning of the twentieth centuries; for two important distinguishing features of imperialism were observed in Great Britain in the middle of the nineteenth century, *viz.,* vast colonial possessions and a monopolist position in the world market. Marx and Engels systematically traced this relation between opportunism in the labour movement and the imperialist features of British capitalism for several decades. For example, on October 7, 1858, Engels wrote to Marx:

"The English proletariat is becoming more and more bourgeois, so that this most bourgeois of all nations is apparently aiming ultimately at the possession of a bourgeois aristocracy, and a bourgeois proletariat *as well as* a bourgeoisie. For a nation which exploits the whole world this is, of course, to a certain extent justifiable." [3]

Almost a quarter of a century later, in a letter dated August 11, 1881, Engels speaks of ". . . the worst type of English trade unions which allow themselves to be led by men sold to, or at least, paid by the bourgeoisie." [3] In a letter to Kautsky, dated September 12, 1882, Engels wrote:

"You ask me what the English workers think about colonial policy? Well, exactly the same as they think about politics in general. There is no workers' party here, there are only Conservatives and Liberal-Radicals, and the workers merrily share the feast of England's monopoly of the colonies and the world market. . . ." [4] (Engels expressed similar ideas in the press in his preface to the second edition of *The Condition of the Working Class in England,* which appeared in 1892.)

---

[1] Henger, *Die Kapitalsanlage der Franzosen (French Investments),* Stuttgart, 1913.

[2] Hourwich, *Immigration and Labour,* New York, 1913.

[3] *Marx-Engels, Briefwechsel, Gesamtausgabe,* 3. *Abteilung,* B. 2, S. 340; B. 4, S. 511.—*Ed. Eng. ed.*

[4] *Cf.* Karl Kautsky, *Sozialismus und Kolonialpolitik,* Berlin, 1907, p. 79; this pamphlet was written by Kautsky in those infinitely distant days when he was still a Marxist.

FACTS AND FIGURES ON THE DECAY OF MODERN CAPITALISM

BELOW we quote additional facts and figures illustrating the exceptional acuteness and specific forms of the decay of post-war capitalism.

I. INABILITY OF CAPITALISM TO UTILISE THE BASIC PRODUCTIVE POWER OF SOCIETY—LABOUR POWER

CHRONIC UNEMPLOYMENT

Before the war most of the unemployed were absorbed during the boom periods. In the post-war period unemployment has remained at an exceedingly high level even at the peak of industrial booms. Severe unemployment has become a constant, chronic factor, as the following tables show:

LOWEST LEVEL OF UNEMPLOYMENT IN BOOM PERIOD OF 1929
(Millions)

U.S.A.	Great Britain	Germany
3 to 4	1.5 to 2	1.5 to 2

HIGHEST AND LOWEST ANNUAL PER CENT UNEMPLOYED AMONG MEMBERS OF TRADE UNIONS BEFORE AND AFTER THE WAR

	1900-1913[2]		1924-1929		1932
	Lowest	Highest	Lowest	Highest	
Great Britain [1]	2.1	7.8	9.7	12.5	22.1
Germany	1.1	2.9	6.7	18.0	43.8

[1] Great Britain, 1924-32—per cent of unemployed among insured workers.
[2] For Germany—1903-13.

SOURCES: *Abstract of Labour Statistics*, pp. 47-48, 68; *Statistisches Jahrbuch für das Deutsche Reich*, 1922-33.

We thus see clearly the causes and effects. The causes are: 1) Exploitation of the whole world by this country. 2) Its monopolistic position in the world market. 3) Its colonial monopoly. The effects are: 1) A section of the British proletariat becomes bourgeois. 2) A section of the proletariat permits itself to be led by men sold to, or at least, paid by the bourgeoisie. The imperialism of the beginning of the twentieth century completed the division of the world among a handful of states, each of which today exploits (*i.e.*, draws super-profits from) a part of the world only a little smaller than that which England exploited in 1858. Each of them, by means of trusts, cartels, finance capital, and debtor and creditor relations, occupies a monopoly position in the world market. Each of them enjoys to some degree a colonial monopoly. (We have seen that out of the total of 75,000,000 sq. km. which comprise the *whole* colonial world, *65,000,000* sq. km., or 86 per cent, belong to six great powers; *61,000,000* sq. km., or 81 per cent, belong to three powers.)

The distinctive feature of the present situation is the prevalence of economic and political conditions which could not but increase the irreconcilability between opportunism and the general and vital interests of the working class movement. Embryonic imperialism has grown into a dominant system; capitalist monopolies occupy first place in economics and politics; the division of the world has been completed. On the other hand, instead of an undisputed monopoly by Great Britain, we see a few imperialist powers contending for the right to share in this monopoly, and this struggle is characteristic of the whole period of the beginning of the twentieth century. Opportunism, therefore, cannot now triumph in the working class movement of any country for decades as it did in England in the second half of the nineteenth century. But, in a number of countries it has grown ripe, over-ripe, and rotten, and has become completely merged with bourgeois policy in the form of "social-chauvinism." [1]

---

[1] Russian social-chauvinism represented by Messrs. Potresov, Chkhenkeli, Maslov, etc., in its avowed form as well as in its tacit form, as represented by Messrs. Chkheidze, Skobelev, Axelrod, Martov, etc., also emerged from the Russian variety of opportunism, namely liquidationism.

DECREASE IN NUMBER OF WORKERS ACTUALLY EMPLOYED IN INDUSTRY IN POST-WAR PERIOD

U.S.A. MANUFACTURING INDUSTRY

Year	No. of workers employed	Average annual change
	(thousands)	
1869........	2,054 [1]	—
1899........	5,306 [1]	+ 108
1899........	4,713 [2]	—
1914........	7,024 [2]	+ 154
1914........	6,888 [3]	—
1919........	8,990 [3]	+ 420
1929........	8,822 [3]	— 17
1931........	6,507 [3]	— 1,158
1933........	6,056 [3]	— 226

[1] Factories, hand and neighbourhood industries.
[2] Establishments with products valued at over $500.
[3] Establishments with products valued at over $5,000.

SOURCES: Census returns in *Statistical Abstract of the United States*, 1935, p. 715.

GERMAN INDUSTRY

Year	No. of workers employed	Average annual change
	(thousands)	
1895........	5,530	—
1907[1]	7,928	+ 199
1907[2]	7,367	—
1925........	9,439	+ 115
1928........	8,678	— 255
1933........	5,718	— 592

[1] Pre-war boundaries.
[2] Post-war boundaries.

SOURCES: Industrial census returns in *Statistik des Deutschen Reichs*, B. 418, S. 200, 203, B. 462, 3, S. 9; for 1928, computed on the basis of factory inspectors' returns with addition of small establishments with less than five employees, in *Jahresberichte der Gewerbeaufsichtsbeamten und Bergbehörden*, 1928, B. III, S. 66-80, 552-53.

INSURED INDUSTRIAL WORKERS AND OFFICE EMPLOYEES ACTUALLY EMPLOYED IN GREAT BRITAIN
(thousands)

	1924	1929	1933	1936
Industry as a [whole...................	7,273	7,234	6,444	7,876
Coal, iron and steel, shipbuilding and textiles	2,919	2,564	2,014	2,084

SOURCES: Computed by the "Konjunktur" Dept. of the Institute of World Economics and World Politics, Moscow, on the basis of the insurance and unemployment figures published in *The Ministry of Labour Gazette*.

15*

CHAPTER IX

THE CRITIQUE OF IMPERIALISM

By the critique of imperialism, in the broad sense of the term, we mean the attitude towards imperialist policy of the different classes of society as part of their general ideology.

The enormous dimensions of finance capital concentrated in a few hands and creating an extremely extensive and close network of ties and relationships which subordinate not only the small and medium, but also even the very small capitalists and small masters, on the one hand, and the intense struggle waged against other national state groups of financiers for the division of the world and domination over other countries, on the other hand, cause the wholesale transition of the possessing classes to the side of imperialism. The signs of the times are a "general" enthusiasm regarding its prospects, a passionate defence of imperialism, and every possible embellishment of its real nature. The imperialist ideology also penetrates the working class. There is no Chinese Wall between it and the other classes. The leaders of the so-called "Social-Democratic" Party of Germany are today justly called "social-imperialists," that is, socialists in words and imperialists in deeds; but as early as 1902, Hobson noted the existence of "Fabian imperialists" who belonged to the opportunist Fabian Society in England.

Bourgeois scholars and publicists usually come out in defence of imperialism in a somewhat veiled form, and obscure its complete domination and its profound roots; they strive to concentrate attention on partial and secondary details and do their very best to distract attention from the main issue by means of ridiculous schemes for "reform," such as police supervision of the trusts and banks, etc. Less frequently, cynical and frank imperialists speak out and are bold enough to admit the absurdity of the idea of reforming the fundamental features of imperialism.

We will give an example. The German imperialists attempt, in the magazine *Archives of World Economy*, to follow the movements for

CONCEALED UNEMPLOYMENT. AGRARIAN OVERPOPULATION

United States

Assistant Secretary of Agriculture, Tugwell, stated at a meeting of economic experts in Philadelphia on December 30, 1933, that two million people had returned to their farms during the crisis. He said that there were now too many farmers, and that probably only half the number of farms that existed today were needed to produce the agricultural produce required.

Poland

Agrarian overpopulation is particularly acute in countries which retain considerable survivals of feudal relations, and where, as a consequence, there is acute land hunger among the peasantry.

According to the calculations of the Polish bourgeois sociologist, Piatkiewicz, the number of persons engaged in agriculture in Poland represents potential labour power equal to 3,890 million workdays a year. The actual requirement in agriculture, however, is estimated at 1,851 million workdays, so that more than half the agricultural labour power of Poland is at present superfluous.

Hungary

According to the very moderate calculations made by the official Hungarian Institute of Economic Research in 1933, "about 24 per cent of the working time of the agricultural population remains unused under the present conditions of land ownership and land tenure and the present size of the population."

SOURCES: *Semi-Weekly Farm News*, 5, I, 1934; *Magyar Gazdaságkutató Intézet*, special number 6, 1933, p. 33.

PAUPERISM

"The lowest sediment of the relative surplus population finally dwells in the sphere of pauperism," wrote Marx (*Capital*, Vol. I, Chap. XXV, Section 4). In Great Britain today the officially registered paupers alone number not less than 1.5 million, according to figures of the Ministry of Labour. In 1929, a boom year, the number of persons receiving poor relief was 320 per 10,000 of the population.

In Germany the number of paupers before the world economic crisis of 1929 was estimated at between one and one and a half million. During the crisis the number increased to over three million.

There are several million paupers in the U.S.A.

SOURCES: *The Ministry of Labour Gazette; Reichsarbeitsblatt.*

national emancipation in the colonies, particularly, of course, in colonies other than those belonging to Germany. They note the ferment and protest movements in India, the movement in Natal (South Africa), the movement in the Dutch East Indies, etc. One of them, commenting on an English report of the speeches delivered at a conference of subject peoples and races, held on June 28-30, 1910, at which representatives of various peoples subject to foreign domination in Africa, Asia and Europe were present, writes as follows in appraising the speeches delivered at this conference:

> "We are told that we must fight against imperialism; that the dominant states should recognise the right of subject peoples to home rule; that an international tribunal should supervise the fulfilment of treaties concluded between the great powers and weak peoples. One does not get any further than the expression of these pious wishes. We see no trace of understanding of the fact that imperialism is indissolubly bound up with capitalism in its present form" (!!) "and therefore also no trace of the realisation that an open struggle against imperialism would be hopeless, unless, perhaps, the fight is confined to protests against certain of its especially abhorrent excesses."[1]

Since the reform of the basis of imperialism is a deception, a "pious wish," since the bourgeois representatives of the oppressed nations go no "further" forward, the bourgeois representatives of the oppressing nation go "further" *backward*, to servility, towards imperialism, concealed by the cloak of "science." "Logic," indeed!

The question as to whether it is possible to reform the basis of imperialism, whether to go forward to the accentuation and deepening of the antagonisms which it engenders, or backwards, towards allaying these antagonisms, is a fundamental question in the critique of imperialism. As a consequence of the fact that the political features of imperialism are reaction all along the line, and increased national oppression, resulting from the oppression of the financial oligarchy and the elimination of free competition, a petty-bourgeois—democratic opposition has been rising against imperialism in almost all imperialist countries since the beginning of the twentieth century. And the desertion of Kautsky and of the broad international Kautskyan trend from Marxism is displayed in the very fact that Kautsky not only did not trouble to oppose, not only was unable to oppose this petty-bourgeois reformist opposition, which is really reactionary in its economic basis, but in practice actually became merged with it.

---

[1] *Weltwirtschaftliches Archiv* (*Archives of World Economy*), Vol. II, pp. 194-95.

OVERPOPULATION IN COLONIAL AND SEMI-COLONIAL COUNTRIES

Overpopulation in China is described by the German Institute of Economic Research in the following manner:

"Approximate estimates relating to 1925 show that out of a total of 305 million self-supporting persons 170 million had no work of any kind. The latest estimates give even higher figures. Although these figures are very unreliable, nevertheless, together with other known facts, they show how low is the standard of living and the purchasing power of the Chinese masses."

In India, according to the bourgeois investigator, Soni, the number of people who are unable to earn a livelihood in the villages and can find no employment in the cities is 110,000,000. Pointing to the fact that India has 100 million unemployed paupers, the author says that "anyone who claims even a superficial acquaintance with the conditions prevailing in India would readily agree that at least a third of the population in the country is badly in need of relief in order to be able to procure the barest necessities of life . . . and that a very large number of people in India constantly live in a state of semi-starvation. . . ."

SOURCES: H. R. Soni, *Indian Industry and its Problems,* Vol. I, Bombay, 1932, pp. 21-23; *Wochenbericht des Instituts für Konjunkturforschung,* 10, II, 1932.

RETARDED INCREASE OF POPULATION

There has been a tremendous increase in unemployment, notwithstanding the fact that the natural increase of population, and consequently the natural increase in labour power, is sharply declining. This decline can be seen from the following table:

AVERAGE ANNUAL INCREASE OF POPULATION
Excess of Births over Deaths per 1,000 of Population

Decade	U.S.A.	England & Wales	Germany	France
1861-70	—	—	10.3	2.7
1871-80	—	15.1	11.9	1.7
1881-90	—	14.0	11.7	1.8
1891-1900	—	12.4	13.9	0.7
1901-10	—	12.4	14.3	1.2
1911-20[1]	—	6.8	3.7	—6.5
1921-30	9.3	5.9	7.7	1.8
1933	5.9	2.1	3.5	0.5
1935	—	3.0	7.0	—0.5

[1] Including those killed in the war.

SOURCES: Official statistical yearbooks of the respective countries.

In the United States, the imperialist war waged against Spain in 1898 stirred up the opposition of the "anti-imperialists," the last of the Mohicans of bourgeois democracy. They declared this war to be "criminal"; they denounced the annexation of foreign territories as being a violation of the Constitution, and denounced the "Jingo treachery" by means of which Aguinaldo, leader of the native Filipinos, was deceived (the Americans promised him the independence of his country, but later they landed troops and annexed it). They quoted the words of Lincoln:

"When the white man governs himself, that is self-government; but when he governs himself and also governs others, it is no longer self-government; it is despotism."[1]

But while all this criticism shrank from recognising the indissoluble bond between imperialism and the trusts, and, therefore, between imperialism and the very foundations of capitalism; while it shrank from joining up with the forces engendered by large-scale capitalism and its development—it remained a "pious wish."

This is also, in the main, the attitude of Hobson in his criticism of imperialism. Hobson anticipated Kautsky in protesting against the "inevitability of imperialism" argument, and in urging the need to raise the consuming capacity of the "people" (under capitalism!). The petty-bourgeois point of view in the critique of imperialism, the domination of the banks, the financial oligarchy, etc., is that adopted by the authors we have often quoted, such as Agahd, A. Lansburgh, L. Eschwege; and among French writers, Victor Bérard, author of a superficial book entitled *England and Imperialism* which appeared in 1900. All these authors, who make no claim to be Marxists, contrast imperialism with free competition and democracy; they condemn the Bagdad railway scheme as leading to disputes and war, utter "pious wishes" for peace, etc. This applies also to the compiler of international stock and share issue statistics, A. Neymarck, who, after calculating the hundreds of billions of francs representing "international" securities, exclaimed in 1912: "Is it possible to believe that peace may be disturbed . . . that, in the face of these enormous figures, anyone would risk starting a war?"[2]

Such simplicity of mind on the part of the bourgeois economists is not surprising. Besides, *it is in their interest* to pretend to be so naive

---

[1] Quoted by Patouillet, *L'impérialisme américain*, Dijon, 1904, p. 272.
[2] *Bulletin de l'Institut International de Statistique*, Vol. XIX, Book II, p. 225.

II. *DIRECT AND INDIRECT DESTRUCTION OF LABOUR POWER*

DESTRUCTION OF LABOUR POWER IN THE WAR OF 1914-18

Killed (registered)....................	9,998,771
Severely wounded.....................	6,295,512
Slightly wounded	14,002,039
Prisoners of war and missing	5,983,600
Died in 1918 from influenza epidemic resulting from war	10,000,000

To the victims of the World War must be added the victims of wars between 1919 and 1936; a list of wars appears on pp. 264-66.

SOURCE: Stuart Chase, *The Tragedy of Waste*, 1927, pp. 58-59.

VICTIMS OF THE WHITE TERROR 1925-35

Arrested	Wounded	Killed	Sentenced to death	Sentenced to imprisonment	Total
5,187,000	3,820,000	3,409,000	243,000	319,000	12,978,000

SOURCES: Figures of the Central Committee of the International Labour Defence.

DESTRUCTION OF LABOUR POWER RESULTING FROM INCREASING POVERTY

Germany

The Hygiene Section of the League of Nations Secretariat appointed a commission to investigate the conditions of the unemployed. In the memorandum submitted by this commission the abject conditions of the unemployed in Germany are depicted. Owing to the fact that the unemployed had some savings and were also able to receive some help from their relatives, their health until the autumn of 1931 was still tolerable. From then on, however, it began steadily to decline. Ailments resulting from malnutrition began to manifest themselves: "children showed signs of stunted growth, anæmia, jaundice, tape-worm, ailments caused by uncleanliness (due to curtailed use of soap), tooth ailments and nervous derangements. In the working class districts of Berlin the children of the unemployed are considerably below normal in weight and height, and, as a consequence, show a disposition to tuberculosis, skin diseases, and nervous disorders. Among the adult unemployed who visited the Kreuzberg Clinic a loss of weight was observed of 7 to 10 pounds in a few months."

In Gelsenkirchen an investigation showed that the number of children treated for tuberculosis increased in the year 1931 alone by 38 per cent.

and to talk "seriously" about peace under imperialism. But what remains of Kautsky's Marxism, when, in 1914-15-16, he takes up the
same attitude as the bourgeois reformists and affirms that "everybody
is agreed" (imperialists, pseudo-socialists and social-pacifists) as regards peace? Instead of an analysis of imperialism and an exposure of
the depths of its contradictions, we have nothing but a reformist "pious
wish" to wave it aside, to evade it.

Here is an example of Kautsky's economic criticism of imperialism.
He takes the statistics of the British export and import trade with Egypt
for 1872 and 1912. These statistics show that this export and import
trade has developed more slowly than British foreign trade as a whole.
From this Kautsky concludes that:

> "We have no reason to suppose that British trade with Egypt would have been
> less developed simply as a result of the mere operation of economic factors, without
> military occupation. . . . The urge of the present-day states to expand . . . can be
> best promoted, not by the violent methods of imperialism, but by peaceful democracy."[1]

This argument, which is repeated in every key by Kautsky's Russian
armour-bearer (and Russian protector of the social-chauvinists), Mr. Spectator, represents the basis of Kautskyan criticism of imperialism and
that is why we must deal with it in greater detail. We will begin with
a quotation from Hilferding, whose conclusions, as Kautsky on many
occasions, and notably in April 1915, declared, have been "unanimously
adopted by all socialist theoreticians."

> "It is not the business of the proletariat," writes Hilferding, "to contrast the more
> progressive capitalist policy with that of the now by-gone era of free trade and of
> hostility towards the state. The reply of the proletariat to the economic policy of
> finance capital, to imperialism, cannot be free trade, but socialism. The aim of
> proletarian policy cannot now be the ideal of restoring free competition—which has
> now become a reactionary ideal—but the complete abolition of competition by the
> vanquishment of capitalism." [2]

Kautsky departed from Marxism by advocating what is, in the period of finance capital, a "reactionary ideal," "peaceful democracy,"
"the mere operation of economic factors," for *objectively* this ideal drags
us back from monopoly capitalism to the non-monopolist stage, and is a
reformist swindle.

Trade with Egypt (or with any other colony or semi-colony)
"would have grown more" *without* military occupation, without imperialism, and without finance capital. What does this mean? That

---

[1] Karl Kautsky, *Nationalstaat, imperialistischer Staat und Staatenbund (National
State, Imperialist State and Union of States)*, Nuremberg, 1915, pp. 72, 70.

[2] Hilferding, *op. cit.*, pp. 471-72.

Great Britain

Infant mortality in Great Britain as a whole was 65 per 1,000 in 1932. The rate is much higher, however, in the working class districts of the large cities. This is shown in the following table:

INFANT MORTALITY IN 1932

Glasgow			Leeds		
Dalmarnock	127	per 1,000	West Street	137	per 1,000
Calton	140	,, ,,	Ayles Lane	141	,, ,,
Exchange	150	,, ,,	London		
Liverpool			Bethnal Green	88	,, ,,
Exchange	117	,, ,,	Paddington	116	,, ,,
Abercromby	133	,, ,,	St. Pancras	139	,, ,,

Speaking at a meeting in Bermondsey, a working class district in London, Field Marshal Lord Milne declared that he was shocked at the number of young people who did not come up to the comparatively low standard of physique now required for entrance into the army. He also declared that the managers of boys' and girls' clubs who are well acquainted with the younger generation as a whole are greatly disturbed over the poor physique of the youth of the present day. The physique of the nation is poor.

United States

According to figures of the New York Department of Health for 1932, 21.1 per cent of the children of school age were sick as a result of malnutrition. Compared with 1927, the number of sick children increased 55 per cent. In 1930 more than six million children in the U.S.A. failed to receive sufficient nourishment because their parents had either no work or no money; later this number rose considerably.

According to figures of the senior statistician of the U.S. Department of Health, as a result of the crisis, sickness has increased among the unemployed by 55 per cent, compared with 1929.

SOURCES: *Internationale Rundschau der Arbeit,* Feb., 1933, pp. 173, 176-77; *Daily Worker,* London, 16, IX, 1933; *Times,* 2, III, 1934; *Pravda,* 13, IX, 1933 (TASS); *Daily Worker,* New York, 28, XII, 1933; *New York Times,* 26, XI, 1933; *Statistical Abstract for the U. K.,* 1935, p. 34.

capitalism would develop more rapidly if free competition were not restricted by monopolies in general, by the "connections" or the yoke (*i.e.*, also the monopoly) of finance capital, or by the monopolist possession of colonies by certain countries?

Kautsky's argument can have no other meaning; and *this* "meaning" is meaningless. But suppose, for the sake of argument, free competition, without any sort of monopoly, *would* develop capitalism and trade more rapidly. Is it not a fact that the more rapidly trade and capitalism develop, the greater is the concentration of production and capital which *gives rise* to monopoly? And monopolies have *already* come into being—precisely *out of* free competition! Even if monopolies have now begun to retard progress, it is not an argument in favour of free competition, which has become impossible since it gave rise to monopoly.

Whichever way one turns Kautsky's argument, one will find nothing in it except reaction and bourgeois reformism.

Even if we modify this argument and say, as Spectator says, that the trade of the British colonies with the mother country is now developing more slowly than their trade with other countries, it does not save Kautsky; for it is *also* monopoly and imperialism that is beating Great Britain, only it is the monopoly and imperialism of another country (America, Germany). It is known that the cartels have given rise to a new and peculiar form of protective tariffs, *i.e.*, goods suitable for export are protected (Engels noted this in Vol. III of *Capital*). It is known, too, that the cartels and finance capital have a system peculiar to themselves, that of "exporting goods at cut-rate prices," or "dumping," as the English call it: within a given country the cartel sells its goods at a high price fixed by monopoly; abroad it sells them at a much lower price to undercut the competitor, to enlarge its own production to the utmost, etc. If Germany's trade with the British colonies is developing more rapidly than that of Great Britain with the same colonies, it only proves that German imperialism is younger, stronger and better organised than British imperialism, is superior to it. But this by no means proves the "superiority" of free trade, for it is not free trade fighting against protection and colonial dependence, but two rival imperialisms, two monopolies, two groups of finance capital that are fighting. The superiority of German imperialism over British imperialism is stronger than the wall of colonial frontiers or of protective tariffs. To use this as an argument *in favour* of free trade and "peaceful democ-

INCREASE OF SUICIDES

Year	Number of suicides			Suicides per 100,000 population			
	U.S.A.	Great Britain	Germany	U.S.A.	Great Britain [3]	Germany	
						All Germany	Berlin
1913....	9,988	3,791	15,564 [1]	15.8	8.3	23.4 [1]	38.5
1925....	12,495	4,531	15,273 [2]	13.1	10.1	24.5 [2]	—
1929....	16,260	5,529	16,665	15.6	12.1	26.1	42.2
1932....	20,927	6,314	18,934	19.3	13.6	29.2	53.1
1934....	19,993 [4]	6,148	18,801	17.5 [4]	13.2	28.3	—

[1] Within pre-war boundaries.   [3] Computed from official statistics.
[2] Within post-war boundaries.   [4] 1933.

SOURCES: U.S.A.—*Statistical Abstract of the United States*; Great Britain— *Statistical Abstract for the United Kingdom*; Germany—*Wirtschaft und Statistik*, No. 14, 1932, No. 13, 1934; *Statistisches Jahrbuch für das Deutsche Reich.*

DESTRUCTION OF LABOUR POWER AS A RESULT OF SPEED-UP

The American bourgeois investigator, Dr. H. Mayer-Daxlander, in his report to the Labour Bureau of the League of Nations, states in regard to conditions of labour in New York and its vicinity that his observations and investigations disclose that work on a conveyor relatively increases the number of accidents and occupational diseases. This is a characteristic result of the excessive speed at which conveyors are run in capitalist industry under the "speed-up" system. A fact which becomes more and more noticeable each year is the growth of mental diseases among industrial workers. From 1920 to 1924 a total of 441,830 cases of accidents and occupational diseases were reported to the New York State Commission on Accidents. This gives an average of 88,366 cases per annum. The figure for 1928 rose to 95,365. By that time industry in the State of New York had been rationalised to the extent of 85 per cent. A certain private company shows the following increase in registered cases:

Year	No. of accidents	No. of nervous breakdowns	No. of mental cases
1926.....	2,535	696	39
1927.....	2,553	768	35
1928.....	2,693	870	40
1929.....	2,931	—	55

One factory employing 3,000 workers showed the following percentage of nervous breakdowns to the total cases of sickness and accidents:

1926	1927	1928	1929
12	18	29	34

racy" is banal, is to forget the essential features and qualities of imperialism, to substitute petty-bourgeois reformism for Marxism.

It is interesting to note that even the bourgeois economist, A. Lansburgh, whose criticism of imperialism is as petty-bourgeois as Kautsky's, nevertheless got closer to a more scientific study of trade statistics. He did not compare merely one country, chosen at random, and a colony, with the other countries; he examined the export trade of an imperialist country: 1) with countries which are financially dependent upon it, which borrow money from it; and 2) with countries which are financially independent. He obtained the following results:

EXPORT TRADE OF GERMANY
(million marks)

Countries Financially Dependent on Germany	1889	1908	Per cent increase
Rumania	48.2	70.8	47
Portugal	19.0	32.8	73
Argentina	60.7	147.0	143
Brazil	48.7	84.5	73
Chile	28.3	52.4	85
Turkey	29.9	64.0	114
Total	234.8	451.5	92

Countries Financially Independent of Germany	1889	1908	Per cent increase
Great Britain	651.8	997.4	53
France	210.2	437.9	108
Belgium	137.2	322.8	135
Switzerland	177.4	401.1	127
Australia	21.2	64.5	205
Dutch East Indies	8.8	40.7	363
Total	1,206.6	2,264.4	87

Lansburgh did not draw *conclusions* and therefore, strangely enough, failed to observe that *if* the figures prove anything at all, they prove that *he is wrong*, for the exports to countries financially dependent on Germany have grown *more rapidly*, if only slightly, than those to the countries which are financially independent. (We emphasise the "if," for Lansburgh's figures are far from complete.)

Tracing the connection between export trade and loans, Lansburgh writes:

"In 1890-91, a Rumanian loan was floated through the German banks, which had already in previous years made advances on this loan. The loan was used chiefly for purchases of railway materials in Germany. In 1891 German exports to Rumania amounted to 55,000,000 marks. The following year they fell to 39,400,000

In another factory, out of 1,200 girl employees, 312 wore glasses at the time of enrolment. A year later this number had increased to 731.

The author concluded his report with the statement that work on the conveyor daily causes the exhaustion of industrial workers and that women suffer relatively more than men.

In its report for 1930, the Association of Physicians in Germany states: "The most important cause of the deterioration of health of the insured ... is the disposition to sickness caused by the more intense utilisation of the labour power of the insured person. ... The rationalisation of economy primarily affects the nervous system and the mental state of the insured person."

According to Kuczinsky, in Germany the percentage of accidents among insured persons resulting from the speeding up of labour increased as follows:

1924	1925	1926	1929
6	7	9	10

SOURCES: U.S.A.—Dr. H. Mayer-Daxlander, *Fliessarbeit, Rationalisierung und Gesundheit des Arbeiters*, New York, 1931; Germany—*Gewerkschaftszeitung*, 1931, No. 45 and *Finanzpolitische Korrespondenz*.

III. *GROWTH OF UNPRODUCTIVE LABOUR*

RELATIVE DECLINE IN NUMBER OF WORKERS EMPLOYED IN INDUSTRY

We have already quoted figures showing the decline in the percentage of productively employed workers among the population of Great Britain. The same phenomenon is observed in the post-war period in Germany and the United States. This is seen from the following figures:

UNITED STATES

Year	Population	No. of workers employed in mfg. industry	Per cent of population
		(millions)	
1899	74.8	4.71 [1]	6.3
1914	97.9	7.02 [1]	7.2
1914	97.9	6.90 [2]	7.0
1919	105.0	9.00 [2]	8.6
1929	121.5	8.84 [2]	7.3
1933	125.7	6.06 [2]	4.8

[1] In establishments with products valued at over $500 per annum.
[2] In establishments with products valued at over $5,000 per annum.

marks; then with fluctuations, to 25,400,000 in 1900. Only in very recent years have they regained the level of 1891, thanks to several new loans.

"German exports to Portugal rose, following the loans of 1888-89, to 21,100,000 (1890); then fell, in the two following years, to 16,200,000 and 7,400,000; and only regained their former level in 1903.

"German trade with the Argentine is still more striking. Following the loans floated in 1888 and 1890, German exports to the Argentine reached, in 1889, 60,700,000 marks. Two years later they only reached 18,600,000 marks, that is to say, less than one-third of the previous figure. It was not until 1901 that they regained and surpassed the level of 1889, and then only as a result of new loans floated by the state and by municipalities, with advances to build power stations, and with other credit operations.

"Exports to Chile rose to 45,200,000 marks in 1892, after the loan negotiated in 1889. The following year they fell to 22,500,000 marks. A new Chilean loan floated by the German banks in 1906 was followed by a rise of exports in 1907 to 84,700,000 marks, only to fall again to 52,400,000 marks in 1908."[1]

From all these facts Lansburgh draws the amusing petty-bourgeois moral of how unstable and irregular export trade is when it is bound up with loans, how bad it is to invest capital abroad instead of "naturally" and "harmoniously" developing home industry, how "costly" is the *backsheesh* that Krupp has to pay in floating foreign loans, etc! But the facts are clear. The increase in exports is *closely* connected with the swindling tricks of finance capital, which is not concerned with bourgeois morality, but with skinning the ox twice—first, it pockets the profits from the loan; then it pockets other profits from the *same* loan which the borrower uses to make purchases from Krupp, or to purchase railway material from the Steel Syndicate, etc.

We repeat that we do not by any means consider Lansburgh's figures to be perfect. But we had to quote them because they are more scientific than Kautsky's and Spectator's, and because Lansburgh showed the correct way of approaching the question. In discussing the significance of finance capital in regard to exports, etc., one must be able to single out the connection of exports especially and solely with the tricks of the financiers, especially and solely with the sale of goods by cartels, etc. Simply to compare colonies with non-colonies, one imperialism with another imperialism, one semi-colony or colony (Egypt) with all other countries, is to evade and to tone down the very *essence* of the question.

Kautsky's theoretical critique of imperialism has nothing in common with Marxism and serves no other purpose than as a preamble to propaganda for peace and unity with the opportunists and the social-chauvinists, precisely for the reason that it evades and obscures the very

---

[1] *Die Bank*, 1909, Vol. II, pp. 826-27.

GERMANY

Year	Population	No. of workers employed in industry	Per cent of population
	(millions)		
1895............	52.0	5.5	10.6
1907............	62.0	7.9	12.7
1925............	62.4	9.4	15.1
1928............	63.6	8.7	13.7
1933............	65.2	5.7	8.8

The figures on the number employed in 1928 are taken from factory inspectors' returns. To these we have added the number of workers employed in small enterprises with less than 5 employees. The other figures are taken from the censuses; the figures for 1895 and 1907 in the pre-year boundaries. The figures for subsequent years relate to present boundaries (not including the Saar).

Sources: U.S.A.—*Statistical Abstract of the U.S.* 1931-35; Germany—*Statistisches Jahrbuch für das Deutsche Reich*, 1934, S. 7; *Statistik des Deutschen Reichs*, B. 418-1, S. 200, 203; *Jahresberichte der Gewerbeaufsichtsbeamten und Bergbehörden*, 1928, B. III, S. 66-80, 552-53.

INCREASE IN RELATIVE NUMBER OF PERSONS ENGAGED IN THE SPHERE OF DISTRIBUTION AND PERSONAL SERVICE

The decline in the percentage of productively occupied persons among the gainfully occupied population in the post-war period of capitalism is accompanied by an increase in the percentage of persons engaged in the sphere of distribution and personal service, etc. This is illustrated by the following figures:

UNITED STATES: INCREASE IN NUMBER OF NON-PRODUCTIVELY EMPLOYED PERSONS AMONG THE GAINFULLY OCCUPIED POPULATION

Occupation	1910	1920	1930	1910	1920	1930
	(thousands)			(%)		
Agriculture, forestry and fishing..............	12,630	10,936	10,723	33.1	26.3	21.9
Mining and manufacturing	11,622	13,922	15,095	30.5	33.5	30.9
Transportation and communications...........	2,665	3,097	3,843	7.0	7.4	7.9
Total of productively occupied population	26,917	27,955	29,661	70.6	67.2	60.7

(*Continued on p. 243*)

profound and radical contradictions of imperialism: the contradictions between monopoly and free competition that exists side by side with it, between the gigantic "operations" (and gigantic profits) of finance capital and "honest" trade in the free market, the contradictions between cartels and trusts, on the one hand, and non-cartelised industry, on the other, etc.

The notorious theory of "ultra-imperialism," invented by Kautsky, is equally reactionary. Compare his arguments on this subject in 1915, with Hobson's arguments in 1902.

Kautsky:

"Cannot the present imperialist policy be supplanted by a new, ultra-imperialist policy, which will introduce the common exploitation of the world by internationally united finance capital in place of the mutual rivalries of national finance capital? Such a new phase of capitalism is at any rate conceivable. Can it be achieved? Sufficient premises are still lacking to enable us to answer this question." [1]

Hobson:

"Christendom thus laid out in a few great federal empires, each with a retinue of uncivilised dependencies, seems to many the most legitimate development of present tendencies, and one which would offer the best hope of permanent peace on an assured basis of inter-imperialism." [2]

Kautsky called ultra-imperialism or super-imperialism what Hobson, thirteen years earlier, described as inter-imperialism. Except for coining a new and clever word, by replacing one Latin prefix by another, the only progress Kautsky has made in the sphere of "scientific" thought is that he has labelled as Marxism what Hobson, in effect, described as the cant of English parsons. After the Anglo-Boer War it was quite natural for this worthy caste to exert every effort to *console* the British middle class and the workers who had lost many of their relatives on the battlefields of South Africa and who were obliged to pay higher taxes in order to guarantee still higher profits for the British financiers. And what better consolation could there be than the theory that imperialism is not so bad; that it stands close to inter-(or ultra-) imperialism, which can ensure permanent peace? No matter what the good intentions of the English parsons, or of sentimental Kautsky, may have been, the only objective, *i.e.*, real, social significance Kautsky's "theory" can have, is that of a most reactionary method of consoling the masses with hopes of permanent peace being possible under capitalism, distracting their

[1] *Die Neue Zeit*, April 30, 1915, p. 144.
[2] Hobson, *op. cit.*, p. 351.

Occupation	1910	1920	1930	1910	1920	1930
		(thousands)			(%)	
Professional service	1,711	2,171	3,254	4.5	5.2	6.7
Commerce, banking, etc....	5,352	7,369	10,107	14.0	17.7	20.7
Domestic & personal service	3,756	3,380	4,952	9.8	8.1	10.1
Public service............	431	739	856	1.1	1.8	1.8
Total non-productively occupied population	9,539	11,488	15,915	24.9	27.6	32.6
Total gainfully occupied	38,167	41,614	48,830	100.0	100.0	100.0

SOURCE: *Fifteenth Census of the United States*, 1930, Occupation Statistics, p. 8.

GREAT BRITAIN: PRODUCTIVELY AND NON-PRODUCTIVELY OCCUPIED INSURED EMPLOYEES

	1923	1929	1933	1923	1929	1933
		(thousands)			(%)	
Productively occupied (industry, building, transportation).....	7,879	7,927	7,110	77.6	73.4	69.2
Non-productively occupied (commerce, banking, finance, etc.)	2,272	2,875	3,165	22.4	26.6	30.8
Total	10,151	10,802	10,275	100.0	100.0	100.0

SOURCES: Computations of the "Konjunktur" Dept. of the Institute of World Economics and World Politics, Moscow, based on unemployment insurance figures in *The Ministry of Labour Gazette*.

*GERMANY: INCREASE IN PERCENTAGE OF PERSONS OCCUPIED IN COMMERCE, FINANCIAL INSTITUTIONS AND PERSONAL SERVICE

Occupation	1907	1925	1933	1907	1925	1933
		(thousands)			(%)	
Industry......................	9,839	12,693	8,999	78.0	75.9	68.2
Commerce, insurance, banking, hotels, etc.	2,776	4,032	4,205	22.0	24.1	31.8
Total	12,615	16,725	13,204	100.0	100.0	100.0

SOURCES: 1907 and 1925—*Statistik des Deutschen Reichs*, Bd. 413, Teil 1, S. 246; 1933—*Statistik des Deutschen Reichs*, Bd. 462, S. 6-9.

attention from the sharp antagonisms and acute problems of the present era, and directing it towards illusory prospects of an imaginary "ultra-imperialism" of the future. Deception of the masses—there is nothing but this in Kautsky's "Marxian" theory.

Indeed, it is enough to compare well-known and indisputable facts to become convinced of the utter falsity of the prospects which Kautsky tries to conjure up before the German workers (and the workers of all lands). Let us consider India, Indo-China and China. It is known that these three colonial and semi-colonial countries, inhabited by six to seven hundred million human beings, are subjected to the exploitation of the finance capital of several imperialist states: Great Britain, France, Japan, the U.S.A., etc. We will assume that these imperialist countries form alliances against one another in order to protect and extend their possessions, their interests and their "spheres of influence" in these Asiatic states; these alliances will be "inter-imperialist," or "ultra-imperialist" alliances. We will assume that all the imperialist countries conclude an alliance for the "peaceful" division of these parts of Asia; this alliance would be an alliance of "internationally united finance capital." As a matter of fact, alliances of this kind have been made in the twentieth century, notably with regard to China. We ask, is it "conceivable," assuming that the capitalist system remains intact—and this is precisely the assumption that Kautsky does make—that such alliances would be more than temporary, that they would eliminate friction, conflicts and struggle in all and every possible form?

This question need only be stated clearly enough to make it impossible for any other reply to be given than that in the negative; for there can be no other conceivable basis under capitalism for the division of spheres of influence, of interests, of colonies, etc., than a calculation of the *strength* of the participants in the division, their general economic, financial, military strength, etc. And the strength of these participants in the division does not change to an equal degree, for under capitalism the development of different undertakings, trusts, branches of industry, or countries cannot be *even*. Half a century ago, Germany was a miserable, insignificant country, as far as its capitalist strength was concerned, compared with the strength of England at that time. Japan was similarly insignificant compared with Russia. Is it "conceivable" that in ten or twenty years' time the relative strength of the imperialist powers will have remained *unchanged*? Absolutely inconceivable.

Therefore, in the realities of the capitalist system, and not in the

GERMANY: INCREASE IN PERCENTAGE OF PERSONS OCCUPIED IN COMMERCE, FINANCIAL INSTITUTIONS AND PERSONAL SERVICE

(Establishments employing over 5 persons)

Occupation	1928	1932	1928	1932
	(thousands)		(%)	
Industry	9,073	5,191	87.9	82.5
Commerce, banking, insurance, hotels, restaurants, etc.	1,254	1,098	12.1	17.5
Total	10,327	6,289	100.0	100.0

SOURCE: *Wirtschaft und Statistik*, No. 21, 1933, S. 654-57.

IV. RETARDED RATE OF INCREASE OF PRODUCTION

PER CENT INCREASE OR DECREASE IN VOLUME OF INDUSTRIAL PRODUCTION

Year	U.S.A.	Great Britain	Germany	France	Whole capitalist world [1]	Index of world production of industry & agriculture
1897-1913 (16 yrs.)	+ 100.0	+ 35.1	+ 79.5	+ 58.7	+ 81.8	+ 68.2
1913-29 (16 yrs.)	+ 69.8	— 0.9	+ 3.0 [2]	+ 38.0 [2]	+ 46.6	+ 31.1
1929-33 (4 yrs.)	— 36.1	— 11.8	— 31.3	— 22.9	— 28.8	—

[1] 1897-1913 includes Russia; 1913-33 exclusive of U.S.S.R.
[2] Post-war boundaries.

SOURCES: 1897-1929—*Vierteljahrshefte zur Konjunkturforschung*, Sonderheft 31; 1929-33—*Monthly Bulletin of Statistics of the League of Nations*, No. 10, 1934; *Wochenbericht des Instituts für Konjunkturforschung*, No. 12, 1934.

PER CENT INCREASE OR DECREASE IN WORLD PRODUCTION OF IMPORTANT INDUSTRIES

Year	Coal	Pig Iron	Steel	Shipbuilding	Cotton consumption
1897-1913 (16 years)	+ 112.0	+ 139.6	+ 254.1	+ 150.4	+ 64.7
1913-29 (16 years)	+ 15.8	+ 27.3	+ 61.6	— 17.1	+ 8.8
1929-33 (4 years)	— 31.4	— 57.5	— 47.4	— 82.4	— 18.1 [1]

[1] 1929-31.

SOURCES: The table is computed on the basis of official statistics. The figures for 1897-1913 include Russia; those for 1913-33 do not include the U.S.S.R.

banal philistine fantasies of English parsons, or of the German "Marxist," Kautsky, "inter-imperialist" or "ultra-imperialist" alliances, no matter what form they may assume, whether of one imperialist coalition against another, or of a general alliance embracing *all* the imperialist powers, are *inevitably* nothing more than a "truce" in periods between wars. Peaceful alliances prepare the ground for wars, and in their turn grow out of wars; the one is the condition for the other, giving rise to alternating forms of peaceful and non-peaceful struggle out of *one and the same* basis of imperialist connections and the relations between world economics and world politics. But in order to pacify the workers and to reconcile them with the social-chauvinists who have deserted to the side of the bourgeoisie, wise Kautsky *separates* one link of a single chain from the other, separates the present peaceful (and ultra-imperialist, nay, ultra-ultra-imperialist) alliance of *all* the powers for the "pacification" of China (remember the suppression of the Boxer Rebellion) from the non-peaceful conflict of tomorrow, which will prepare the ground for another "peaceful" general alliance for the partition, say, of Turkey, on the day after tomorrow, etc., etc. Instead of showing the vital connection between periods of imperialist peace and periods of imperialist war, Kautsky puts before the workers a lifeless abstraction solely in order to reconcile them to their lifeless leaders.

An American writer, Hill, in his *History of Diplomacy in the International Development of Europe*,[1] points out in his preface the following periods of contemporary diplomatic history: 1) The era of revolution; 2) The constitutional movement; 3) The present era of "commercial imperialism." Another writer divides the history of Great Britain's foreign policy since 1870 into four periods: 1) The first Asiatic period (that of the struggle against Russia's advance in Central Asia towards India); 2) The African period (approximately 1885-1902): that of struggles against France for the partition of Africa (the Fashoda incident of 1898 which brought France within a hair's breadth of war with Great Britain); 3) The second Asiatic period (alliance with Japan against Russia), and 4) The European period, chiefly anti-German.[2] "The political skirmishes of outposts take place on the financial field," wrote Riesser, the banker, in 1905, in showing how French finance capital operating in Italy was preparing the way for a political alliance of these countries, and how a conflict was develop-

---

[1] Vol. I, p. X.
[2] Schilder, *op. cit.*, Vol. I, p. 178.

V. RETARDATION OF TECHNICAL PROGRESS

The following examples show that on a background of rapid technical progress the *"tendency* to stagnation and decay, which is the feature of monopoly" (Lenin) continued in the post-war period with increasing effect, particularly owing to the fact that fixed capital is being chronically utilised below capacity.

High pressure boilers. As electric power stations are chronically working below capacity, high pressure boilers cannot be widely employed under modern capitalism. In this connection, the well-known scientist, Professor Münzinger, writes:

"Owing to the fact that electric power stations are working much below capacity, the general opinion prevails today that changing from 20 to 100 atm. pressure would not pay in the majority of German central stations, notwithstanding the fact that an additional investment of 7 per cent capital would result in a 15 per cent saving in specific fuel expenditure per effectively delivered kilowatt hour at full load."

The case of the Douglas la Monte high-pressure forced circulation boiler serves as a characteristic example. "Notwithstanding the fact that great experts like Professor Eberle, D'Huart and others, have admitted the superiority of this new type of boiler, notwithstanding the revolution in power engineering the wide application of the Douglas la Monte principles would bring about, and finally, notwithstanding the fact that some of the biggest boiler manufacturers in Europe have obtained rights to manufacture this type of boiler, actually it is still being ignored. . . . Fear of the obsolescence of existing capital investments and the sharp diminution of the profitableness of the new improvements and achievements of technique on account of the crisis, are the principal factors which compel manufacturers to withhold these and a number of other patents from the market."

The unified high-tension transmission sytem cannot be introduced under the conditions of capitalism, although the technical problems connected with the introduction of this system have been solved, and separate high-pressure power rings have achieved large dimensions. Hence the numerous pronouncements against the unified system. The following are examples of such pronouncements:

a) The discussion in 1931-32, especially in the journal "ETZ," on the subject of "Grosskraft oder Einzelkraft"; in particular, the paper by R. Franck (1929) and the articles by Schräder and Block, written in

ing between Great Britain and Germany over Persia, between all the European capitalists over Chinese loans, etc. Behold, the living reality of peaceful "ultra-imperialist" alliances in their indissoluble connection with ordinary imperialist conflicts!

Kautsky's toning down of the deepest contradictions of imperialism, which inevitably becomes the embellishment of imperialism, leaves its traces in this writer's criticism of the political features of imperialism. Imperialism is the epoch of finance capital and of monopolies, which introduce everywhere the striving for domination, not for freedom. The result of these tendencies is reaction all along the line, whatever the political system, and an extreme intensification of existing antagonisms in this domain also. Particularly acute becomes the yoke of national oppression and the striving for annexations, *i.e.*, the violation of national independence (for annexation is nothing but the violation of the right of nations to self-determination). Hilferding justly draws attention to the connection between imperialism and the growth of national oppression.

"In the newly opened up countries themselves," he writes, "the capitalism imported into them intensifies contradictions and excites the constantly growing resistance against the intruders of the peoples who are awakening to national consciousness. This resistance can easily become transformed into dangerous measures directed against foreign capital. The old social relations become completely revolutionised. The age-long agrarian incrustation of 'nations without a history' is blasted away, and they are drawn into the capitalist whirlpool. Capitalism itself gradually procures for the vanquished the means and resources for their emancipation and they set out to achieve the same goal which once seemed highest to the European nations: the creation of a united national state as a means to economic and cultural freedom. This movement for national independence threatens European capital just in its most valuable and most promising fields of exploitation, and European capital can maintain its domination only by continually increasing its means of exerting violence." [1]

To this must be added that it is not only in newly opened up countries, but also in the old, that imperialism is leading to annexation, to increased national oppression, and, consequently, also to increasing resistance. While opposing the intensification of political reaction caused by imperialism, Kautsky obscures the question, which has become very serious, of the impossibility of unity with the opportunists in the epoch of imperialism. While objecting to annexations, he presents his objections in a form that will be most acceptable and least offensive to the opportunists. He addresses himself to a German audience, yet he obscures the most topical and important point, for instance, the annexation by Germany of Alsace-Lorraine. In order to appraise this "lapse of mind" of Kautsky's

---

[1] Hilferding, *op. cit.*, p. 406.

opposition to the introduction of a unified system in Germany. The main argument advanced against it was that it would not pay from the point of view of private capital.

b) The report of H. V. Liversidge, President of the Philadelphia Electric Company, at the annual general meeting of the N.E.L.A. His main argument was that the area which a single central station can cover cannot be very large, and in all probability will diminish.

Some of the principal motives that prompt this opposition are fear of strikes and military expediency. For example, G. Dehne writes:

"A further obstacle in the present case is the important fact that the power supply in an enormous territory passes into the hands of a few persons and is produced in a single centre. Consequently, in the event of war, or during a strike or disorders, large industrial regions may be cut off from the centres of power supply."

The electrification of railways is still in a rudimentary stage, as the following table shows:

PER CENT OF ELECTRIFIED RAILWAYS IN THE BEGINNING OF 1936

U.S.A.	1.1
Great Britain	3.9
Germany	4.1
France	6.1
Western Europe as a whole	4.5

Only Italy, Sweden, and Switzerland show a greater percentage of railway electrification, owing to their poverty in coal and abundance of water resources. In Italy 4,846 kilometres, or 21.1 per cent of the railways, are electrified; in Sweden 2,450 kilometres, or 14.6 per cent, and in Switzerland 2,081 kilometres, or 71 per cent. The following indicates some of the causes that retard the growth of railway electrification:

In Great Britain, the Committee on Railway Electrification, set up by the government, issued its report (the Weir Report) in 1930. Although the plan proposed by the Committee was a very modest one, spread over twenty years, it met with great hostility and was effectively squashed. Particularly sharp objections were raised by the coal and transport interests (a series of articles in *Modern Transport* and a fierce attack by Robert Smith, one of the leaders of these interests). Among the arguments used in opposition to the scheme were the following:

we will take the following example. Let us suppose that a Japanese is condemning the annexation of the Philippine Islands by the Americans. Will many believe that he is doing so because he has a horror of annexations as such, and not because he himself has a desire to annex the Philippines? And shall we not be constrained to admit that the "fight" the Japanese is waging against annexations can be regarded as being sincere and politically honest only if he fights against the annexation of Korea by Japan, and urges freedom for Korea to secede from Japan?

Kautsky's theoretical analysis of imperialism, as well as his economic and political criticism of imperialism, are permeated *through and through* with a spirit, absolutely irreconcilable with Marxism, of obscuring and glossing over the most profound contradictions of imperialism and with a striving to preserve the crumbling unity with opportunism in the European labour movement at all costs.

a) Electrification will cause a sharp reduction in the sale of coal, as the efficiency of electric power stations is much higher than that of steam locomotives.

b) Hence, there will be a sharp reduction in railway freight traffic (approximately one-third of the freight revenue of British railways is derived from the transportation of coal).

c) And consequently there will be a considerable reduction in the demand for labour and an increase of unemployment.

d) Fear of strikes.

e) Fear of war.

"From a national point of view it is clear that an electrified railway system *is more vulnerable to attack and disorganisation by a foreign foe or malcontent wreckers than a system served by independent traction units. This is certainly the most serious aspect of the matter"* (our italics).

Gasification of coal in the mines. This idea was advanced by Sir William Ramsay as far back as the nineties of the last century, but, as Lenin predicted, it has not yet found practical application in capitalist countries.

The liquefaction of coal by the Bergius method (manufacture of synthetic gasoline) has not received wide application during the post-war period, although the technical problem connected with it has long been solved. The reasons for this are the monopolisation of the patents and the resistance of the oil monopolies. The agreement between the Standard Oil Company and the German I. G. Farbenindustrie, restricting the utilisation of the Bergius patents, is a matter of common knowledge. It was only during the world economic crisis that interest in synthetic gasoline was greatly aroused in connection with war preparations, and a number of plants were constructed for this purpose.

SOURCES: Prof. W. Weitz, *Modern Development of Electrification in Capitalist Countries* (in Russian), Leningrad, 1933, pp. 107-09, 115, 121-36; *Elektrizitätswirtschaft*, 1931; G. Dehne, *Deutschlands Grosskraftversorgung*, Berlin, 1929; *Elektrotechnische Zeitschrift*, 4, I, 1934; Report of the Weir Committee on the Electrification of British Railways, 1930.

CHAPTER X

THE PLACE OF IMPERIALISM IN HISTORY

WE have seen that the economic quintessence of imperialism is monopoly capitalism. This very fact determines its place in history, for monopoly that grew up on the basis of free competition, and precisely out of free competition, is the transition from the capitalist system to a higher social-economic order. We must take special note of the four principal forms of monopoly, or the four principal manifestations of monopoly capitalism, which are characteristic of the epoch under review.

Firstly, monopoly arose out of the concentration of production at a very advanced stage of development. This refers to the monopolist capitalist combines, cartels, syndicates and trusts. We have seen the important part that these play in modern economic life. At the beginning of the twentieth century, monopolies acquired complete supremacy in the advanced countries. And although the first steps towards the formation of the cartels were first taken by countries enjoying the protection of high tariffs (Germany, America), Great Britain, with her system of free trade, was not far behind in revealing the same basic phenomenon, namely, the birth of monopoly out of the concentration of production.

Secondly, monopolies have accelerated the capture of the most important sources of raw materials, especially for the coal and iron industries, which are the basic and most highly cartelised industries in capitalist society. The monopoly of the most important sources of raw materials has enormously increased the power of big capital, and has sharpened the antagonism between cartelised and non-cartelised industry.

Thirdly, monopoly has sprung from the banks. The banks have developed from modest intermediary enterprises into the monopolists of finance capital. Some three or five of the biggest banks in each of the foremost capitalist countries have achieved the "personal union" of industrial and bank capital, and have concentrated in their hands the disposal of thousands upon thousands of millions which form the greater part of the capital and income of entire countries. A financial oligarchy, which throws a close net of relations of dependence over all the

252

VI. *THE CHRONIC BELOW-CAPACITY UTILISATION OF MEANS OF PRODUCTION*

PRODUCTION OF INDUSTRY IN PER CENT OF CAPACITY

GERMANY

(Hours actually worked compared with possible hours of normal shift)

	1929	1932
Industry as a whole	67	36
Production of means of production	68	30
Production of means of consumption	67	43
Production of iron and steel	80	35
Production of non-ferrous metals	78	35
Engineering	68	27
Textiles	72	50
Superphosphates	53	40
Nitrogen industry	51	37

U.S.A.[1]

	1929	1932
Coal (bituminous)	78	57 [3]
Steel	87	19
Copper	78	19
Automobile [2]	54	14
Portland Cement	67	28
Paper	86	55
Nitrogen	68	30

GREAT BRITAIN [1]

	1929	1932
Pig iron	52 [4,5]	30 [5,6]
Steel	59 [4]	42 [6]
Sulphuric acid	69	63
Nitrogen	67 [4]	66

FRANCE [1]

	1929	1932
Superphosphates	61	39 [7]
Nitrogen	45 [4]	41

It must be borne in mind that for most industries official and bourgeois unofficial statistics take 100 per cent of capacity to mean the full utilisation of equipment during one shift. If we based our calculations on two or three shifts, the percentage would be much lower than that shown in the above tables.

[1] Actual production in per cent of production capacity.

[2] Production capacity of automobile industry in 1929-32 taken at 10 million cars per annum.

[3] 1931.　　　　　[4] 1930.

[5] Production capacity exclusive of blast furnaces that have been idle for long periods. If the latter are taken into account, the percentage of utilisation will be reduced to 48 in 1929 and 27 in 1932.

[6] Calculated on basis of production capacity of 1930.

[7] Calculated on basis of production capacity of 1929.

SOURCES: *Konjunkturstatistisches Handbuch*, 1933; *Glückauf*; *Survey of Current Business*; *Statistical Tables Relating to British and Foreign Trade and Industry*; *Statistical Yearbook*, L. of N., 1930-34.

economic and political institutions of contemporary bourgeois society without exception—such is the most striking manifestation of this monopoly.

Fourthly, monopoly has grown out of colonial policy. To the numerous "old" motives of colonial policy, finance capital has added the struggle for the sources of raw materials, for the export of capital, for "spheres of influence," i.e., for spheres for profitable deals, concessions, monopolist profits and so on; in fine, for economic territory in general. When the colonies of the European powers in Africa, for instance, comprised only one-tenth of that territory (as was the case in 1876), colonial policy was able to develop by methods other than those of monopoly— by the "free grabbing" of territories, so to speak. But when nine-tenths of Africa had been seized (approximately by 1900), when the whole world had been divided up, there was inevitably ushered in a period of colonial monopoly and, consequently, a period of particularly intense struggle for the division and the redivision of the world.

The extent to which monopolist capital has intensified all the contradictions of capitalism is generally known. It is sufficient to mention the high cost of living and the oppression of the cartels. This intensification of contradictions constitutes the most powerful driving force of the transitional period of history, which began from the time of the definite victory of world finance capital.

Monopolies, oligarchy, the striving for domination instead of the striving for liberty, the exploitation of an increasing number of small or weak nations by an extremely small group of the richest or most powerful nations—all these have given birth to those distinctive characteristics of imperialism which compel us to define it as parasitic or decaying capitalism. More and more prominently there emerges, as one of the tendencies of imperialism, the creation of the "bondholding" (rentier) state, the usurer state, in which the bourgeoisie lives on the proceeds of capital exports and by "clipping coupons." It would be a mistake to believe that this tendency to decay precludes the possibility of the rapid growth of capitalism. It does not. In the epoch of imperialism, certain branches of industry, certain strata of the bourgeoisie and certain countries betray, to a more or less degree, one or other of these tendencies. On the whole, capitalism is growing far more rapidly than before. But this growth is not only becoming more and more uneven in general; its unevenness also manifests itself, in particular, in the decay of the countries which are richest in capital (such as England).

VII. DESTRUCTION OF FIXED CAPITAL

During the World War

Precise figures on the value of the fixed capital destroyed in the course of military operations during the period of 1914-18 are not available. There is no doubt, however, that it must have been enormous.

Post-War Years

INCREASE OR DECREASE IN TOTAL NUMBER OF SPINDLES (INCLUDING IDLE SPINDLES) IN COTTON INDUSTRY OF CAPITALIST EUROPE AND U.S.A.

	(Millions)		
	1908-13	1924-28	1928-36
Great Britain	+3.7	+0.3	—15.7
Germany	+1.5	+1.7	— 1.0[1]
United States	+4.5	—2.3	— 7.4

[1] 1928-34.

SOURCES: *Annuaire Statistique, Statistique Générale de la France*, 1932-33, p. 385; *International Cotton Statistics*, Oct. 1934, p. 104, Sept, 1936, pp. 8, 11-12, 26.

During the period 1924-30 ninety-nine blast furnaces were built or reconstructed in the United States. The total pig iron production capacity of the country, however, remained unchanged owing to the fact that 109 blast furnaces were dismantled.

In Great Britain, the total blast furnace capacity dropped in the same period from 16.3 million tons per annum to 14.7 million tons.

From 1929 to July 1933 ninety-two blast furnaces were dismantled or abandoned in the United States. In Great Britain, 72 blast furnaces were dismantled between 1930 and October 1934. In Germany, 28 furnaces were scrapped in the same period and in France 10.

In the United States in 1932, steel furnaces of a total capacity of 4 million tons per annum were dismantled.

In the same year the Hartmann Engineering Works in Saxony were dismantled. In the boom years these works employed 15,000 workers.

In Great Britain a special company was formed known as the National Shipbuilders' Securities, Ltd., which is financed by the big shipbuilding companies, and the business of which is to buy up and dismantle so-called "superfluous" shipbuilding yards.

There is a rapid increase in the tonnage of merchant ships that are being broken up, as will be seen from the following table:

In regard to the rapidity of Germany's economic development, Riesser, the author of the book on the big German banks, states:

"The progress of the preceding period (1848-70), which had not been exactly slow, stood in about the same ratio to the rapidity with which the whole of Germany's national economy, and with it German banking, progressed during this period (1870-1905) as the mail coach of the Holy Roman Empire of the German nation stood to the speed of the present-day automobile...which in whizzing past, it must be said, often endangers not only innocent pedestrians in its path, but also the occupants of the car."[1]

In its turn, this finance capital which has grown so rapidly is not unwilling (precisely because it has grown so quickly) to pass on to a more "tranquil" possession of colonies which have to be seized—and not only by peaceful methods—from richer nations. In the United States, economic development in the last decades has been even more rapid than in Germany, and *for this very reason* the parasitic character of modern American capitalism has stood out with particular prominence. On the other hand, a comparison of, say, the republican American bourgeoisie with the monarchist Japanese or German bourgeoisie shows that the most pronounced political distinctions diminish to an extreme degree in the epoch of imperialism—not because they are unimportant in general, but because in all these cases we are discussing a bourgeoisie which has definite features of parasitism.

The receipt of high monopoly profits by the capitalists in one of the numerous branches of industry, in one of numerous countries, etc., makes it economically possible for them to corrupt certain sections of the working class, and for a time a fairly considerable minority, and win them to the side of the bourgeoisie of a given industry or nation against all the others. The intensification of antagonisms between imperialist nations for the division of the world increases this striving. And so there is created that bond between imperialism and opportunism, which revealed itself first and most clearly in England, owing to the fact that certain features of imperialist development were observable there much earlier than in other countries.

Some writers, L. Martov, for example, try to evade the fact that there is a connection between imperialism and opportunism in the labour movement—which is particularly striking at the present time—by resorting to "official optimistic" arguments (à la Kautsky and Huysmans) like the following: the cause of the opponents of capitalism would be hopeless if it were precisely progressive capitalism that led

---

[1] Riesser, *op. cit.*, third ed., p. 354.—*Ed.*

TONNAGE OF MERCHANT SHIPS BROKEN UP IN THE PRINCIPAL CAPITALIST COUNTRIES
(Thousand register tons)

1913	87.7
1929	943.6
1930	848.5
1931	1,018.2
1932	1,346.1
1933	2,415.2
1934	1,740.9
1935	1,151.3

The U.S. Department of Merchant Marine ordered the scrapping of 124 ships comprising a total of 1,000,000 reg. tons.

In Germany, ships comprising a total of 400,000 reg. tons have been scrapped.

SOURCES: Gt. Britain—*Industrial and Labour Information*, 16, V, 1932, p. 239. Tonnage of the principal capitalist countries—Lloyd's *Register of Shipping*, 1936-37; U.S.A.—*The Journal of Commerce*, 5, X, 1932; Germany—*New York Times*, 26, VIII, 1932.

U.S.A. REDUCTION OF THE TOTAL LENGTH OF RAILWAY LINES
(Miles)

Year	Newly completed lines	Abandoned lines	Net increase or decrease of lines in operation
1929	666	475	+191
1930	513	694	—181
1931	748	795	—47
1932	163	1,452	—1,289
1933	24	1,876	—1,852
1934	76	1,995	—1,919
1935	45	1,843	—1,798
1936	93	1,519	—1,426

According to *The Railway Age* the length of abandoned railways in the period 1930-36 exceeded the length of newly constructed lines by over 8,500 miles. As a result, the total length of railways in the U.S.A. at the end of 1936 was lower than at any time since 1910 and almost 13,500 miles less than in 1916.

An important factor in the destruction of fixed capital during the world economic crisis was the reduction of replacements below the level necessary to cover annual wear and tear. For example, on the United States railways, at the beginning of 1934, there were about five million tons of old rail and about ninety million ties which should normally have been replaced, but were not.

SOURCES: *The Railway Age*—Annual Statistical Number, January 2, 1937, pp. 53-55.

to the increase of opportunism, or, if it were precisely the best paid
workers who were inclined towards opportunism, etc. We must have no
illusion regarding "optimism" of this kind. It is optimism in regard
to opportunism; it is optimism which serves to conceal opportunism.
As a matter of fact the extraordinary rapidity and the particularly re-
volting character of the development of opportunism is by no means a
guarantee that its victory will be durable: the rapid growth of a malig-
nant abscess on a healthy body only causes it to burst more quickly and thus
to relieve the body of it. The most dangerous people of all in this respect
are those who do not wish to understand that the fight against imperialism is a sham and humbug unless it is inseparably bound up with the
fight against opportunism.

From all that has been said in this book on the economic nature of
imperialism, it follows that we must define it as capitalism in transition,
or, more precisely, as moribund capitalism. It is very instructive in this
respect to note that the bourgeois economists, in describing modern
capitalism, frequently employ terms like "interlocking," "absence of
isolation," etc.; "in conformity with their functions and course of development," banks are "not purely private business enterprises; they are
more and more outgrowing the sphere of purely private business regulation." And this very Riesser, who uttered the words just quoted, declares
with all seriousness that the "prophecy" of the Marxists concerning
"socialisation" has "not come true"!

What then does this word "interlocking" express? It merely ex-
presses the most striking feature of the process going on before our
eyes. It shows that the observer counts the separate trees, but cannot
see the wood. It slavishly copies the superficial, the fortuitous, the
chaotic. It reveals the observer as one who is overwhelmed by the mass of
raw material and is utterly incapable of appreciating its meaning and importance. Ownership of shares and relations between owners of private
property "interlock in a haphazard way." But the underlying factor of
this interlocking, its very base, is the changing social relations of production. When a big enterprise assumes gigantic proportions, and, on
the basis of exact computation of mass data, organises according to plan
the supply of primary raw materials to the extent of two-thirds, or
three-fourths of all that is necessary for tens of millions of people;
when the raw materials are transported to the most suitable place
of production, sometimes hundreds or thousands of miles away, in a
systematic and organised manner; when a single centre directs all the
successive stages of work right up to the manufacture of numerous

VIII. *DESTRUCTION OF STOCKS OF COMMODITIES IN THE PERIOD OF THE WORLD ECONOMIC CRISIS* [1]

Grain in U.S.A.—Owing to the low price of wheat the educational authorities in Colfax County, Nebraska, decided to purchase wheat to be used as fuel for heating the public schools. (Reported in *The Montreal Gazette*, Sept. 12, 1932.)

Fish in France.—In the port of Douarnenez an entire haul of fish was thrown into the sea because the buyers refused to pay the minimum price of 20 francs per 100 kilograms. (*Humanité*, May 5, 1933.)

Vegetables in Holland.—120 carloads of cauliflower, spinach, onions and cabbage were destroyed by Dutch farmers because there were no purchasers for this quantity. (*Daily Worker*, June 2, 1933.)

Sheep in Chile.—225,000 sheep were slaughtered in Chile and instead of being exported in the form of mutton, they were used for the production of lubricating grease and tallow, and for other industrial purposes. (*Daily Worker*, June 28, 1933.)

Sheep in Argentina.—Owing to the fact that receipts from the sale of hides and fat did not cover the cost of transporting the sheep to the slaughter houses (there was no demand whatever for the wool and mutton), hundreds of thousands of old sheep were slaughtered in the mountain pastures in order to make room for the young sheep. (*Wirtschaftsdienst*, July 7, 1933.)

Grain in Bulgaria.—Six thousand tons of grain, purchased for export by the Khranioiznos grain company, rotted in the granaries. (*Echo*, November 9, 1933.)

Hops in Great Britain.—At one of the hearings of the Hops Commission, Mr. Stewart May, a Kent farmer, declared that during the period 1925-29 about 1,000,000 cwts. of hops, valued at £2,000,000, had been destroyed in Great Britain with the object of raising prices. (*The Morning Post*, Sept. 13, 1933.)

Cotton in the U.S.A.—According to returns of the Department of Agriculture, 10,403,000 acres out of a total of 40 million acres of cotton sown in 1933 were ploughed under. (*Pravda*, Sept. 14, 1933, quoted from a correspondence in *New York Times* by Charles Packet.)

---

[1] Materials taken from E. Varga, *New Phenomena of the World Economic Crisis*, (Russian), Partizdat, 1934.

varieties of finished articles; when these products are distributed according to a single plan among tens and hundreds of millions of consumers (as in the case of the distribution of oil in America and Germany by the American "oil trust")—then it becomes evident that we have socialisation of production, and not mere "interlocking"; that private economic relations and private property relations constitute a shell which is no longer suitable for its contents, a shell which must inevitably begin to decay if its destruction be delayed by artificial means; a shell which may continue in a state of decay for a fairly long period (particularly if the cure of the opportunist abscess is protrac-. ted), but which will inevitably be removed.

The enthusiastic admirer of German imperialism, Schulze-Gaevernitz, exclaims:

"Once the supreme management of the German banks has been entrusted to the hands of a dozen persons, their activity is even today more significant for the public good than that of the majority of the Ministers of State." (The "interlocking" of bankers, ministers, magnates of industry and rentiers is here conveniently forgotten.). . . "If we conceive of the tendencies of development which we have noted as realised to the utmost: the money capital of the nation united in the banks; the banks themselves combined into cartels; the investment capital of the nation cast in the shape of securities, then the brilliant forecast of Saint-Simon will be fulfilled: 'The present anarchy of production caused by the fact that economic relations are developing without uniform regulation must make way for organisation in production. Production will no longer be shaped by isolated manufacturers, independent of each other and ignorant of man's economic needs, but by a social institution. A central body of management, being able to survey the large fields of social economy from a more elevated point of view, will regulate it for the benefit of the whole of society, will be able to put the means of production into suitable hands, and above all will take care that there be constant harmony between production and consumption. Institutions already exist which have assumed as part of their task a certain organisation of economic labour: the banks.' The fulfilment of the forecasts of Saint-Simon still lies in the future, but we are on the way to its fulfilment—Marxism, different from what Marx imagined, but different only in form." [1]

A crushing "refutation" of Marx, indeed! It is a retreat from Marx's precise, scientific analysis to Saint-Simon's guesswork, the guesswork of a genius, but guesswork all the same.

January-July, 1916.

---

[1] Schulze-Gaevernitz, in *Grundriss der Socialökonomik*, pp. 145-46.

Coffee in Brazil.—Approximately 22 million bags of coffee were destroyed in Brazil up to September 1933, and it has been proposed to destroy an additional 20 million bags of a round crop of 30 million in 1934 (*Deutsche Allgemeine Zeitung*, Sept. 27, 1933.)

Oranges in England.—In August 1933, about 1,500,000 Spanish oranges were to be dumped into the sea. (*El Sol,* Aug. 1, 1933; *Mundo Obrero,* Aug. 3, 1933.)

Hops in Czechoslovakia.—The Hops Syndicate is taking measures to destroy 7,000 tons of hops in the district of Saatz. (*Sozial-Demokrat,* Sept. 12, 1933.)

Cattle in Denmark.—According to the returns of the Ministry of Agriculture up to October 1, 1933, a total of 117,000 head of cattle have been destroyed in Denmark. This destruction was carried out with the sanction of the government.

Hogs in U.S.A.—In 1933, 6,400,000 hogs were destroyed.

Milk in U.S.A.—Twenty thousand quarts of milk were poured into the sewers in Los Angeles in May 1933.

Tea in Ceylon.—A hundred million pounds of tea were destroyed.

Peaches in U.S.A.—The big fruit growers destroyed 80,000 peach trees. (*Economic Notes,* Vol. 2, No. 3, March 1934.)

IX. INCREASE IN DISTRIBUTION COSTS

This increase is seen from the following:

The number of persons engaged in the sphere of distribution and their proportion to the total population has risen sharply (see tables on pp. 241 and 243).

Stuart Chase cites facts showing that the U.S.A. spends annually over 1.25 billion dollars on advertising. About 600,000 persons are engaged in the advertising business, directly or indirectly. Of the total amount of paper used by the newspapers, 58 per cent is used up in advertising space.

According to figures by the *Electrical World* (March 2, 1934), direct and indirect expenditure connected with the sale of an automobile priced at $4,500 may amount to $2,000. The selling cost of an electric refrigerator priced at $200 may amount to $100.

(*New Data continues on p. 262 et seq.*)

Stuart Chase asserts that "at the present time the price of commodities doubles in the passage from the producer to the consumer," and in particular "the joint Commission on Agriculture arrived at the conclusion that fifty cents out of every dollar the consumer pays for bread goes in distribution costs."

According to Warren and Pearson, in April 1933 the index of cost of distribution (the difference between the price paid by the consumer and the price received by the producer) of food products was 38 per cent higher than the pre-war level (1910-14=100) while the index of prices paid to the farmers for the same products had dropped 42 per cent below the pre-war level.

It must be borne in mind that this increase in the difference between the price paid by the consumer and that received by the producer is not only due to the increase in the cost of distribution, but also to the monopoly price policy.

SOURCES: Stuart Chase, *Tragedy of Waste*, 1927, pp. 109, 111, 214; G. A. Warren and F. Pearson, *Prices*, 1933, pp. 187-88.

X. *ARMAMENTS, WARS, INCREASE OF POLICE FORCE*

BUREAUCRACY IN THE U.S.A.[1]

Index, 1910=100

	1910	1920	1930
All civil service employees	100	138	199
Police	100	132	213

BUREAUCRACY IN GREAT BRITAIN

Index, 1922=100

1922	100
1930	106
1933	118

[1] Civil service employees, municipal employees and police.

SOURCES: U.S.A.—*Fifteenth Census of the U.S.*, Occupation Statistics, p. 16; Great Britain—*Statistical Abstract for the U.K.*, 1933.

GROWTH OF EXPENDITURE ON ARMAMENTS

The German Institute for Economic Research gives the following figures comparing the changes in world production (industry and agriculture) with those in world expenditure on armaments.

INDEX OF WORLD EXPENDITURE ON ARMAMENTS AND WORLD PRODUCTION

(Monetary values: 1913=100)

	Expenditure on armaments	World production
1913	100	100
1925	135	133
1929	157	145
1936	300-350	121

Thus, in 1936, expenditure on armaments in 53 countries was from three to three and a half times that of 1913, whereas world production was a little over twenty per cent higher than in 1913.

SOURCE: *Vierteljahrshefte zur Konjunkturforschung*, Heft 3, 1937, Teil A, S. 281.

OFFICIAL BUDGET EXPENDITURE ON ARMAMENTS [1]

(1912-13 = 100)

Countries	1912-13	1928-29	1932-33	1934-35	1937-38
U.S.A.	100	235.7	238.7	278.1	325.0 [3]
Japan.......	100	259.1	343.9	471.9	706.2
Great Britain	100 [2]	147.0	133.3	147.1	374.0

[1] Not including indirect and secret appropriations.
[2] 1913-14.
[3] 1936-37.

SOURCES: *Annual Report of the U.S. Treasury*, 1935; *Résumé Statistique de l'Empire du Japon*, 1916-36; *Statistical Abstract for the United Kingdom*, 1935; *Japan Chronicle*, 4, III, 1937.

WARS AND ARMED CONFLICTS SINCE THE WORLD WAR
OF 1914-18

Counter-Revolutionary Wars
Against the Land of the Soviets

1918....German troops invade Soviet Russia and Soviet Ukraine. Occupation of Soviet Ukraine.
1918....Seizure of Bessarabia by Rumania.
1918....Landing of British troops at Murmansk.
1918....Landing of French troops in Odessa.
1918-22 .Japanese intervention in the Far East.
1919....*Spring.* First Allied Expedition against Soviet Russia (Poland, Kolchak, Denikin, Yudenich and mixed Anglo-Russian Whiteguard detachments in Turkestan and Archangel).
1919....*Autumn.* Second Allied Expedition against Soviet Russia (Denikin, Yudenich, Poland).
1920....Third Allied Expedition against Soviet Russia (Poland, Wrangel).
1921-22 .Finnish attempt to seize Soviet Karelia.
1929....Attack on the Chinese Eastern Railway by Chinese militarists.
1931-38.Continuous violations of the Soviet-Manchurian frontier by Japano-Manchurian troops.

Since the imperialist war a number of so-called small wars have taken place.

Europe

1919....Intervention of Allies, Czechoslovakia and Rumania against the Hungarian Soviet Republic.
1919....Seizure of Fiume by Italian volunteers under the leadership of Gabriele d'Annunzio.
1920....Occupation of Frankfurt and Darmstadt by French troops.
1920....Poland occupies Vilno.
1921....Polish insurrection in former German Upper Silesia.
1923....France occupies the Ruhr.
1923....Lithuania occupies Memel region.
1923....Italy temporarily seizes Corfu.
1925....Greece invades Bulgaria.
1936-38 .Military-fascist mutiny and Italian-German intervention in Spain.
1938....Germany seizes Austria.

Africa

1919-26 .Spanish war against the Riffs in North Africa.
1925-26 .Franco-Spanish military expeditions against North-African tribes.
1929-32 .French military operations in Morocco.
1930....Italy establishes control over the whole of Tripolitania.
1934-35 .Invasion of Abyssinian territory by Italian troops.
1935-36 .Italo-Abyssinian War and seizure of Abyssinia by Italy.

South America

1928....War between Bolivia and Paraguay.
1928-32 .United States intervention in Nicaragua.
1932-33 .War between Peru and Colombia.
1932-34 .Second war between Bolivia and Paraguay.

India and Indo-China

1919....War between Great Britain and rebels on the Northwest frontier of British
    India.
1927....Dutch punitive expedition in Indonesia.
1930....French punitive expedition against the Annamites in Indo-China.
1930-31 .British colonial war in Burma on the Northwest frontier of India.
1930-37 .Continuous struggle between British troops and tribes in Northwest Prov-
    inces of India.

Near and Middle East

1919....Anglo-Afghan war.
1918-22 .Greco-Turkish war.
1919-22 .British punitive expedition against Arabian tribes in Iraq, Transjordania
    and Central Arabia.
1919-26 .French punitive expedition against rebels in Syria.
1925....War between Nejd and Hejaz in Arabia.
1928-29 .Civil war in Afghanistan provoked by agents of British imperialism.
1930....Attack on Hejaz-Nejd by border tribes operating with the support of
    British imperialists.
1932....British air forces operate against the independent Kurdish tribes in Iraq.
1934....War between Yemen and Saudi Arabia.
1936-38 .Armed collisions between British troops and insurgent Arabs in Palestine.

Far East

1925....Intervention of imperialist powers in China.
1927....International imperialist intervention in Shanghai. Bombardment of Nan-
    king.
1928....Occupation of Shantung by Japan.
1930....Bombardment of Changsha while occupied by the Chinese Red Army.
1930....First Nanking expedition against the Soviet regions and the Chinese Red
    Army.
1931-37 .Japanese war on China. Seizure of Manchuria and part of North China.
1931....*April.* Second Nanking expedition against Chinese Soviet territories begins.
1931....*May.* Failure of second expedition.
1931....*August.* Third Nanking expedition begins.
1931....*September.* Failure of third expedition.
1932....Attack on Shanghai by Japan.
1932....*February.* Fourth Nanking expedition against Chinese Soviet territories
    begins.
1932....*May.* Failure of fourth expedition.
1932....*June.* Fifth Nanking expedition begins.
1933....*July.* Failure of fifth expedition.
1933....*October.* Beginning of sixth campaign of Nanking government against Soviet
    districts of China.
1933.... Seizure of Jehol and northeastern parts of Hopei by Japan.
1933....France seizes nine Coral Islands in the Pacific.
1934....Japan seizes a great part of Chahar (Inner Mongolia).
1934....*November.* End of the sixth expedition of the Nanking government against
    the Soviet districts of China.
1934-35 .Forces of the Chinese Red Army move from south and central China to
    northwestern China.

1935....*November.* Formation of the puppet "anti-Communist" government in Eastern Hopei occupied by Japanese troops.

1936....*June-August.* Armed action by troops of Kwangtung and Kwangsi groups against Nanking government.

1936....*October.* Unification of the main forces of the Chinese Red Army in the provinces of Kansu and Shensi.

1936....*October-December.* Invasion of Suiyuan by Mongolian-Manchurian troops.

1936....Chan Hsueh-liang's mutiny against Nanking goverment in Sian-fu.

1935-36 .Invasions of territory of Mongolian People's Republic by Japano-Manchurian troops.

1937-38 .Predatory war of Japan against China.

CONCERNING NEW DATA FOR

V. I. LENIN'S

"IMPERIALISM, THE HIGHEST STAGE OF CAPITALISM"

By

LEO   MENDELSSOHN

CONCERNING NEW DATA FOR
V. I. LENIN'S
"IMPERIALISM, THE HIGHEST STAGE OF CAPITALISM"

LENIN wrote *Imperialism, the Highest Stage of Capitalism* in the first half of 1916. Since then more than twenty years have elapsed. Measured in terms of history, this is a very short period. But human history has never marched so rapidly, and the changes in social life have never been so profound as they have been during this period. We shall enumerate the most important historical events of this period: the World War, which gave rise to the general crisis of capitalism; the Great October Socialist Revolution in 1917, which ushered in the first round of revolutions all over the world; the heroical years of Civil War in the Soviet Republic; the relative stabilisation of capitalism; the Chinese revolution, the gigantic achievements of the two Five-Year Plans in the Land of the Soviets and the prolonged and acute economic crisis in the lands of capitalism; the world-historical victory of socialism in the U.S.S.R. embodied in the Stalin Constitution; the collapse of capitalist stabilisation and the opening of a new round of revolutions and wars—these are the outstanding landmarks of this period. And the whole of this rich experience of the period, all these processes and changes of world-historic importance and worldwide dimensions, brilliantly corroborate the truth of Lenin's theory of imperialism, not only in its main outline, but in all its "details." This theory is one of the foundation stones of the programme of the Communist International; it is a mighty weapon in the struggle of the oppressed of the whole world for their emancipation.

In his *Imperialism,* Lenin quotes facts and figures of the pre-war period. But the facts and figures of capitalist economy during the subsequent twenty years not only corroborate the tendencies that were indicated in the data quoted by Lenin; they also reveal that these tendencies have become more marked and developed. In the first place, they reveal the further immense growth of the power and oppression of monopolies, and the resulting growth of the parasitism and decay of capitalism. By that they lay bare one of the most decisive factors in the exceptional acuteness of the contradictions of the capitalist system which is particularly characteristic of the epoch of the general crisis of capitalism.

269

I. THE GROWTH OF CONCENTRATION OF PRODUCTION

Lenin's theory of imperialism proceeds from the premise that "the tendency towards monopoly arises from the very dimensions of the enterprises."[1]

"Economically imperialism (or the 'epoch' of finance capital, it is not a matter of words) is the highest stage in the development of capitalism, namely, the stage at which production is carried on on such a large and very large scale that *free competition is superseded by monopoly*. This is the *economic* quintessence of imperialism."[2]

This is precisely why Lenin starts his analysis of imperialism with the careful examination of the data on the concentration of capitalist production. The very latest data then available to Lenin were the industrial census of 1907 for Germany, and that of 1909 for the United States. Now, however, we have the German censuses for 1925 and 1933, and also the United States censuses for 1929 and 1933. Moreover, contemporary statistics also throw light on the process of concentration in France and Japan, with which Lenin did not deal, but which are of great interest because of the considerably more important role these two countries now play in the ranks of the imperialist powers. Finally, in 1934, figures became available for the first time on the concentration of production in British industry as a whole.

A comparison of the figures on the concentration of production quoted by Lenin with the latest figures shows that during the intervening twenty to twenty-five years, the level of concentration has risen to an enormous degree. This is one of the decisive factors which determined the immense growth of the power and oppression of monopolies.

The most important facts indicating the enormous rise in the level of capitalist concentration of production are the following:

In *Germany*, during the eighteen years from 1907 to 1925, the proportion of persons occupied in large establishments (*i.e.*, those with not less than 50 occupied) to the total number of persons occupied in industry[3] increased from 39.4 per cent to 47.6 per cent. The number of giant enterprises (with over 1,000 occupied each) almost doubled (from 586 to 1,122), and their share of the total motive power used increased from 32 per cent to 41.2 per cent.

---

[1] *Cf.* p. 18 in this volume.

[2] *Cf. Collected Works.* Vol. XIX, Russ. ed., "A Caricature of Marxism and 'Imperialist Economism,'" part 3, p. 207.

[3] In the broad sense, *i.e.*, including commerce, transportation, etc.

"Tens of thousands of large-scale enterprises are everything; millions of small ones are nothing."[1] This is the conclusion Lenin arrived at after analysing the German industrial census of 1907. Today, it is no longer tens of thousands of large-scale enterprises that occupy the decisive place, but a much smaller number. This is proved by the following glaring fact: In German industry in 1925 there were only 67 establishments which employed 5,000 workers or over. But the aggregate motive power used in these *three-score or so* establishments was twice that of 1,600,000 small establishments. Here are the exact figures: [2]

Establishments employing:	No. of establishments:	Aggr. motive power (thousand h.p.)
1 to 5 persons	1,614,069	1,368
5,000 persons and over	67	2,738

The figures of the 1933 census of German industry show a further increase in the concentration of production. During the period of 1925 to 1933 the average motive power per establishment increased by no less than 26 per cent.[3] This is evidence of a very considerable increase in the average size of German industrial establishments. During the same period approximately 124,000 small enterprises in eleven industries were closed down chiefly as a result of the economic crisis. True, in eight other industries, a total of 65,000 new enterprises were established, so that the net decrease in the number of enterprises in German industry during the period was only 58,600. The increase in the number of small enterprises in certain branches of German industry in the period of the world economic crisis is a peculiar result of the immense increase in unemployment. It reflects the attempts of a very small section of the unemployed to escape from starvation by setting up small repair shops and workshops of the domestic industry type. This, however, does not imply that the position of small industry has become stronger. On the contrary, the crisis has accelerated its ruin.

In the *United States*, during the twenty years intervening between the census of 1909 and that of 1929, the share of the total value of products of the manufacturing industry produced by the big establishments with a production valued at $1,000,000 per annum and over, increased from 43.8

---

[1] *Cf.* p. 14 in this volume.

[2] *Statistik des Deutschen Reichs*, B. 413, I. Teil, S. 274.

[3] The figures refer to industry in the narrow sense and also to the building industry; they do not include plumbing or water, gas and electricity supply.

per cent to 69.3 per cent. The number of giant establishments (employing over 1,000 workers) increased from 540 to 996; their aggregate motive power reached nearly 12,000,000 h.p. This means that less than one thousand of the biggest American establishments own approximately two-thirds of the motive power that was at the disposal of the whole of German industry (in the broad sense) in 1925, consisting as it did of over three million establishments, including the giant enterprises referred to above.

The world economic crisis gave an added impetus to the concentration of American industry. The scale on which small industry was wiped out in the United States during the crisis is indicated by the following figures:

PER CENT INCREASE OR DECREASE IN NUMBER OF ESTABLISHMENTS IN U.S. MANUFACTURING INDUSTRY

1925-29	+12.3
1929-31	—17.1
1931-33	—18.4
1929-33	—32.4

Commenting on the figures for 1931-33, *The Conference Board Bulletin*[1] justly observes that perhaps there is hardly a figure that more strikingly reveals the severity of the crisis than that showing the reduction in the number of industrial establishments by 18 per cent. As a result of the ruin of small industry, the average number of workers employed per establishment in the United States in the period 1931-33 *increased* 11.4 per cent, notwithstanding the fact that the total number of employed workers *declined* by 8.8 per cent.

In *France*,[2] in the period between 1906 and 1926, the proportion of persons occupied in large industrial establishments (with over 50 occupied) to the total number of persons engaged in industry increased from 30.6 per cent to 44.8 per cent. The number of giant industrial establishments (with 1,000 occupied and over) increased from 207 to 362, and the proportion they employed of the total number of persons engaged in industry almost doubled (from 8.1 per cent to 13.4 per cent).

---

[1] *Conference Board Bulletin*, October 10, 1934.
[2] Exclusive of Alsace-Lorraine, for otherwise the figures for 1906 and 1926 would not be comparable. The level of concentration of production in Alsace-Lorraine is somewhat higher than in the rest of France.

In *Japan*, particularly important successes have been achieved in the field of the concentration of capital and production. During the eighteen years from 1909 to 1927, the number of very large commercial and industrial companies, each having a capital exceeding 5,000,000 yen, increased eighteen-fold (from 38 to 687); their aggregate capital increased from 495,000,000 yen to 8,113,000,000 yen, and their share of total paid-up capital increased from 36.2 per cent to 64.2 per cent. Out of every hundred workers employed in Japanese industry (taking only industrial establishments employing not less than five persons), the giant establishments (employing over 1,000 workers) employed 17 in 1914, and 27 in 1925. In the period of the world economic crisis, however, the number and proportion of the industrial establishments employing over 1,000 workers diminished somewhat, for owing to the curtailment of production in many of these enterprises the number of workers they employed was reduced below 1,000.

In *Great Britain*, also, considerable success has been achieved in concentrating capital and production. According to the returns of the industrial census of 1930 there are in the textile industry and in the smelting and working-up of metals[1] alone, 353 giant establishments, each employing over 1,000 persons. This figure is very much below the figure for the United States (667), but it is not much below the German figure (430). In regard to the proportion of the total number of persons engaged in industry employed by these giant industrial establishments, a number of branches of British industry in 1930 (textiles, mechanical engineering, electrical engineering, etc.) were approximately on the same level as those in Germany in 1925 and some were even higher. All this shows that the level of concentration of production in British industry is much higher than has been usually described in world economic literature. This has been the decisive factor in the rapid growth of British monopolies in the post-war period.

In examining the progress of capitalist concentration, Lenin laid special emphasis on the outstanding importance of the growth of combination in capitalist production. In this sphere, too, enormous changes have taken place in the post-war period. Not only have the dimensions of the combined plants in those branches of industry in which they existed before the war increased several fold, but the data quoted show that the achievements of chemistry and electricity created new opportunities for combining processes in production, and gave rise to combined plants of a new

---

[1] Including mechanical engineering, electrical engineering, shipbuilding, automobile and aircraft industries.

type; they widened the sphere in which combined processes can be employed. At the same time, the combined process method has been widely adopted in several branches of industry which manufacture consumers' goods, for example, the Bata Shoe Plant in Czechoslovakia, meat packing plants, etc.

This enormous (although very uneven) progress in the concentration of production does not require special explanation. It provides fresh, brilliant confirmation of the laws of capitalist development as laid down by Marx, and which Lenin developed and took as the starting point for his analysis of the latest phase of capitalism. Mention must be made, however, of the specific conditions which have facilitated the process of concentration during the past twenty years. These include:

a) The world imperialist war, which accelerated the process of concentration. During the war the unevenness of development as between the heavy and the light industries, and the "new" and the "old" industries, became extremely marked; and it was precisely those branches of industry in which the level of concentration of production was lowest that found themselves in the worst position. Simultaneously, the enormous demand for standardised production created by the war owing to the shortage of labour power, gave a powerful impetus to the introduction of machinery and of mass production even in such industries as clothing, boots and shoes, etc., in which small production had been particularly prevalent before. These processes have been still further developed in the post-war period.

b) The increase in the productive forces of post-war capitalism—which in general has been slower than before the war, and extremely uneven—was in the main more rapid in those countries (United States) and branches of industry (heavy industry and the "new" industries) which were formerly distinguished for their high level of concentration of production. As a result, the relative importance of these countries and branches of industry in world capitalist industry has increased; and this in itself implies a higher level of concentration.

c) The important technical changes that have taken place: the increase in the dimensions of main installations such as blast furnaces, open hearth furnaces and rolling mills in the iron and steel industry, turbines in power stations, etc., and the introduction of so-called "American" methods in industry which can be employed effectively only in large-scale enterprises.

d) And finally, the fact that the competitive struggle has become exceptionally more fierce under post-war capitalism owing to the problem of markets having become more acute and to the growth of monopoly. This has intensified the struggle between large-scale and small production, and has thus accelerated the process of concentration. The shrinking of markets, which accelerates the bankruptcy of small and medium enterprises and their absorption by the larger ones, naturally leads to the acceleration of concentration. Monopoly, which grew out of the concentration of production, in its turn, affects the process of concentration; it accelerates it by its specific methods of competition, *viz.*, by "strangling" its competitors with the aid of the peculiar influence it exercises on the character and rate of technical progress, etc. The enormous growth of monopoly during the past twenty years has therefore also been an important factor in the acceleration of the process of concentration.

However, the difficulty of finding markets, the fact that the plant is chronically working below capacity, and the retarded rate of growth of the productive forces of post-war capitalism resulting from this, while accelerating the process of concentration, simultaneously create additional obstacles to capitalist concentration of production, cause all its contradictions to become extremely acute and lay bare the relative narrowness of its limits. Lenin directly points to a certain dependence of the rate of concentration of production upon the general rate of development of capitalism. He writes: ". . . the more rapidly trade and capitalism develop, the greater is the concentration of production and capital . . . ."[1] It is not an accident that the process of concentration during the past decades has been most marked in the countries (United States) and branches of industry (heavy industry, the "new" industries) which have developed most rapidly. On the other hand, Great Britain, for example, has not been able to remedy the relatively scattered nature of her iron and steel industry. To do so would have meant constructing a number of new gigantic works; but the stimulus to this was lacking owing to the fact that even the existing works have been working at their lowest capacity. Even in the United States giant automobile works like the Ford plant feel the effects of the restrictedness of markets very acutely, particularly during the crisis, when the plant was operating at low capacity, insufficient to make it pay. Hence Ford's sudden discovery that it is necessary to decentralise industry. The European countries cannot even dream

---

[1] *Cf.* p. 236 in this volume.

of having works on this scale, for with the present capacity of the markets, no one of them could be sure of working even 20 per cent of capacity, even if all other automobile plants were closed down. The rate and scale of concentration of production under modern capitalism are increasing, but they lag behind the requirements and opportunities created by modern technique. They also lag very considerably behind the rate and scale of centralisation of capital. Capitalism makes insufficient use of the great opportunities of combined production processes which the present level of technique provides. The relative narrowness of the limits of capitalist concentration of production is brought out in striking relief on the background of the achievements of the U.S.S.R., which in a short period was transformed from a country of small and dwarf agriculture into a country of the largest scale mechanized agriculture in the world, and which has built, and is still building giant industrial enterprises on a scale unknown in capitalist Europe.

The growing difficulties of the capitalist process of concentration of production, which reflect the increased decay of capitalism, did not, however, prevent this process from being very marked in the post-war period, including the period of the economic crisis. But these difficulties cause the contradictions of capitalist concentration to become more acute and determine the peculiar form it has assumed. The narrowness of the limits of the concentration process is expressed first of all in the fact that it is not proceeding on the lines of constructing new giant enterprises and extending old enterprises by the installation of new equipment to the same degree that it did before the war; and this means that the productive forces of capitalism are now increasing at a slower rate than was the case before the war. On the other hand, a much more rapid liquidation of smaller enterprises and a corresponding increase of production in larger enterprises are observed. This form of concentrating production is to be observed particularly within trustified monopolies, and in these cases the buying up of outsiders for the purpose of closing them down is widely practised. It goes without saying that concentration of production without the extensive construction of new giant enterprises, without the extensive installation of new equipment in the old enterprises, bears evidence of deep decay, and its possibilities are relatively limited. Nevertheless, this form of concentration provides a solid basis for the further growth of monopolist rule.

Secondly, the narrowness of the limits of capitalist concentration of production is expressed in the fact that the restricted capacity of the markets limits the possibilities of erecting giant enterprises such as the

Ford automobile plant and the Gary iron and steel plant, because it pays better to build smaller enterprises which have a prospect of being operated at 60 to 70 per cent of capacity than giant enterprises which can be operated at only 20 to 40 per cent of capacity.

The growth of the contradictions in the process of concentration under modern capitalism is expressed first of all in the extreme increase of its unevenness. Unevenness has always been an attribute of capitalism; it assumes particularly large dimensions in the period of the rule of monopoly. Its increase in the post-war period is a natural expression of the extreme acuteness of the competitive struggle. The unevenness of capitalist concentration explains why monopoly does not embrace all branches of industry but serves merely as a super-structure resting upon a broad base of non-monopolised production. "Not in every branch of industry are there large-scale enterprises," said Lenin,[1] emphasising the unevenness of the process of concentration. The fact that the process of concentration is becoming more and more uneven causes the gulf between the economic might of the small stratum of giant enterprises and the hundreds of thousands and millions of medium and small enterprises to become rapidly wider; and among the medium enterprises are now included such as were regarded as giants twenty or thirty years ago. But it is precisely this rapid growth of the supremacy of a few giant enterprises over all the rest that serves as a mighty factor in increasing the yoke of monopoly.

II. THE GROWTH OF INDUSTRIAL MONOPOLIES

A comparison of the data on the growth of monopolies quoted by Lenin with the latest data *not only reveals the enormous growth of monopolies, but also the obvious acceleration of the rate of growth in the war and post-war periods compared with the pre-war period.*

This is indicated by the following facts: The increase in the number of cartel agreements in Germany in the period 1896 to 1911 amounted to 300-350 (from 250 to 550-600) but in the period 1911 to 1930 the increase amounted to 1,500-1,550 (from 550-600 to 2,100). As examples of powerful monopolies Lenin mentioned the Rhine-Westphalian Coal Syndicate, the Gelsenkirchen Mining Co., the chemical combine in Germany, the U.S. Steel Corp. and Standard Oil in the United States, etc. But the present steel trust in Germany is four to five times larger than the Gelsen-

---

[1] *Cf.* p. 28 in this volume.

kirchen Co. was before the war. The capital of the present German chemical trust is twenty times larger than either of the two groups of chemical concerns to which Lenin referred. The output capacity of the United States Steel Corp. is 27,000,000 tons of steel per annum, compared with 14,000,000 tons in 1908.

Thus the United States Steel Corp. can now produce one and a half times more steel than Great Britain, Germany, France and Italy put together could produce in 1932. Nevertheless, the United States Steel Corp.'s share of the total steel output of America has dropped, for other monopolies have arisen, primarily, the Bethlehem Steel Corp., which can produce 10,000,000 tons of steel per annum, i.e., more than Great Britain produced in her best post-war years. The capital of Standard Oil (which in 1911 formally broke up into a number of independent companies in order to evade the anti-trust laws) has increased approximately twenty-fold compared with what it was in 1910; the market value of the stock of the companies it controls has reached the enormous total of over $5,000,000,000. All this indicates the tremendous growth in the size of monopolies and their economic power during the period since Lenin wrote *Imperialism*.

The increase in the power of monopolies is also strikingly illustrated by their profits. The following are a few examples: The profits of the General Motors Corp. even in the best pre-war years never exceeded $10,000,000; in 1928 they exceeded a quarter of a billion ($272,000,000). The Bethlehem Steel Corp., the second largest iron and steel trust in the United States, made as much profit in 1929 as it made during the whole of the last ten years preceding the war. In a period of six years, from 1922 to 1928, the Radio Corporation of America increased its profits sevenfold. These figures are most likely an understatement, for a large part of the profits is distributed in a concealed form. The tribute which monopolies impose upon society can be seen from the following striking examples: The net profits the United States Steel Corp. obtained in the period 1901 to 1930 amounted to about $4,500,000,000; during the period 1912 to 1930 Standard Oil made profits amounting to over $4,000,000,000; the profits of General Motors in the period 1909 to 1932 amounted to about $1,600,000,000; in the period 1915 to 1932 duPont de Nemours & Co. made profits amounting to over $1,100,000,000; the profits of the American Telephone & Telegraph Co. in the period 1900 to 1932 together with those of its subsidiary, the Bell Telephone Co., in the period 1915 to 1932, amounted to over $4,200,000,000, etc.

Combined approximate data on the level achieved in the monopolisation of production are given in the following table:

APPROXIMATE DEGREE OF MONOPOLISATION OF PRODUCTION
(Not including cartel and syndicate agreements)

Industry	Year	No. of monopolist enterprises taken into account	Degree to which they cover given industry (%)	Degree to which the largest monopoly covers given industry (%)
UNITED STATES OF AMERICA				
Anthracite	—	6	90	45
Iron ore	1931	4	60	43
Oil	1932	1	45-50	45-50
Steel	1932	3	60	40
Copper	1933	5	98	37
Aluminium	1928	1	95-100	95-100
Explosives	1917	1	65-80	65-80
Sodium	1930	1	60	60
Artificial silk	1933	6	80	33
Automobiles	1933	3	89	50
Agricultural machinery	1918	1	65	65
Electrical engineering	1923	2	75-80	40-50
Telephone and telegraph	1930	1	75	75
Radio	1930	1	95-100	95-100
Meat packing	1929	4	70	—
Sugar	1928	2	46	—
Baking	1928	3	18	—
Tobacco	1930	4	79	41
Railways	1930	14	86	12
Electric power	—	8	74	23
GREAT BRITAIN				
Iron and steel	1934	10	70-75	16
Aluminium	1928	1	100	100
Automobiles	1933	1	50	50
Shipbuilding	1926	10	66	—
Basic chemicals	1928	1	95	95
Synthetic nitrogen	1928	1	100	100
Synthetic dyes	1928	1	40	40
Artificial silk	1930	1	80	80
Cement	1926	2	60-70	—
Cotton	1932	1	20-25	20-25
Thread	1926	1	80	80
Tobacco	1923	1	60-70	60-70
Beer and spirits	1926	1	80	80
Soap	1926	1	90	90
Margarine	1932	1	90	90
Rubber tires	1926	1	90	90
Wallpaper	1926	1	90	90
Railways	1931	4	95	—
Shipping	1932	6	50	—

Industry	Year	No. of monopolist enterprises taken into account	Degree to which they cover given industry (%)	Degree to which the largest monopoly covers given industry (%)
GERMANY				
Coal	1933	10	45	17-20
Pig iron	1932	5	86	53
Steel	1932	5	73	38
Aluminium	1928	1	80-85	80-85
Automobiles	1932	4	71	30
Electrical engineering	1932	2	60-80	—
Synthetic dyes	1928	1	95-100	95-100
Synthetic nitrogen	1932	1	80	80
Mineral acids	1928	1	90	90
Artificial silk	1930	3	70	—
Potassium	1932	6	100	41
Margarine	1928	1	75-80	75-80
Shipbuilding	1929	3	75	36
Shipping	1930	1	61	61
FRANCE				
Iron and steel	1933	10	72	16
Aluminium	1928	2	100	90
Basic chemicals	1928	1	70	70
Synthetic nitrogen	1928	1	40	40
Synthetic dyes	1928	1	80	80
Electrical engineering	1931	1	60	60
Electricity supply	1931	2	90-100	50
Railways	1931	4	70	—
Automobiles	1932	3	75	33
JAPAN				
Coal	1930	2	50	30
Iron and steel	1929	3	75	42
Copper	1927	5	87	23
Synthetic nitrogen	1928	2	79	43
Cement	1932	2	70	50
Cotton	1929	5	54	14
Paper	1928	1	76	76
Flour milling	1929	2	82	45
Sugar	1928	2	78	44
Electricity supply	1930	5	50	—
Artificial silk	1933	4	73	24

SOURCES: Laidler, *Concentration of Control in American Industry*, 1931; *Handbuch der Internationalen Petroleumindustrie*, 1933-34; *American Iron and Steel Institute*, 1932; *Yearbook of the American Bureau of Metal Statistics*, 1933; *Die wirtschaftlichen Kräfte der Welt*, Dresdner Bank, 1930; *Commercial and Financial Chronicle*, 1934; American Telephone & Telegraph Co. Annual Reports, *Chicago Daily Tribune*, 18, V, 1934; Neumann, *Economic Organisation of the British Coal Industry*, 1934; *Financial News*, 1933-34; *Economist*, 11, VI, 1934, 4, VIII, 1934; Fitzgerald, *Industrial Combination in England*, 1927; *Chemische Industrie*, 1933-34; *Returns of the Railway Cos. of Great Britain*, 1931; *The Stock Exchange Yearbook*, 1933-34; *Grünbuch der Aktiengesellschaften*, 1934; *Deutsche Bergwerkszeitung*, 2, VIII, 1933; *Der Deutsche Volkswirt*, 1934; *Wirtschaftskurve der Frankfurter Zeitung*, 1931; *Statistique des Chemins de fer Français*, 1931; Inomata Tsuneo, *Financial Capital in Japan*; Takahashi Kamekiti, *Investigation of Investments of Big Concerns* (in Japanese) and periodicals for respective branches.

The actual degree of monopolisation of production is much higher than that indicated in the table. In the first place, the table does not contain all branches of industry that are monopolised. Secondly, in the branches that are given, only the biggest monopolies have been taken into account. Thirdly, a number of industries given separately in the table are often controlled by one and the same monopolies. Fourthly, a great many monopolies are closely interlocked and this fact is not brought out in the table. Fifthly, the table only deals with the biggest trusts and concerns, and entirely leaves out cartel and similar agreements.

The latter is particularly important, as is strikingly illustrated by the following example: In the German coal industry there are about ten monopolies of the trust type, and the biggest of these monopolies, the Steel Trust, controls from 17 to 20 per cent of the coal output of the country. But if we take into account monopolies of the cartel-syndicate type we shall find that the Rhine-Westphalian Coal Syndicate alone controls 99.6 per cent of the coal output of the Ruhr and 74.5 per cent of the total coal output of the country.

The degree to which separate spheres of production are controlled by cartels in Germany today [1] is illustrated by the following:

Manufactures Controlled by Cartels	Degree of Control (%)
Potassium, pig iron, coal, iron bars, tin plate, drawn wire, electric metres, pottery, synthetic nitrogen, sugar, lime, wire netting, soap, glass, cement, cigarettes, automobile tires, tobacco, chemicals, drugs...	95-100
Machinery, boilers, apparatus, railway cars, newsprint, flax yarn, jute fabrics, silk, artificial silk..................................	80-95
Alloy steels, salt, fabric belts	60-70
Window glass, cotton fabrics	40-50

---

[1] It is difficult to make a similar computation for other countries. The number of industrial cartels in France and Great Britain, however, is approximately as follows:

	France	Great Britain
Total number of cartels	87	181
Cartels in:		
Heavy industry (mining, iron and steel, mechanical engineering, electrical engineering, chemicals)	64	109
Light industry (textiles, leather, paper, food products)............................	16	42
Building and building materials	5	29

SOURCES: Wagenführ, *Kartelle in Deutschland;* Fischer-Wagenführ, *Kartelle in Europa (ohne Deutschland);* *Kartellrundschau,* 1928-34; *Wochenbericht des Instituts für Konjunkturforschung,* 22, VIII, 1934; *Frankfurter Zeitung,* 23, IX, 1934.

The degree of monopolisation indicated in the above table is an underestimation; nevertheless, it gives an idea of the enormous power wielded by the monopolies, uneven though that power is in the different industries and countries.

How is the fact that the power of monopolies is growing at such an extremely accelerated rate in the midst of the general crisis of capitalism to be explained? The most important factor in the growth of monopoly was the progress made in the concentration of capitalist industry during the war and in the post-war period. Simultaneously, the following factors were particularly effective in accelerating the growth of monopoly during the last decades:

a) The imperialist war, which greatly accelerated the growth of monopolies. Speaking of monopolies, Lenin said: "The war increased their number, role and importance tenfold."[1] The monopolies became the core of the state-capitalist organisations which during the war controlled industry, and distributed orders and raw materials (the war corporations and munition industry combines in Germany, United States and other countries). This greatly strengthened the position of the monopolies, and the latter took advantage of this not only for the purpose of making huge super-profits out of the war, but also for the purpose of widening their spheres of domination by eliminating outsiders, in order to capture new branches of industry, etc. In this they were directly assisted by the state, which not infrequently created monopolies by compulsory and semi-compulsory methods. The whole system of war-time state-monopoly capitalism, which grew out of the domination of the monopolies, was at the same time a powerful lever for increasing this domination.

b) Never in the history of capitalism has the process of centralisation of capital been so rapid as it was during the war and the post-war periods. This could not but accelerate the growth of monopolies. The war and the huge super-profits it provided for a handful of monopolists, thus causing universal impoverishment; inflation in the first years of the post-war period, when colossal fortunes were made within a few months causing the ruin of the broad masses of the people; the exceptionally acute competitive struggle that broke out in the post-war period; and finally, the exceptionally acute and prolonged world economic crisis—all this served to accelerate the centralisation of capital and thus facilitated and accelerated the growth of monopolies.

c) The growth during the war and post-war periods of the "new" industries, which from the start were always on the highest level of

---

[1] Lenin, *Collected Works*, Vol. XXI, p. 187, Russ. ed.

monopolisation, also served to accelerate the growth of monopolies. The most rapid growth of monopolies was observed in the chemical, automobile, oil, aluminium, artificial silk industries, etc. This was facilitated by the high level of concentration of production and of the organic composition of the capital in these industries. In those countries where these industries were introduced for the first time, they immediately assumed the form of powerful monopolies. The table on pages 279-80 in this volume shows that these industries hold first place in regard to the level of monopolisation.

d) The fact that the industrial apparatus is chronically working below capacity, and the specific difficulties in obtaining markets that arose in the post-war period, have also helped to accelerate the growth of monopolies. For example, one of the most important factors which stimulated the creation of the German Steel Trust in 1926 was the effort to concentrate the largest possible number of enterprises under a single ownership in order to close down the smaller and more backward enterprises and thus to run the larger and technically better equipped enterprises at fuller capacity. Another stimulus was the effort to create conditions for introducing greater specialisation for the various enterprises. This example is very typical of the rapid trustification movement that assumed very large proportions in the period of capitalist stabilisation, and which became inseparably interwoven with the so-called "rationalisation" of industry. The expansion and strengthening of monopolies, the transition from the lower to the higher forms of monopoly (particularly to combines of the trust type), these were the lines on which the monopolies strove to increase their super-profits when markets were hard to find, when enterprises were working below capacity, and when the struggle for world markets assumed unprecedented acuteness.

e) As a result of the particular severity of the struggle for world markets, the growth of monopoly was greatly accelerated even in those countries which had formerly lagged behind in this respect. This applies primarily to Great Britain, where this acceleration was due in a large degree to the growth of the "new" industries. But important changes also took place in the "old" industries, particularly immediately before the crisis and during the crisis. It is sufficient to mention the formation of the Lancashire Cotton Corporation, one of the largest monopolies in the world cotton industry, to illustrate this point. The data quoted on pages 37, 39, 41, 43 in this volume show that the growth of British monopolies, which increased in the period 1926-29, assumed particularly large dimensions during the period of the world economic crisis. Of course, this does not mean that Great Britain has already caught up with Germany and the United States in regard to the degree of monopolisation of industry. Great Britain still lags behind in this respect, and the principal obstacle that hinders the growth of British monopolies is the fact that the "old" British industries lag behind the corresponding industries in Germany and the United States in regard to degree of concentration of production.

f) A by no means unimportant factor in the acceleration of the growth of monopoly was that the unevenness of capitalist development became extremely marked in the post-war period. The rapid growth of French industry in Europe, and the still more rapid growth of Japanese industry in Asia, were accompanied by an accelerated growth in the power of monopoly in those countries.

The power of the Japanese monopolies is strikingly illustrated by the fact that the four biggest concerns in that country control about half of the total paid-up capital of all companies in Japan. The fact that the colossal growth of Japanese monopolies is taking place when relations of a feudal type still play an important role in the country merely serves to increase the oppression exercised by these monopolies.

During the period of the economic crisis we witnessed the collapse of a number of big monopolies owing to their failure to withstand the competition of their more powerful rivals. Taken as a whole, however, the period of crisis was a period in which the role of monopolies, and the oppression they exercised, increased to a considerable extent.

The following figures, although incomplete, are nevertheless sufficient to indicate the changes that have taken place in the sphere of cartelisation during the period of the world economic crisis:

NATIONAL CARTELS IN PERIOD OF ECONOMIC CRISIS [1]

(January 1930 to August 1934)

	11 European countries	Germany only
Cartels revived	132	61
Collapsed	89	49
Newly formed	277	142

The period of crisis witnessed the collapse of numerous cartels, many of which were subsequently revived. But the number of newly formed car-

---

[1] Calculated by the "Konjunktur" Dept. of the Institute of World Economics and World Politics, Moscow, on the basis of data published in *Kartellrundschau*, 1930-34.

tels exceeds the number that collapsed, even if allowance is made for the fact that many cartels which actually ceased to function in the first years of the crisis were not officially dissolved, and therefore were not included in the figures of dissolved cartels. As a matter of fact, as a result of the crisis, the degree of cartelisation increased to a considerable extent. It is characteristic also that in Germany, the country in which the cartel system is most highly developed, the rate of *collapse* of cartels sharply diminished during the two years from July 1932 to August 1934, whereas the rate at which new cartels were formed has greatly increased compared with the first years of the crisis. This is shown in the following table:

NATIONAL CARTELS IN GERMANY[1]

	Annual Averages for Period:	
	Jan. 1930 to June 1932	July 1932 to July 1934
Cartels revived.............	13	14
Collapsed	15	5
Newly formed..............	18	47

The considerable acceleration of the process of cartelisation during these two years was due to the crisis passing into the "depression of a special kind," and particularly to the policy of compulsory cartelisation pursued by the fascist government of Germany.

An important instrument for strengthening monopolies during the crisis was the buying up of the shares of competing enterprises which had depreciated as a result of Stock Exchange slumps. It is also extremely characteristic that during the crisis the monopolies very widely utilised the authority, and particularly the treasury, of the state in order to strengthen their position.

In all countries during the crisis, the monopolies, threatened with bankruptcy, obtained billions in subsidies with the aid of which they brought about what was called the "reconstruction" of their enterprises. For example, the reconstruction of the Dresdner Bank alone cost the German government more than half a billion marks. On preceding pages the reader will find characteristic examples of the manner in which state funds were widely used for the purpose of saving the monopolies from bankruptcy. There were other ways, too, by which the monopolies extracted funds from the state treasury: for example, subsidies for the

---

[1] *Ibid.*

building of munition works, government orders, particularly orders for armaments, etc. Taxation, which inexorably reduces the standard of living of the toilers, serves here as a material source for the enrichment of the monopolists.

In the process of the struggle for a capitalist way out of the crisis, measures were adopted in several countries which, directly or indirectly, led to the strengthening of the domination of monopolies. Among these were the so-called "codes of fair competition" introduced by Roosevelt in United States industry; compulsory curtailment of production (the most striking example of which was the closing of oil wells by armed force in the United States); the compulsory syndication and cartelisation of enterprises, or compelling outsiders to join existing syndicates or cartels (compulsory membership of the wire cartel, the cement syndicates, cigarette cartel, paper cartel, glass cartel, salt cartel, dairy produce syndicates, etc., in Germany, the compulsory cartelisation of the iron and steel industry in Italy, the cartelisation of a number of industries with the aid of the state in Japan, etc.); the introduction of state control over new industrial construction and the direct prohibition of such construction in various industries in Germany, Italy and other countries, and a number of other measures of a similar kind. In a number of cases, the measures facilitating the strengthening of the monopolies were camouflaged by demagogic phrases about "restricting" the sphere of operation of monopolies. This applies particularly to the policy pursued by the government of fascist Germany. The case of the German Steel Trust is characteristic in this respect. In 1932, when the directors of the trust were in financial difficulties, the German government purchased the control block of shares of the Gelsenkirchen Mining Co., by which the state obtained control over the Steel Trust. The shares were purchased at a price far exceeding the market price on the pretext that it was done to prevent them from passing into foreign hands. In 1933, the fascist government, under pressure of the manufacturers, brought about the "reorganisation" of the trust, as a result of which the government lost the position in the trust which it had acquired by purchasing the shares. The reorganisation, which took the form of technical and production decentralisation and the formation of thirteen separate companies, actually increased the role of the leading men in the trust. Thyssen, the actual head of the trust, is a member of the board of every one of these companies; these boards have no power to deal with questions of finance, investments and the purchase of raw materials; these matters are dealt with by the central body. The outcome of these two operations, each of which was carried out on the plea of protecting "public interests," was that the government made a present to the leaders of the steel trust of the nice round sum of 100,000,000 marks.

The Social-Democrats, misinterpreting the real position, tried to make it appear that the government's measures for the purpose of strengthening the positions of monopolist capital signified that capitalism was entering into a new era, *i.e.*, the era of state capitalism, in which, they alleged, the private interests of the monopolies are subordinated to the interests of the state. But it is precisely the growth of the tendencies towards state capitalism in the period of the crisis and of the depression of a special kind which, by increasing the oppression of finance capital, more glaringly than ever proves that "state monopoly in capitalist society is nothing more than a means of increasing and guaranteeing the income of millionaires on the verge of bankruptcy in one branch of industry or another."[1]

III. THE GROWTH OF BANK MONOPOLIES AND OF THE FINANCIAL OLIGARCHY

The much higher level attained in the concentration of capitalist production and the even greater increase in the dimensions, number and importance of industrial monopolies, brilliantly confirm the truth of Lenin's theory of imperialism. Lenin's thesis that: "the rise of monopolies, as the result of the concentration of production, is a general and fundamental law of the present stage of development of capitalism,"[2] is here put to an excellent historical test. Similarly, the new data on the concentration of banks and the growth of bank monopolies also confirm the truth of this theory.

In Lenin's opinion, one of the most important indices of the degree of concentration of banks and of the change which their role in capitalist economics has undergone, was the enormous increase in bank deposits. But never, perhaps, has this increase been so rapid as it has been in the post-war period. In order to illustrate the rapid increase in bank deposits Lenin points to the increase in the deposits of the German banks during the last five years before the war by 2,800,000,000 marks, or by almost 40 per cent. In the period of inflation, deposits in German banks catastro-

---

[1] *Cf.* p. 92 in this volume.
[2] *Cf.* p. 38 in this volume.

phically declined, and in 1924 they dropped to about one-fifth of the level of 1912-13. During the three subsequent years (1924 to 1927), however, deposits increased sevenfold, and exceeded the level of 1912-13 by almost 40 per cent. During the next two years there was a further increase in deposits of about 3,500,000,000 marks; and it was only during the crisis that this rapid increase ceased and a decline set in. During the thirty-three years preceding the war (1880 to 1913) the total deposits in banks and savings banks in the four biggest imperialist countries—*i.e.*, Great Britain, Germany, France and the United States—increased by an equivalent of 127,000,000,000 marks, and during the subsequent fifteen years (1913 to 1928) they increased by an equivalent of 183,000,000,000 marks. This shows that during the period of the general crisis of capitalism, the process of concentration of social wealth in the hands of the magnates of finance capital was accelerated to an enormous degree.

The increase of the role and importance of the big monopolies in the banking system was even more rapid. From 1914 to 1933, six existing German banks (of which three were Berlin banks) absorbed 191 banks having 1,699 branches. The very diminution of the number of big banks controlling the credit resources of the country is in itself instructive. For 1912-13. Lenin gives the figure of nine big Berlin banks, of which six were very big banks; but as a result of a number of mergers which took place in the post-war period, particularly during the period of the economic crisis, their number was reduced to four, of which three are giant banks of colossal power. But the share of the total bank deposits held by these four banks amounted to 63 per cent in 1931, whereas in 1912-13 the share of nine banks was only 49 per cent. Before the war, the six big Berlin banks had 450 branches, agencies, controlled banks, etc., whereas in 1932, three banks had 844 institutions of this kind.

Data for other countries also corroborates the fact that the power of finance capital is increasing with astonishing rapidity in the post-war period. In the United States, during eleven years (1923 to 1934), the share of total deposits held by banks having a capital of over $5,000,000 each more than doubled (from 22 per cent to 48 per cent). In Japan, during nine years (1926 to 1935), the share of total deposits held by five big banks increased from 24 per cent to 43 per cent. A particularly large increase in the importance of bank monopolies compared with the pre-war period is observed in Great Britain. The share of total deposits held by the five big British banks increased from 27 per cent in 1900 to 40 per cent in 1913, and by 1924 it had increased to 72 per cent. This unexampled growth in the importance of the big banks which led to the formation of what is known as "the Big Five," was brought about as a result of a number of bank mergers and absorptions. Lenin mentions that in 1910 the British banks had 7,100 branches; in 1935, over 5,000 new branches had been added to these.

The number of branches of French banks increased more than 150 per cent compared with the pre-war period.

The enormous concentration of banks is illustrated in the following table:

DEPOSITS OF THE BIGGEST BANK
(millions)

	1913	1936
In Great Britain (£).	89	487 [1]
„ Germany (M)	1,573	2,652 [2]
„ United States ($)	181	2,286 [3]

An important factor in this astonishingly rapid concentration of the banks was the world economic crisis. During the crisis there was a marked decline in total bank deposits in the majority of countries. The crisis shook the banking system very severely and caused the bankruptcy of such giants as the Danat Bank and the Dresdner Bank in Germany. The credit crisis, among other things, caused the bank monopolies to resort to the state treasuries for the purpose of reinforcing their position; and it also hastened the bankruptcy of the small banks. In the United States, for example, in the period from 1921 to 1929, when the concentration of banks on the whole proceeded at a very rapid rate, about 4,000 small banks failed. During the period of the crisis, 1,352 banks failed in 1930, 2,294 in 1931 and 1,456 in 1932. From 1929 to December 1933 the total number of banks in the United States was reduced from 25,000 to 15,000.

A similar but more rapid process took place in Japan, where the number of banks diminished from 2,155 in 1914 to 1,001 in 1929, and to 563 in 1935.

The crisis of 1929, and the years immediately preceding this crisis witnessed the largest bank mergers. This was a reflection of the enor-- mous growth of industrial monopolies, and was at the same time an important instrument for the further acceleration of this growth.

Simultaneously with the growth of the power of bank monopolies, there was an increase in the process of coalescence of the latter with the indus-

---

[1] Midland Bank, Ltd.
[2] Deutsche Bank–Disconto-Gesellschaft.
[3] Chase National Bank.

trial monopolies. In proof of the high degree of this coalescence, Lenin quotes Jeidels, according to whom, in 1903, the six Berlin banks had their representatives in 751 companies. As a result of mergers the number of banks had been reduced by half in 1932, and the number of companies in which they had representatives was at least doubled. These figures give only a faint idea of the real extent to which the connection between the banks and industry has grown during the past decades.

Lenin wrote: "The supremacy of finance capital over all other forms of capital means the predominance of the rentier and of the financial oligarchy."[1] It is obvious that the enormous acceleration of the growth of industrial and bank monopolies which occurred during the war and in the post-war period could not but have been accompanied by an unprecedented growth of the power of the financial oligarchy and of the rentier. As important evidence of the growth of finance capital and of the financial oligarchy Lenin quoted the enormous increase in total capital issues in the first decade of the twentieth century, during which they increased from 100 billion francs to 193 billion francs. But in the period 1921 to 1930, this total had increased to about 550 billion francs of pre-war parity. In the five years 1926 to 1930 alone, new securities were issued amounting to 333 billion pre-war francs, which is a threefold increase compared with the pre-war level. Total current securities also increased to a large extent, and it is instructive to note in this connection that the total value of securities quoted on the *New York Stock Exchange alone* in January 1929 (calculated in pre-war francs) was greater than the total value of securities current in the *whole of the capitalist world in 1910.*

The growth of the financial oligarchy implies an increase in the tribute which this oligarchy imposes upon society. First of all, promoters' profits have increased enormously compared with those in the pre-war period. Lenin quotes data showing that bank profits derived from the issue of industrial shares in Germany constituted on an average 50 per cent. But the total issue of securities has increased enormously, and with that the income from the issue of securities must have increased also. In particular, the considerable "watering" of the capital of the big monopolies in the post-war period is evidence of the enormous increase in the profits of the financial oligarchy. The watering of capital is a favourite method of obtaining promoters' profits and of concealing from the public the actual amount of profits obtained.

An important source of profit for the financial oligarchy is stock

----

[1] *Cf.* p. 132 in this volume.

exchange speculation. This has grown very rapidly in the post-war period. It is sufficient to state that in the United States, in the two and a half years preceding the crisis, the price of stocks increased 2.3 times, and that in the period of the crisis the price of stocks fluctuated twenty, thirty, forty per cent and more in the course of weeks or even days. This tremendous fluctuation in the price of stocks provided the big stock exchange sharks with opportunities to make huge profits by ruining large numbers of small investors. The loss in stock exchange values during the period of the crisis in the United States alone amounted to scores of billions of dollars; but by the very nature of stock exchange speculation, the loss of some is a source of profit for others. In particular, stock exchange failures were widely utilised by the big monopolies for the purpose of buying up the shares of a great number of enterprises for next to nothing. Lenin wrote:

". . . The development of capitalism has arrived at a stage when, although commodity production still 'reigns' and continues to be regarded as the basis of economic life, it has in reality been undermined and the big profits go to the 'geniuses' of financial manipulation. At the basis of these swindles and manipulations lies socialised production; but the immense progress of humanity, which achieved this socialisation, goes to benefit the speculators."[1]

During an economic crisis, when the catastrophic diminution of the number of workers exploited cannot be fully compensated by increasing the rate of their exploitation, the proportion of profits obtained from speculation to total monopoly income increases with particular rapidity. On the basis of the general increase in speculation "legitimate" forms of income from stock exchange speculation and stock exchange swindling are supplemented by frauds like the Stavisky affair in France, which came to light in the beginning of 1934 and involved a sum of about a billion francs. The parasitic nature of the financial oligarchy reveals itself here in all its nakedness.

One of the most important bases of the power of the financial oligarchy is the holding system. A comparison between the data quoted by Lenin and the new data shows that in this sphere, also, monopoly has made enormous progress. The role of joint stock companies has greatly increased. The variety of organisational forms which the control and holding systems assume has increased considerably. The data quoted on preceding pages shows that with the aid of a multiple storey system of holdings, the monopolists obtain control over a group of joint stock companies, even if they own only an insignificant share (one per cent and less) of their

---

[1] *Cf.* p. 58 in this volume.

capital. The control of the capital of numerous enterprises by a single centre by means of the holding system has reached enormous dimensions. For example, in his book, *The House of Morgan,* L. Corey calculates that the capital controlled by Morgan and his partners on the eve of the crisis amounted to $74,000,000,000; they held in their hands 72 corporations with assets amounting to a total of $20,000,000,000. According to the figures published in May 1929 by the American Bankers' Association, twenty-four New York bankers are directors of 438 enterprises, of which 297 are industrial and commercial enterprises; one of these bankers heads 47 concerns, etc. An official document submitted to the United States Congress points out that in the public utility companies alone there are 90 persons each of whom is a member of the board of directors, or supervisory board, of no less than 50 enterprises, and fifteen of whom are directors of 2,117 enterprises. The same is the case in other countries, although on a smaller scale.

Thus, it can be said that the number of persons who actually control the wealth of capitalist society is steadily diminishing. Lenin referred to three hundred capitalists who governed Germany; but under post-war capitalism their number is much smaller. The pro-fascist writer Ferdinand Fried, in analysing the "oligarchy of wealth" points out that 100 to 140 persons hold the economic key positions in Germany. The former United States ambassador in Berlin, Gerard, gives a list of 64 persons who control the wealth of the United States. *Bergwerkszeitung,* the organ of German heavy industry, points out that only 100 persons control the joint stock companies in France, and that at the head of this 100 there are two men who are the embodiment of the whole might of finance capital in the country.

IV. THE EXPORT OF CAPITAL

The latest data on the export of capital also prove that the principal features of the economics of imperialism that were revealed by Lenin have undergone further development. This is extremely important, for, according to Lenin, the export of capital is "one of the essential economic bases of imperialism." A comparison between the data on capital exports quoted by Lenin and later data reveals the following:

1. *A large increase in total foreign investments.* For the four countries, Great Britain, United States, Germany and France, the increase in 1930 compared with 1914 amounts to an equivalent of 20 to 40 billion pre-war francs. This increase took place in spite of the fact that a con-

siderable amount of foreign investments were lost as a consequence of
the imperialist war and the October Revolution. Germany lost all her foreign investments (about 44 billion francs), France lost 23 billion francs,
Great Britain was compelled to dispose of one-fourth of her foreign investments in order to finance the war, etc.

2. *Important changes in the roles of various countries in the capital
export market.* The most important of these are the passing of the role of
principal exporter of capital from Great Britain to the United States, and
the cessation of capital exports from Germany. The United States has increased her foreign investments 8 to 9 fold, and has almost caught up
(if war loans are included, has actually caught up) with Great Britain,
whose foreign investments accumulated over a long period of years.
It is important to note that the increase of the United States' foreign
investments occurred at a time when Great Britain and France (not to
speak of Germany) have evidently not exceeded their pre-war total of
foreign investments to any extent, notwithstanding the large capital exports
in the period of stabilisation.

3. *Important changes in the direction of capital exports.* First of all,
Russia has dropped out as a sphere of investment and as a source of
super-profit. Secondly, Germany has now entered the list of countries
which import capital. The technically and economically most advanced
country in Europe has now become a source of super-profit obtained
from capital exports. Thirdly, owing in the main to United States expansion, the importance of Central and South America as spheres of
foreign investments has increased. Taking advantage of her financial and
economic superiority, the United States is utilising her increased investments in these countries, in addition to other economic and extra-economic
measures, to squeeze Great Britain out of these markets, and to strengthen
her own position on the American continent. Fourthly, the importance
of China as a sphere of investment has greatly increased. According to
Remer (*cf.* page 139 in this volume), from 1914 to 1929-30, foreign investments in China increased from $1,610,000,000 to $3,243,000,000. Of this
total, Japanese investments account for an increase from $220,000,000 to
$1,137,000,000; British investments increased from $608,000,000 to
$1,189,000,000 and those of the United States from $49,000,000 to
$197,000,000. The figures for the U.S.A. are obviously an underestima-
tion.

4. *A tendency towards retardation of the rate of capital exports.*
While the rate of capital exports from the United States (and from several
other countries during the period of stabilisation) was accelerated, the

export of capital from imperialist countries as a whole (except for certain years) was undoubtedly slower compared with the pre-war rate. It is sufficient to mention that during the period 1902 to 1914, the increase in foreign investments from four countries ranged from 70 to 100 billion francs of pre-war parity, as against an increase of 20 to 40 billion francs during the period 1914 to 1930.

The slowing down of the rate of capital exports cannot be explained by the fact that Germany has dropped out as an exporter of capital, for the difference thus caused is more than compensated for by increased capital exports from the United States.

Nor is it possible to speak of the diminution of the role of capital exports as a weapon in the struggle for spheres of influence in general, and for markets in particular. The post-war period has witnessed a particularly sharp increase in the acuteness of this struggle, and this necessarily served as an increased stimulus to the export of capital. Evidently also, the diminution in the rate of capital exports cannot be ascribed to the diminution in the resources for such exports. It is generally known that Great Britain, France and other countries have had large amounts of free capital in the post-war period. A large portion of this free capital flows from country to country in the form of short-term investments, and thus serves as a contributory factor in the instability of the world money market and in the growth of stock exchange speculation. The fact that investors are less eager today to invest in long-term investments than they were before the war is due to the unstable position of capitalism in the midst of its general crisis, to the shrinking of the realm of capital as a consequence of the formation of the Soviet Union, and to the growth of colonial revolutions. An important factor that served to retard the export of capital during the period of the world economic crisis was the disorganization of world economic intercourse as a result of the depreciation of currency, the ban on gold exports, refusal to meet foreign debts and commercial obligations, etc.

The Great Socialist Revolution deprived western capitalism of billions of money invested in tsarist Russia. This huge country no longer serves as a profitable market for export capital.

The growth of colonial revolutions, particularly of the Chinese revolution, is causing the imperialists to become concerned about the safety of their investments in backward countries and thereby lessens the stimulus to make new investments. Nor are investors sure of the safety of their investments in European countries owing to the instability of the

political situation in those countries and their severe economic position.
The greatly enhanced danger of a new world war on the part of the fascist aggressors and the wars carried on by them in China, Spain and Abyssinia are a particularly great hindrance to the export of capital. Finally it
must be borne in mind that during twelve or fifteen years of the past two
decades specific obstacles to the export of capital have existed. First of all,
there was the period of the war, when the belligerent countries were largely
cut off from the outside world. Secondly, there was the period of post-war
inflation, which greatly hindered long-term foreign investments. Thirdly,
there was the period of the world economic crisis. The latter led to the
bankruptcy of a number of states which were unable to pay interest and
sinking fund payments on foreign obligations. During the period of the
crisis, a large portion of foreign investments depreciated in value and the
incomes received from them appreciably declined; the export of new capital greatly diminished. All these were factors that hindered the export of
capital.

The tendency towards the retardation of the rate of capital exports
from a number of European countries in the post-war period does not
imply, as we shall show below, that the role of capital exports as
a form of the parasitic degeneration of capitalist economy ("the export
of capital is parasitism squared," as Lenin wrote) and as a weapon in
the struggle for the repartition of the world, is diminishing.

V. THE GROWTH OF INTERNATIONAL MONOPOLIES

In regard to international cartels and the growth of gigantic "super-
monopolies" which bring about the economic partition of the world, the
new data not only brilliantly corroborate Lenin's theory, but also show
that the features of imperialism which Lenin revealed have become
very much more marked.

The war, which greatly strengthened monopolies at home, struck
a severe blow against international cartels and caused the collapse
of the overwhelming majority of them. This collapse was not by any
means caused by the patriotism of the monopolists in the belligerent
countries. In fact, some of the international combines continued to operate
in one form or another during the war. Among these were the International
Carbide Syndicate, the Nobel Dynamite Trust, etc., which operated in
spheres of industry of enormous military importance. Nevertheless, the
countries which were fighting against each other continued to participate

in them. But firstly, the war dislocated the world market. Secondly, the basic industries in the belligerent countries ceased to supply the world market as they were entirely loaded up with war orders. Under these circumstances, the international agreements for the division of foreign markets lost all significance for them.

In the first years of the post-war period the international cartels revived very slowly. Their revival was hindered by inflation, owing to which many countries did not want to bind themselves by agreements that would prevent them from resorting to dumping on the world market with the aid of depreciated currency. International cartels began to grow again only in the period of the stabilisation of capitalism. The more astonishing is it therefore, that by 1931 the number of international cartel agreements had reached 320, i.e., had exceeded the level of 1910 more than threefold. This is evidence of the exceptionally rapid development of international cartels in the period of the stabilisation of capitalism. The following is a list of the most important international cartels and syndicates that have arisen in the past decade, showing the share of world production they each controlled in the respective years.

APPROXIMATE SHARE OF CAPITALIST WORLD PRODUCTION CONTROLLED BY INTERNATIONAL CARTELS

	Year	Share of world output (%)
European Steel Cartel	{ 1929	32
	{ 1936	45
Copper Cartel	1932	90
Rail Cartel	1932	over 85
European Rolled Wire Cartel...........	1931	39
The Lead Pool	1929	40
The Tin Cartel.......................	1932	83
International Synthetic Nitrogen Syndicate	1932	67
Potassium Syndicate	1932	91
Artificial Silk Cartel	1929	70
Electric Bulb Cartel	1934	90
Rubber Producers' Convention	1936	97

SOURCES: *Statistisches Jahrbuch für die Eisen- und Stahlindustrie*, 1930-32; Palot, *Strukturwandlungen in der Internationalen Kupferwirtschaft*, 1932; *Statistisches Jahrbuch für das Deutsche Reich*, 1930-33; *Report of the British Federation of Sulphate of Ammonia Producers; Chemische Industrie*, 1930-34; *The Times*, Trade and Engineering Supplement, 1931.

The crisis brought about the collapse of several of these cartels (copper cartel, the lead pool, etc.). The reasons for this were: the extremely acute competition, the dislocation of the world market, inflation in a number of countries, the unprecedented development of dumping in all its forms and the extreme increase in the uneven development of capitalism during the crisis, as a result of which conditions of production in the various countries and the relation of forces between them changed so rapidly that more or less durable international cartel agreements, which are based on this relation of forces, became less possible. But the temporary decrease in international cartelisation does not imply a *decrease* in the economic partition of the world among monopolies. In the first place, the collapse of some international cartels was immediately compensated for to some extent by the rise of others. This collapse of some and formation of other international combines is due to the change in the relation of forces between the various members of the international cartels. As we have seen, on the whole, there is now a large increase in the number of international cartels compared with pre-war times. Secondly, international cartels are only a *part*, and in a number of leading industries by no means the decisive part, of those super-monopolies which partition the world markets among themselves. In analysing the economic partition of the world, Lenin did not concentrate attention on international cartels, but on trusts and concerns of world-wide importance, such as the General Electric Co., Standard Oil, etc.

The changes in these trusts and concerns reveal even more distinctly the enormous progress that has been made in regard to the partition of the world markets among the monopolists in the post-war period. The following are a few examples: by 1929, the General Electric Co. had increased its turnover nearly sixfold compared with 1910. By purchasing 30 per cent of the shares of the A.E.G. it subordinated to itself the second largest electrical engineering trust in the world with which it had, in a "friendly" way, shared the world since 1907. Its influence extends to the largest electrical concerns in Great Britain, France and other countries.

At the present time all the big electrical engineering firms in the world are interlocked by the holding system and agreements. This, however, does not prevent them from fiercely competing with each other. In the oil industry, as is well known, all the oil sources and markets (except those in the Soviet Union) are divided among three world trusts. Although engaged in fierce competition, these trusts conclude agreements with each other for certain definite purposes. In the chemical industry, three monopolist groups, in the main, share the world market; in addition, however, they have concluded a number of local agreements. Many more examples of a similar nature could be cited.

The growth of the power of the monopolies which divide the world

market among themselves is not the only new feature of the economic
partition of the world among super-monopolies; the number of objects
that are divided has increased also, particularly the "new" industries.
Under pre-war capitalism there were no powerful world monopolies in
automobiles, synthetic nitrogen, artificial silk, etc., such as exist now.
There were no world giants like Unilever, the margarine concern which combines 400 companies in 51 countries, of which the combined capital of
38 companies alone amounts to over £200,000,000. Before the war there
was nothing to equal the Kreuger Match Trust, which collapsed during
the crisis. It owned 150 match factories in 35 countries; it had the match
monopoly, or a share in the state match monopoly, in 15 countries, and
had holdings in iron, gold, silver, copper and phosphorus mining companies, in wood-pulp, electrical engineering, railway and other companies.

On the other hand, the following circumstances are particularly important in principle. Firstly, the October Revolution deprived the international monopolies of the enormous market of the U.S.S.R. as an object
for division. Secondly, the whole policy of the Soviet Union in entering
the world market as an independent factor hinders the international
monopolies from carrying out their policy of economically dividing
the world among themselves in those spheres of world trade in which Soviet exports play a prominent role.

VI. THE DIVISION OF THE WORLD AMONG THE IMPERIALIST COUNTRIES

A comparison of the data quoted by Lenin on the partition of the
world among the great powers with the latest data on this subject not
only shows the further development of the fundamental features of imperialism that were revealed by Lenin, it not only shows that Lenin's
theory of imperialism has stood the test of history; it also reflects those
decisive features of the present epoch which determine its character as
the epoch of the general crisis of the capitalist system, the epoch of the
world proletarian revolution. The most important changes that have
taken place in regard to the partition of the world are the following:

1. Tsarist Russia has dropped out of the fold of imperialist powers.
This "prison of nations," as it was called, has been transformed into a
free union of nationalities enjoying equal rights, which, on the basis of an
enormous increase in the productive forces, are developing a culture that
is national in form and socialist in content. Hence, the great changes that

are taking place in the colonial world. According to the data quoted by Lenin, on the threshold of the twentieth century, 56.6 per cent of the area of Asia consisted of colonies (not including semi-colonies or Korea). In 1932 the colonial area had been reduced to 20.6 per cent (including Korea, but not the provinces in China recently occupied by Japan). This indicates a reduction in the area of colonial possessions on the continent of Asia by 64 per cent compared with that at the beginning of the twentieth century. This enormous reduction is due to the emancipation of the Asiatic part of Russia—Siberia and Central Asiatic Russia, which were included in the category of colonies in Lenin's figures.

2. In the tables quoted by Lenin, China is included in the category of semi-colonies. The Chinese revolution and the anti-Japanese national united front established in China introduced in these tables an amendment of world-historical importance. The Chinese people are courageously and successfully fighting against the attempts of Japanese imperialism to turn China into its colony and for the complete emancipation of their country. The Mongolian and Tanna Tuva People's Republics have also freed themselves from imperialist subjection.

3. In the data quoted by Lenin, Turkey, Iran and Afghanistan are also included in the category of semi-colonies. Today, however, Turkey has achieved her independence as a result of her war of liberation, and Iran (Persia) and Afghanistan have made considerable progress in the same direction.

All these changes, taken together, signify that the colonial monopoly of imperialism has been undermined to an enormous extent. The liberation of the tsarist colonies was the direct result of the October Revolution; but the revolution in China, the liberation of Turkey, etc., were also the result of the direct influence of the October Revolution. This became possible only because the October Revolution transformed Russia from a bulwark of world reaction which crushed the national liberation struggle, into the principal bulwark of this struggle. The erection on the territory of the former tsarist colonies of gigantic industrial enterprises equal to the largest in the world, the enormous successes in socialist construction achieved by the formerly oppressed nationalities of the U.S.S.R., and the rapid development of their national culture, are mobilising the toilers of the East for the decisive battle with imperialism. The Chinese nation is in the vanguard of this gigantic struggle.

4. On the other hand, a comparison of the data quoted by Lenin with that of 1932 also reveals that the sphere of colonial rule is expanding mainly as a result of the transformation of semi-colonial and semi-de-

pendent countries into colonies. On preceding pages we gave a list of
the important colonial conquests in modern times; but this expansion of
the sphere of colonial rule is most strikingly illustrated by the conquest
of Abyssinia by Italy and the conquest of Manchuria and parts of Northern and Central China by Japan. The noteworthy thing about this is the
fact that Lenin's forecast that the future attempts of imperialism to
enlarge its colonial possessions will proceed primarily along the lines
of a struggle to bring about the final partition and subjugation of China,
has been brilliantly corroborated. Japan is conducting a predatory war
against China with the object of turning her into a colony. However,
there is every reason to believe that the imperialist plans of Japan will
prove an utter failure in view of the ever growing heroic resistance of the
Chinese people.

5. Finally, the latest data reveals the important regrouping that has
taken place in the distribution of colonies among the imperialists. The
repartition of the world, which was brought about on the basis of the
relation of forces created in the process of the World War, eliminated
Germany from the list of colonial powers and increased the colonial
possessions of Great Britain, France, Italy and Japan. Today, we are on
the threshold of a new world war for a new repartition of the world;
Japan's invasion of China, Italy's invasion of Abyssinia and Italo-German
intervention in Spain mark the beginning of this war. Through the
medium of their fascist agents, the magnates of finance capital in Germany, who are dreaming of *revanche*, are feverishly preparing for war.
German fascism is the principal instigator of the impending world war.
The extent to which the new conflicts for the repartition of the world
have matured is indicated by the fact that today the distribution of
colonies is more uneven than ever, and corresponds to the economic and
military might of the respective powers still less than was the case in
1914. To prove this it is sufficient to point to the fact that Great Britain,
which has lost a number of important positions in world economy during
the past two decades, has more colonies today than she had before the
war, and that Japan, whose technical and economic development is not
only very much below that of the United States but also of that of the
big imperialist states in Europe, is striving, by the conquest of Manchuria
and North China, to become one of the first colonial powers in the world.
But the peculiar feature of the impending imperialist struggle for the
redistribution of the colonies is that it must necessarily become interwoven with the struggle against the Chinese revolution—which has shaken
the world system of colonial rule to its foundations—and primarily with

the struggle against the U.S.S.R., which is the cradle of the revolutionary struggle all over the world. The peace policy steadily pursued by the Soviet Union and the growing might of the latter are postponing the outbreak of the war towards which the Japanese militarists, and the German and Italian fascists, aided by the more reactionary sections of the British bourgeoisie, are directing all their efforts. The first world war and the October Revolution caused irreparable damage to the world imperialist colonial system; but the result of the impending war will be still more disastrous for world imperialism.

VII. UNEVENNESS OF CAPITALIST DEVELOPMENT BECOMES MORE MARKED

The immediate danger of a new imperialist war provides further historical confirmation of the correctness of the Lenin-Stalin doctrine of the uneven development of capitalism under imperialism, and proves once again that under the rule of monopoly "the periodical repartition of the already *partitioned world* by means of military conflicts and military disasters" (Stalin), is inevitable. The enormous successes achieved in socialist construction in the U.S.S.R. have brilliantly confirmed another decisive thesis of this doctrine, *viz.*, that it is possible to build socialism in one country. The counter-revolutionary "theories" of Kautsky, Trotsky, Zinoviev, Kamenev, Bukharin and others, against which Lenin and Stalin have always waged a relentless struggle, have suffered utter bankruptcy. Lenin and Stalin have developed and added keenness to their doctrine on the particular nature and particular role which the uneven development of capitalism plays in the epoch of the rule of monopolies. But history has not only confirmed the fundamental conclusions of this doctrine; it has also confirmed all its individual elements. During the past twenty years, the discrepancy in the rate of development of the important capitalist countries has increased, and the uneven development of various branches of industry has assumed unprecedented dimensions. This has caused important changes in the relation of economic forces between countries as well as between branches of industry. The increase in uneven development has accelerated the levelling-up process as between countries and industries. This has caused the struggle between them to become more acute, and this, in turn, has caused the unevenness of their development to become still more marked. On the other hand, the difference in the level of other industries and countries has greatly increased. The difference in degree of economic, military, political and colonial power of various countries has increased enormously, and this serves as one of the decisive factors that are causing the extreme tension in international relations in the post-war period, and are accelerating the maturing of a new imperialist war. Finally, the unevenness in the *political* development of various capitalist countries has manifested itself in new and immeasurably more striking and sharp forms in the post-war period. We shall examine several of these points:

Difference in "rapidity of growth of various countries" (Lenin). In the following table we examine three fundamentally different periods in the development of capitalism: 1) the period 1860 to 1880, *i.e.*, the period when free competition still reigned; 2) the period 1890 to 1913, *i.e.*, the period in which monopoly had already assumed a decisive role in the economics of the important capitalist countries (in order distinctly to separate this period from the preceding one, we have left out the decade 1880 to 1890, which was the transition period from the reign of free competition to the reign of monopoly); 3) the period 1914 to 1929, *i.e.*, the period of the World War and of the general crisis of the capitalist system.

INCREASE OR DECREASE IN INDUSTRIAL PRODUCTION (%)[1]

Country	1860 to 1880	1890 to 1913	1913 to 1929
Japan..................	—	—	+197
Canada	—	+245	+120[2]
British India...........	—	—	+81
Russia	+113	+270	—
U.S.A.	+113	+156	+70
Italy..................	—	+150	+76
Germany	+78	+148	+13
France................	+65	+79	+38
Great Britain	+56	+61	—1
Poland................	—	—	—10
Capitalist world.........	+86	+133	+47
Relative rapidity of development of fastest and slowest developing countries:	113:56=2:1	270:61=4.4:1	+197:—10
Relative rapidity of development of United States and Great Britain:....	113:56=2:1	156:61=2.5:1	+70:—1

The table shows that with the change of historical epochs the differ-

---

[1] Computed on the basis of the indices of industrial production of the German Institut für Konjunkturforschung in *Vierteljahrshefte zur Konjunkturforschung.* Sonderheft 31, Berlin, 1933.
[2] 1910 to 1929.

ence in the rapidity of development of various countries increased and the discrepancy between their rapidity of growth became wider.

We do not claim that the figures quoted in the table are absolutely exact in so far as the indices compiled by the Berlin Institut für Konjunkturforschung, on the basis of which the table was compiled, are by no means exact. Nevertheless, they enable us to obtain an idea of the main trends in the development of capitalist industry. What are these trends?

As can be seen from a comparison of the rapidity of development in the period 1860 to 1880 and 1890 to 1913, with the change from the reign of free competition to the reign of monopoly, the general rate of increase of world industrial output was somewhat accelerated. During the twenty years from 1860 to 1880, world capitalist production increased 86 per cent; during the twenty-three years from 1890 to 1913, however, it increased 133 per cent. Simultaneously, the unevenness of development of various countries became much more marked. The difference between maximum and minimum rapidity became twice as wide, the ratio being 2:1 in 1860 to 1880, and 4.4:1 in 1890 to 1913. The slowest rate of increase in both stages occurred in Great Britain. All this excellently illustrates Lenin's thesis that: "On the whole, capitalism is growing far more rapidly than before. But this growth is not only becoming more and more uneven in general; its unevenness also manifests itself, in particular, in the decay of the countries which are richest in capital (such as England)."[1]

The World War and the general crisis of capitalism brought about a sharp change in the development of industrial production in the capitalist world. The rapidity of growth of world industry as a whole sharply declined. During the sixteen years from 1913 to 1929, the increase in output of capitalist industry amounted to only 47 per cent, *i.e.*, an average of 2.4 per cent per annum, as against 3.7 per cent per annum in the period 1890 to 1913.[2] In the subsequent five years, production, as is known, declined. On the background of the general retardation of the growth of capitalist industry, the unevenness of development of various countries became more marked. This was expressed in the following:

First, amidst the general slowing down of rates of development, certain countries (Japan and Canada) showed rates which were exceptional even in the period of the most rapid development of capitalism.

Second, and this is of still more decisive importance, even the wealthi-

---

[1] *Cf.* p. 254 in this volume.
[2] Average annual per cent = geometrical mean.

est country in Europe, Great Britain, not to speak of Poland, showed a fluctuation of output during the whole of the post-war period about a level that did not to any extent exceed that of 1913. This is one of the symptoms of the exceptionally deep decay of post-war capitalism. Of course, this marking time is *relative*: certain industries in these countries are developing rather rapidly; there is a considerable growth in the apparatus of production in almost *all* industries in Great Britain, while technique is making marked progress. But this relative stagnation of industrial production in some of the countries in capitalist Europe marks a new and higher stage in the unevenness of development of individual countries; it shows that it has become more marked. The fact that the rate of growth of several countries is close to zero cannot but mean that the difference in rapidity is becoming wider even if the rate of growth of the most rapidly developing countries is also diminishing. Indeed the post-war rapidity öf growth of the United States is markedly below pre-war. But while the pre-war rapidity of growth of the United States was approximately equal to that of Germany and two and a half times greater than that of Great Britain, since the war the rapidity of growth of the United States is from fifteen to twenty times greater than that of Germany; and its ratio to that of Great Britain is + 70:—1. The unevenness of development of industry as between Japan and Poland has become still more marked.

Third, the following facts are extremely important for the purpose of characterising the great increase in the unevenness of development of industrial production in various countries: in the period 1890 to 1913, of the six countries under review, three, *viz.*, the United States, Italy and Germany, developed at an almost equal rate, and there was only a slight difference between the rates of France and Great Britain, although both considerably lagged behind the other countries. In the period 1913 to 1929, only the United States and Italy developed at an approximately equal rate. This indicates that the difference in the conditions of development in the various countries is much greater than it was before the war.

Fourth, spasmodic regrouping took place in the relative rates of development of the various countries. The most important of these is Germany's passing in 1919-29 from the group of countries in which industrial production increased *most rapidly*, to the group of countries in which industrial production increased at the *slowest* rate. The position of France changed in the opposite direction, although to a much smaller degree.

The uneven development of various branches of industry has also become much more marked in the post-war period.

The following table shows the capitalist world output of various industries in 1929 compared with 1913 (%). [1]

Shipbuilding	83	Nitrogen (sulphate of ammonia)	286
Cotton (consumption)	111	Oil	411
Coal and lignite	116	Aluminium	424
Pig iron	126	Automobiles	892
Steel	160	Artificial silk	1172

The important industries, pig iron, coal and cotton, developed extremely slowly, although their positions vary in the different countries. On the other hand, the new industries developed very rapidly. This caused a rapid evening-up of the level attained and economic might as between the "new" and "old" industries, which caused the competitive struggle to become more acute and the unevenness of their development more marked (compare coal and oil, cotton consumption and production of artificial silk, shipbuilding and automobiles, pig iron and aluminium). The difference in the development of industries producing means of production and those producing consumers' goods, and also as between monopolised and non-monopolised industries, is also extremely great.

A still more important symptom of the growing unevenness of development in the various spheres of economy is the increased lag as between agriculture and industry. This is expressed first of all in the fact that whereas there has been a revival of industry in the post-war period (although a brief and by no means universal one), since 1921 agriculture has been experiencing a prolonged agrarian crisis, which subsided somewhat in the period of capitalist stabilisation, but which became extremely acute in the period of the world economic crisis.

The fundamental reasons for this sharp increase in the unevenness of development during the past twenty years are the following:

1. During the World War, the conditions of economic development were very different in the various countries, and this caused a very profound unevenness in the rate of their growth. The most striking example of this is the development of the United States and Germany in the period 1914 to 1918. After the war, conditions were created by the whole system of peace treaties which favoured the economic development of some countries, and hindered the economic development of others.

---

[1] For sources see p. 307.

2. The enormous growth of monopolies, and the increase in the spasmodic character of technical progress due to the latter, also greatly increased the unevenness of capitalist development.

3. The formation of the Soviet Union, while restricting the general possibilities for expansion of world capitalism, and depriving it of an enormous source of raw materials and of a market for goods and the investment of capital nevertheless affected the various capitalist countries in varying degrees. The influence the Soviet Union exercises on the political development of various countries is still more uneven.

4. The decisive factor in the increase of the unevenness of development of post-war capitalism, however, is the increased decay of the capitalist system, which is characteristic of the period of the general crisis of capitalism. At a time when the possibilities for the growth of productive forces have sharply contracted, the competitive struggle waged by enterprises, industries and countries for the purpose of widening these possibilities at the expense of their rivals becomes more acute. More and more frequently development in one sphere can be ensured under present conditions only by retarding development in another sphere. Hence the continuously growing difference in the rate of development of the various countries and branches of industry.

The regrouping in the relation of economic forces of the important capitalist countries. The enormous increase in the unevenness of development has given rise to spasmodic changes in the relation of forces of the imperialist countries. The most important of these changes, which are of decisive importance in determining the fundamental antagonisms within the general system of present-day international imperialist antagonisms, are those that have taken place in the relation of forces as between the United States and Great Britain. These are indicated in the table on the opposite page.

By the end of the last century, the United States had already captured Great Britain's place as the premier industrial country. But the degree of the United States' industrial supremacy over Great Britain at the end of the last century was relatively small, and was more than compensated for by Great Britain's supremacy in world trade, world credit, foreign investments, naval armaments and colonial power. The next spurt was made in the period 1900 to 1913. At the beginning of the imperialist war the United States' steel output was four times as large as that of Great Britain; output of pig iron was three times as large; consumption of cotton 1.4 times as large; coal output 1.7 times as large, etc. On the eve

INDICES OF THE RELATION OF FORCES AS BETWEEN GREAT BRITAIN AND U.S.A.

	Units of measurement	1880		1913		1929		1936	
		Great Britain	U.S.A.	Great Britain	U.S.A.	Great Britain	U.S.A.	Great Britain	U.S.A.
Motive power in industry......	mill. h.p.	—	3.41	10.75	22.42	14.89	42.93	—	—
Value of production (mining and manufacturing)......	bill.$ (old par.)	3.99 (1888)	5.80[1]	10.59	26.24	13.90 (1930)	76.32	—	—
Steel output......	mill. tons	1.3	1.2	7.7	31.3	9.8	57.3	11.9	47.7
Foreign trade......	bill.$ (old par.)	2.78	1.56	5.76	4.21	8.94	9.47	3.62	48.4
Export of manufactured goods...	" " (old par.)	—	0.09	2.00	0.78	2.79	2.53	1.00	0.68
Issue of foreign securities......	mill.$ (old par.)	—	—	781	44 (1914)	424	671	75	13
Total foreign investments	bill.fr. (current)	22 (1882)	—	75-100 (1914)	9.9 (1912)	94 (1930)	81 (1930)	—	—
Merchant fleet (total tonnage) ..	mill. reg. tons	6.52[2]	3.58[2]	18.70	5.38	20.17	14.38	20.39	12.56
Navy " " ..	mill. reg. tons	—	—	2.22	0.84	1.32	1.28	1.20	1.07
Battleships......	units	—	—	67	34	20	18	15	15
Cruisers......	units	—	—	123	32	54	30[3]	53	25[3]
Official expenditure on armed forces......	mill.$ (current)	137	63	375.3	335.3	552.0	838.2	1381 (1937-38)	1221
Population of colonies......	mill.inhab.	267.9	—	393.5 (1914)	9.7 (1914)	440.6	13.9	466.5 (1932)	14.6 (1932)

[1] Mining—average for 1881-85. Manufacturing industry—1879.
[2] Net tonnage; for other years, gross tonnage. [3] Including 22 obsolete cruisers in 1929; none in 1936.

SOURCES: *Annuaire Statistique, Statistique Générale de la France,* 1932, pp. 559-60; *Board of Trade Journal,* 16, II, 1933; *Statistical Abstract of the U.S.,* 1933; Woytinsky, *Die Welt in Zahlen,* 1928, Bd. IV; *National Federation of Iron and Steel Manufacturers,* 1932; *Statistical Yearbook of the League of Nations,* 1933-34, 1935-36; Customs Returns of Great Britain and U.S.A. in *The World Almanac,* 1934; *The Economist; The Statist; Commercial and Financial Chronicle; Jane's Fighting Ships,* 1936 (figures corrected on basis of latest figures published in the press); *Monthly Bulletin of Statistics,* L. of N., No. 3, 1937.

of the war, the value of United States' industrial production was two and a half times as large as that of Great Britain. The industrial base of the United States was far broader than that of Great Britain; but Great Britain firmly held first place in world trade, in foreign investments and in the world money market. Compared with that of Great Britain the United States' navy was a small one. But the war and post-war periods witnessed a radical change in the situation, and this is a fact of decisive world importance. After the war the United States became a large exporter of capital (*cf*. data on page 141), deprived London of its position as the centre of the world money market, forced Great Britain to second place in volume of foreign trade and came close to her in regard to naval armaments. Simultaneously, the United States' industrial supremacy increased still further, and as we pointed out above, the difference in the rate of development of industry in the two countries increased enormously.

But, notwithstanding the fact that she has completely lost her leading economic position, and that her naval supremacy is being threatened, Great Britain:

a) has retained and even greatly enlarged her colonial possessions, not only absolutely, but relatively to other countries;

b) notwithstanding the fact that she has lost a large share of her markets, the proportion of her home manufactures that she is able to dispose of in foreign markets is five to six times larger than that of the United States, and this, in the main, is due to her enormous colonial possessions;

c) her investments in Asia, Africa and Australia and also in Argentina, Brazil and Uruguay greatly exceed those of the United States.

This shows that the difference in the economic power of the United States and Great Britain, and in their respective share in the exploitation of colonies and foreign markets has increased enormously. This is precisely the basis on which Anglo-American antagonisms are being transformed into the central antagonism of modern imperialism.

The second decisive change in the relation of forces between the imperialist powers is due to the exceptionally rapid growth of Japanese imperialism.

The faster rate of development of Japan compared with that of the United States, Great Britain and other imperialist powers has been even more marked during the past twenty years. This, in turn, has greatly strengthened her economic position, absolutely and relatively, and has

accelerated the levelling-up process as between herself and other imperialist countries. But Japan still lags very much behind the United
States and Great Britain in degree of economic power, as can be seen from
the size of her heavy industry and her share of world production and
world trade. However, even before her seizure of Manchuria, Japan owned
twice as many colonial slaves as the United States. The positions of the
respective countries are illustrated in the following table:

INDICES OF THE RELATION OF FORCES OF JAPAN, U.S.A., AND GREAT BRITAIN

	Years	Units of measurement	Japan	U.S.A.	Great Britain
RATE OF GROWTH:					
Industrial production ..	1913-29	per cent	+197	+70	—1
Electric motors in industry	1913-29	„	+1,450	+300	+363
Exports (change in prices not allowed for)....	1913-29	„	+212	+110	+39
Share of production in world capitalist industry...........	{ 1929	„	2.5	47.0	9.8
	{ 1935	„	3.7	43.4	11.8
Steel output..........	{ 1929	mill. tons	2.3	57.3	9.7
	{ 1936	„ „	5.0	47.7	11.9
Share of world trade ...	{ 1925-29	per cent	3.0	14.0	13.6
	{ 1936	„	3.9	12.1	15.4
Merchant fleet	1936	mill. reg. t.	4.2	12.6	20.4
Navy:					
Total tonnage	1936	thous. reg. t.	841	1,072	1,196
Battleships..........	1936	units	9	15	15
Cruisers	1936	„	41	25	53
Population of colonies: Not including Manchuria	1932	mill. inhab.	28.0	14.6	466.5
Including Manchuria	1932	„ „	60.0	14.6	466.5

SOURCES: *Vierteljahrshefte zur Konjunkturforschung,* Sonderheft 31, Die *Industriewirtschaft,* S. 64-66; *Monthly Bulletin of Statistics of the League of Nations,*
No. 7-8, 1934, No. 3, 1937; *Statistical Yearbook,* L. of N., 1927-33; *Financial and
Economic Annual of Japan,* 1916; *Fourteenth Census of the U. S.,* 1920, *Manufactures,* VIII, General Report; H. Butler, *The United Kingdom,* 1930; *The Economist,*
11, III, 1933; *Report of the National Federation of Iron and Steel Manufacturers,*
1933; Customs returns of the respective countries in *The World Almanac,* 1934;
Jane's Fighting Ships, 1936 (figures corrected).

In 1916 Lenin wrote: "The partition of China is only beginning, and
the struggle between Japan, U.S.A., etc., in connection therewith is continu-

ally gaining in intensity."[1] Today, this struggle has entered into a new phase. The United States is ever so much stronger than Japan economically; but Japan enjoys a number of military strategical advantages over the United States in the struggle for China. Her position is also strengthened by the existence of Anglo-American antagonisms. Utilising these advantages, Japan is striving to transform China into her colony and to squeeze the United States and other imperialist powers out of that country. This is precisely why the Pacific, where war is already being conducted against China by Japan, has become transformed into an important arena of the maturing, new world war.

Finally, the important changes in the relation of forces between France and Germany are also of exceptional significance. As a result of these changes, Central Europe, where the knot of the Versailles contradictions has been tied, has become transformed into the second arena of the impending imperialist war. The change in the relation of forces between Germany and France is indicated in the table given on the next page.

The economic power of France has greatly increased compared with that of Germany, and as a result of the war of 1914-18 France obtained far more favourable conditions for the development of her industry than Germany. The relation of rate of growth of industrial production between France and Germany was as follows:

1890 to 1913	1913 to 1929 (1913 given in present frontiers)
79:148 = 1:1.9	38:13 = 3:1

Before the war Germany's industrial production increased *twice as fast* as that of France; after the war French industrial production increased *three times as fast* as that of Germany. This is evidence of the marked increase in the unevenness of development of these two countries, as the result of which French industrial development has approached the level of Germany. Nevertheless, Germany continues to be the biggest industrial country in Europe, with the most advanced technique, the highest level of concentration of production and the most powerful monopolies. The changes in the industrial apparatus of production (*cf.* data on motive power in industry on preceding page) are much less favourable for France than the increase of industrial output. France still lags behind Germany in world trade, in spite of the fact that the possession of colonies and large resources for the export of capital put her in a

---

[1] *Cf.* p. 206 in this volume.

INDICES OF RELATION OF FORCES BETWEEN GERMANY AND FRANCE [1]

	Units of measurement	1913		1929		1936	
		Germany	France	Germany	France	Germany	France
Population	mill. inhab.	67.0	39.8	64.0	41.2	65.2 (1933)	41.8 (1933)
Motive power in industry ..	mill. h.p.	8.64 (1907)	3.55 (1906)	18.09 (1925)	11.72 (1926)	23.8 (1933)	—
Share of production of capitalist world industry..	per cent	—	—	12.6[2]	7.6[2]	13.2	6.2
Steel output	mill. tons	18.9	4.7	16.2	9.7	19.2	6.2
Export of manufactured goods..............	bill. $ (old par.)	1.61	0.16	2.34	1.23	1.44	0.31
Foreign investments	bill. francs	44 (1914)	60 (1914)	5 (1930)	31.40 (1930)	—	—
Merchant fleet	mill. reg. tons	5.08	2.20	4.09	3.38	3.72	3.00
Navy:							
Total tonnage.........	thous. reg. tons	1033.7	689.2	99.6[3]	522.3	124.9[3]	502.0
Battleships	units	47	24	6[4]	9	6[4]	7
Cruisers.............	"	50	29	5	15	6	14
Army................	thous. men	806.0	770.7	100.5	563.0	1,000	624
Population of colonies.....	mill. inhab.	12.3 (1914)	55.5 (1914)	—	65.1 (1932)	—	65.1 (1932)

[1] The table has been compiled from the following sources: German census returns; Annuaire Statistique, Stat. Générale de la France, 1932; Wochenbericht des Instituts für Konjunkturforschung, No. 41, 1934; The Report of the National Federation of Iron and Steel Manufacturers, 1932; Statistical Yearbook of the League of Nations, 1933-34; The World Almanac, 1934; Jane's Fighting Ships, 1936; Monthly Bulletin of Statistics, L. of N., No. 3, 1937.

[2] 1928.

[3] In 1929-36 there was a considerable qualitative growth of the navy: obsolete tonnage was scrapped and new units, in particular, two battleships, were added.

[4] Including 3 obsolete.

position of great advantage over Germany in foreign markets. Utilising her industrial might and taking advantage of the antagonisms in the camp of her former enemies, Germany broke through the Versailles ban on armaments and is feverishly strengthening her military power. German fascism has turned Austria into a German colony. In conjunction with Italian fascism it is conducting a war of plunder in Spain with the object of enslaving the Spanish people. It is preparing an attack on Czechoslovakia, it is plotting a counter-revolutionary war against the Soviet Union; it is provoking a new world war. German fascism considers it to be its fundamental task to prepare for this war.

We have not by any means enumerated all the forms in which the exceptional increase in the uneven development of capitalism which is characteristic in the post-war period manifests itself. It has found specific expression in the special character of the post-war economic cycles, and in the profound difference in degree to which the economic crisis affects various industries and countries. An indirect illustration of this is contained in the following table:

INCREASE OR DECREASE OF INDUSTRIAL PRODUCTION OF THE CAPITAL-
IST WORLD IN 1932 COMPARED WITH 1929 (%)[1]

Production by countries		World production by industry	
Japan	— 2.2	Artificial silk	+25.9
Great Britain	—16.6	Industrial consumption of cotton	—11.7
Sweden	—20.9	Synthetic nitrogen	—12.8
France	—30.9	Oil	—20.4
Italy	—33.2	Coal and lignite	—30.6
Austria	—35.7	Aluminium	—43.9
Poland	—46.1	Zinc	—46.9
U. S. A.	—46.2	Copper	—52.1
Germany	—46.7	Steel	—61.4
		Pig iron	—64.6
		Automobiles	—69.1

The unevenness of development also manifests itself with exceptional sharpness in the profound difference that exists in the development of the various countries and industries during the period of depression of a special kind. This deserves special examination; but this cannot be undertaken within the limits of the present article. The question of the unevenness of the *political* development of the various countries, which became very much more marked in the period of the general crisis of capitalism owing to the sharp increase in the unevenness of *economic* development, is also worthy of special examination. On the whole, the unevenness of the

---

[1] Compiled from the figures in *Statistical Yearbook of the League of Nations*, 1933-34 and in *Monthly Statistical Bulletin, L. of N.*, 1936.

intense speeding up of labour and the minimum of new capital investments. The weakening of the stimulus for the investment of new capital
in the basic industries leads to an accumulation of capital seeking profitable speculative investment (note for example the enormous flow of capital
to the United States in 1928-29 for speculation on the New York Stock Exchange). At the same time, the share of capital invested in industries of
secondary importance and non-productive spheres increases. The case
of Great Britain illustrates this, as will be seen from the following table:

CAPITAL ISSUES IN GREAT BRITAIN [1]
(thousand £) 1904 — 1933

	Ten Years 1904-13	Ten Years 1924-33	Five Years 1924-28	Five Years 1929-33
Basic industries (iron and steel, metal-working, mechanical engineering, coal mining)......	41,761	27,806	21,405	6,401
Breweries................................	6,029	26,495	14,979	11,516
Hotels, theatres, etc.........................	7,189	28,616	20,424	8,192

The figures of capital issues published in *The Economist,* on the basis
of which the above table has been compiled, are not complete, but they
quite correctly reveal the basic trends. They show that before the World
War, in the period 1904 to 1913, the amount of new capital investments
in the basic industries was seven times as large as that invested in
breweries; and six times as large as that invested in theatres, hotels, etc.;
but the situation radically changed after the war. During the ten years
1924 to 1933, the amount of capital invested in the basic industries was
less than that invested in breweries, hotels, theatres, etc. This was particularly the case in the period of the world economic crisis. These figures
very clearly reveal the enormous acceleration in the decay of British
capitalism.

The same trend is revealed by the changes in the value of building
contracts awarded in the United States. This is seen from the following
table:

VALUE OF BUILDING CONTRACTS AWARDED IN UNITED STATES [2]
(million $)

	1925 to 1929	1930 to 1934
Industrial construction......................................	2,228	660
Commercial enterprises, hotels, etc..........................	4,540	1,300
Religious buildings, monuments, etc..........................	692	209

---

[1] Compiled on the basis of figures published in *The Economist.*
[2] Compiled on the basis of the returns published in *The Statistical Abstract of
the United States,* 1935, p. 787.

During the five years of so-called "prosperity," industrial construction reached the peak of the post-war period; nevertheless the value of such construction was only half that of commercial enterprises, hotels, etc. It is noteworthy that the value of religious buildings, monuments, etc., amounted to nearly one-third of the value of industrial construction. During the world economic crisis and depression the value of industrial construction still further diminished.

Naturally, parasitism connected with export of capital also increased amidst these conditions of the general growth of monopoly and the retarded growth of home industry and commerce. In Lenin's opinion one of the most important features of the parasitism of British capitalism was the fact that already in 1899, Great Britain's income from foreign investments (£100,000,000) exceeded her income from foreign trade by £80,000,000 or fivefold. But in 1929, Great Britain's income from foreign investments amounted to nearly £250,000,000, not including the income from bankers' commissions, interest on short-term foreign investments, etc. If the latter is included, the total income from these sources will amount to nearly £375,000,000 which exceeds the income from foreign trade by more than £300,000,000 or sevenfold. (During the crisis this sum was diminished.) In the period 1924 to 1929, the total national income of Great Britain increased 11 per cent; but her income from foreign investments during the same period increased 55 per cent. This signifies a large increase in the proportion of incomes obtained from the exploitation of colonies compared with that obtained from home industry and commerce. This is a symptom of the further parasitic degeneration of British capitalist economy, of the growth of the features peculiar to Great Britain as a rentier state.

The characteristic feature of the post-war period is that the United States is rapidly overtaking Great Britain as a rentier state. Before the war, United States payments abroad exceeded income from abroad. The war caused a radical change in the situation. In 1922, United States receipts in payment of interest and dividends from foreign investments, together with payments on war debts, amounted to over $500,000,000. In 1929, these receipts had increased to $1,186,000,000, *i.e.*, an increase of 134 per cent, while total national income during the same period increased only 41 per cent. It was only during the period of the crisis that United States income from foreign investments dropped considerably. For eleven years, from 1922 to 1932, United States income from foreign investments, including payment on war debts, amounted to a total of $9,223,000,000.

General increase of rentiers' incomes. Income from foreign investment represents only a part of the parasitic income of the rentiers. We
have already shown above how enormously capital issues and the total
number of securities in circulation have increased in the post-war period
compared with the pre-war period. This implied an enormous increase in
dividends, promoters' profits, and similar incomes. In the United States,
according to official figures, which are obviously an underestimation,
payments on dividends and interest increased 4.5 fold in 1930 compared
with 1913 (from $1,800,000,000 to $8,200,000,000). The total payments
on dividends and interest in the United States in 1931, amounting to
$8,100,000,000, was 40 per cent higher than the *gross* money income of 30
to 31 millions of the farming population in the United States, and three
times as much as the gross income from the harvest of agricultural
produce ($2,700,000,000).[1] For two years alone (1930 and 1931) the
total payments on dividends and interest amounted to $16,000,000,000.
Such is the tribute that the rentiers impose upon society. It is characteristic
that during these two years the income of the rentiers was higher than in
any preceding year. By comparing the index of these incomes with that
of incomes obtained from wages and salaries we get the following
picture:[2]

	1927	1928	1929	1930	1931	1932
			(1923-1925 = 100)			
Total payments on dividends and interest	145	154	180	214	211	182
Total payroll in manufacturing industry	102	102	109	89	68	46

The figures show a steady increase in the incomes of the rentiers in
the period 1923 to 1930. These incomes were particularly large in 1930,
when payments were made on the enormous profits obtained during the
peak of the boom in 1929. In 1931, the income of the rentiers was almost
equal to that in 1930. It is true that profits showed a marked decline, but
accumulated surplus enabled dividends to be kept at a comparatively
high level. Payments of interest even showed a slight rise. It was only in
1932 that the total payments on dividends and interest showed a serious
drop. But the most characteristic thing is that in 1932, rentiers' incomes
were 82 per cent higher than the average for 1923-25, whereas the income of the working class was 54 per cent less than its income for the
same period.

---

[1] Farmers' incomes taken from official returns published in *Crops and Markets*,
No. 8, 1934.

[2] *World Almanac*, 1935, p. 290; *Survey of Current Business*.

An increase in the income of the rentiers, side by side with the growing impoverishment of the proletariat—can a more striking proof of the enormous growth of the parasitism of capitalism be required?

The gowth of the parasitic rentier incomes aus a result of the war of 1914-18 and the preparations for a new war. One of the most important sources from which the incomes of the rentiers were increased in the post-war period were home and foreign war loans. Lenin wrote: "War must be paid for *everywhere,* including 'victor' nations, by interest on loans. And what is this interest? It is billions paid in tribute to messieurs the millionaires for being good enough to permit millions of workers and peasants to kill and maim each other in order to decide how the profits of the capitalists are to be distributed." [1] In France, the national debt (home and foreign) in 1929 has increased threefold compared with pre-war (if the depreciation of the franc is not taken into account—fourteenfold); the national debt of Great Britain has increased ninefold, that of the United States, sixteen to seventeenfold, etc. During the world economic crisis the internal national debt of the United States increased still further owing to the enormous subsidies paid by the state to the banks, to industry and the big farmers. By January 1937, the national debt of the United States had increased to the enormous sum of $34,500,000,000 compared with $16,900,000,000 in June 1929. This increase in the national debt during the crisis was a new factor serving to increase the income of the rentiers. The following table shows the proportion of total budget expenditure paid out in interest on state debts (%):

Great Britain	1914....12.5	1929....44.4
France	1913....19.0	1928....36.5
United States	1912.... 3.3	1929....35.1

From one-third to one-half of total budget expenditure in imperialist countries goes to pay the rentier holders of state bonds! A more than tenfold increase in the proportion of these payments to the total budget of the richest country in the world, the U.S.A., compared with pre-war—such is the statistical evidence of the growing parasitism of the modern rentier state. On the eve of the economic crisis, treasury payments on the national debt in Great Britain amounted to £368,000,000 per annum. In the United States, even in 1932, when a large number of schools had to be closed owing to the lack of appropriations, payments on the national

---

[1] Lenin, *Collected Works,* Vol. XXIV. p. 404, Russ. ed.

debt amounted to over one billion dollars; and this at a time when the federal budget made no provision whatever for unemployment relief.

Most of the payments on the national debt today represent the cost of the *last* war. To these, however, are now added the cost of the wars now being conducted and in the course of preparation. Compared with pre-war, expenditure on armaments has increased in Great Britain almost four-fold, in the United States more than threefold and in Japan more than sixfold. To a still greater extent has it increased in fascist Germany which has entirely stopped publishing its budget. In these countries, expenditure on armaments absorbs the greater part of the budget; but actual expenditure on armaments far exceeds the sums officially allocated in the budget. The total cost of the last war and expenditure on the future war absorbs from 60 to 80 per cent of the budgets of capitalist countries. A large part of the remainder is absorbed by the bureaucratic and police apparatus. Here the state stands forth as a parasitic apparatus which directs the flow of enormous sums into the pockets of the rentiers and the armaments manufacturers. In view of the thoroughly parasitic structure of the budgets of modern capitalist states, the increase in the proportion of budget expenditure to total national income is extremely important. The following table shows this proportion (%):

	1913	1929	1932	1935
United States	2.1	4.7	11.7	14.0
Great Britain	8.8	21.6	22.4	18.5
France	14.1	21.1	25.5 (1931)	32.3
Germany	7.0	10.6	13.0	—

It must be pointed out that only *national* budgets are taken into account in the above table. If to these figures are added local government budgets, the proportion of budget expenditure to total national income will be increased several times. For example, for 1929 it will cause an increase from 10.6 per cent to 28.5 per cent in Germany and from 4.7 per cent to 11.4 per cent in the United States. The latter figure, however, does not take into account the budgets of towns with less than 30,000 population. All this increases the burden of taxation, particularly in agriculture.

The growth of parasitism and the increased lag of agriculture. In Lenin's opinion, one of the most important symptoms of the growth of parasitism is the increased lag of agriculture behind industry. Notwithstanding the very considerable technical progress that has been made in various spheres of world capitalist agriculture, the extreme increase in the lag of agriculture behind industry, and the extreme acuteness of the decay of agriculture, manifest themselves in the fact that the whole of the

post-war period is a period of agrarian crisis. The following table shows
to what extent the position of agriculture is worsened by the increase in
taxation and the increase in the tribute which finance capital extracts
from it directly in the form of interest and sinking fund payments on debts.

ALLOCATION OF FARM INCOME IN THE UNITED STATES [1]
(per cent of gross money income)

	1923	1929	1931	1932
Property tax	8.5	7.0	11.8	14.7
Interest on debts	10.3	7.5	12.7	17.1
Total taxes and interest	18.8	14.5	24.5	31.8
Machinery	4.9	6.0	4.0	3.4
Fertilisers	2.7	3.0	3.6	3.8
Improvements	6.3	4.7	3.7	2.9

Payment of property tax (this does not include indirect taxes)
together with interest is several times larger than expenditure on machinery (six times larger in 1931 and nine times larger in 1932). With
certain modifications, the figures for the United States are typical of other
countries. In Japan, for example, where the methods of exploitation employed by finance capital in agriculture are interwoven with feudal relationships, the burden of taxation and interest payment on debts are still
greater. There is no need to dwell on the position of agriculture in
colonial countries. The tribute finance capital extracts from agriculture
is one of the important factors in the increase in the severity of the
post-war world agrarian crisis.

The influence of the growth of parasitism on the composition of the
population. The diminution in the proportion of the productive section
of the population, which Lenin noted, continued at a rapid rate in the post-
war period, particularly owing to the enormous amount of unemployment.
Simultaneously, there has been an increase in the percentage of the population engaged in the sphere of distribution, thus causing a reduction in the
percentage engaged in the sphere of production. For Great Britain, the
following data are available: during the period 1923 to 1929 the number
of insured persons engaged in industry remained almost stationary
(1923—7,208,000; 1929—7,234,000). The number engaged in commerce,
banks, insurance, financial and similar institutions, however, increased by
26.6 per cent. This implies a considerable diminution in the proportion of
the productive section of the population and an increase in the proportion

---

[1] Computed on the basis of data published in *Yearbook of Agriculture*, 1933, p.
704. The averages are computed on the basis of farmer-owned evaluation of income
returns. Of such returns 11,805 were made in 1920, 6,228 in 1930, 7,437 in 1931 and
6,383 in 1932.

of the non-productive section. During the crisis, this process was greatly accelerated. Thus, in 1932 the number of persons engaged in industry declined by over one million compared with 1929, whereas the number of persons engaged in commerce, banks, etc., increased by 200,000 in the same period. The diminution in the proportion of the industrial proletariat to the whole population, which Lenin regarded as one of the symptoms of the growth of parasitism, proceeds unevenly in the various countries and assumes distinct form in different periods. Whereas this process was already observed in Great Britain in the period from 1850 to 1900, it began to develop in Germany and in the United States only in the post-war period; but then it was interwoven with a new phenomenon, *viz.*, not only a relative, but also an absolute diminution in the number of industrial workers (counting the employed, but not the unemployed).

In Germany, the proportion of industrial workers to the total population *increased* from 10.6 per cent in 1895 to 15.1 per cent in 1925. From 1925 to 1928, however, the proportion dropped from 15.1 per cent to 13.5 per cent. During the economic crisis, the proportion was still further reduced (from 13.5 per cent in 1928 to 8 per cent in 1932), owing to the enormous increase in unemployment.

Simultaneously, the proportion of the population engaged in industry diminished, while there was an increase in the proportion engaged in the sphere of distribution. This is illustrated in the following table computed on the basis of census returns.

NUMBER OF PERSONS OCCUPIED IN GERMANY

	Engaged in industry		Engaged in trade[1]	
	thous.	% inc. or dec.	thous.	% inc. or dec.
1907	9,839		2,776	
1925	12,693	+ 29.0	4,032	+ 45.2
1933	8,999	— 29.1	4,205	+ 4.3

This process assumed particularly large proportions during the economic crisis. Of the total number of persons occupied in establishments under the supervision of a factory inspector (those employing 5 persons and over), the number engaged in industry declined 46.5 per cent in the period from 1928 to 1932, while the number of those engaged in commerce declined only 12.4 per cent, which meant a considerable increase in the proportion engaged in commerce. The same trend is observed in the United States. Thus, the number of workers engaged in the manu-

---

[1] Including insurance, banks, hotels, etc.

facturing industry per thousand of the population was as follows: 1899
—63; 1914—70; 1919—73; 1931—52; 1933—48.

During the crisis; the proportion of the population in the U.S.A. engaged in industry naturally declined very sharply and in 1933 had dropped
to 48 per thousand as against 73 per thousand in 1929. Another trend that
is characteristic of the growth of parasitism clearly revealed itself in the
United States, *viz.*, an increase in the proportion of the population engaged
in the sphere of distribution with a simultaneous decrease in the proportion
of the population engaged in the sphere of production. Thus, the proportion of those engaged in the mining and manufacturing industries to the
total self-supporting population in the United States *declined* from 33.5
per cent in 1920 to 30.9 per cent in 1930. The proportion of those engaged
in commerce, the civil service and commercial offices, domestic and professional service, etc., *increased* in the same period from 32.8 per cent to
39.3 per cent.

We have not by any means enumerated all the concrete forms in which
the decay and parasitism of modern capitalism manifest themselves. But
we think that what we have said is sufficient to prove the exceptional rapidity with which these features of modern capitalism, which Lenin
revealed, are growing. The growth of these features is particularly striking against the background of the successes achieved in socialist construction in the U.S.S.R. The antithesis of the laws of development of
these two systems stands out in striking relief.